ADDING
VALUE

Carin Werner,

all the best.

Mcclurie

1-25-01

ADDING VALUE

The Joseph M. Bryan Story
from Poverty to Philanthropy

NED CLINE

The Joseph M. Bryan Foundation,
Greensboro, N.C.

ISBN 1-878086-88-x

Library of Congress Control Number 00-133227

Printed in the United States of America

Book design by Elizabeth House

Jacket design by Tim Rickard

Jacket portrait by Tom Edgerton

The Joseph M. Bryan Foundation
P.O. Box 14829
Greensboro, N.C. 27415

Published in association with
Down Home Press
P.O. Box 4126
Asheboro, N. C. 27204

Distributed by
John F. Blair, Publisher
1406 Plaza Dr.
Winston-Salem, N.C. 27103

To the many people who have been willing to share their resources

to add value to the lives of those with special needs

ACKNOWLEDGEMENTS

No research and writing project like this one could be done without the help and cooperation of many people. Certainly no author could ever do it alone.

Grateful thanks are due hundreds of people. The more than 125 individuals interviewed are listed at the back of the book, as is attribution for sources quoted in each chapter. Appreciation is expressed to all because each added to the value of the story.

A special thank you is owed to Jim Melvin, president, and Carole Bruce, legal counsel, of the Joseph M. Bryan Foundation. They provided full access of their own knowledge of Joe Bryan's life as well as documentation of his benevolence over many decades. They did the same with records of his foundation. That information and material were key ingredients during the many months of research before writing was begun.

Melvin and Bruce read an early draft of the manuscript — but not the final one — and, thankfully, pointed out some factual errors that needed correction. But they did not attempt to alter a single word on the unpleasant aspects of Mr. Bryan's life concerning the early struggles with a dysfunctional family, his later difficulties with his own children and grandchildren or his corporate disappointments.

Telling the full story, warts and all, Melvin and Bruce readily agreed, was essential to telling it accurately and putting it in perspective. These personal problems, Bruce accurately surmised, may well have helped explain many of Bryan's later acts of kindness and generosity toward those outside his family and laid the groundwork for his vast philanthropy. I especially appreciate their openness and acceptance of full disclosure without even a hint of omission or suggestion of changes that would have created a distorted view.

Fortunately, Bryan and his siblings were pack rats when it came to holding onto family historical records and documents, some predating 1900 and some not of a pleasant nature involving family members. But all were of utmost importance in telling a thorough family history. Thank goodness those records were saved as part of Bryan's in-depth official papers that are now part of the archives at the University of North Carolina at Greensboro.

A very special thank you is also owed to the staff in the Special Collections Section of Jackson Library at UNCG, where Bryan's family and historical papers are on file. Betty Carter, Janis Holder, Linda Jacobson and Carolyn Smith were professional, cooperative, understanding and extremely patient throughout more than 15 months of plowing through tedious records and files. Never once did they flinch at a request, no matter how mundane. They made what would have been a difficult, if not impossible, task, relatively easy. I shall be forever indebted to them.

More than six hours of interviews with Bryan's dear friend Greta Tilley Medlin and his dedicated staff assistant Ann Rambeaut presented a view of the man that no one else had. He told them things about himself and showed them a side of his personality that no one else knew. Their respect for and devotion to him were bountiful. They were willing to share their feelings, albeit reluctantly at first, and their assistance has added a warmth to his story that deserved to be included.

I was fortunate enough to spend an inspirational morning with former governor and Duke University President Terry Sanford and an afternoon with Charlotte broadcast executive Charles Crutchfield in the twilight of their lives. Each shared their invaluable intimate thoughts on Joe Bryan's life, even though each was ill and in pain. They helped make this a better book, and for their cooperation under adverse circumstances I am grateful. Sadly, each died within a few months of our talks.

Retired Jefferson Standard leader Seth Macon, the unofficial company historian and devoted community supporter, was a treasure of information. His own knowledge of the company, its people and personalities, and his ability to point me toward others with special knowledge of local history and events was a significant contribution. His enthusiastic cooperation was critical to thoroughness.

I am also appreciative of members of the Bryan family who were willing to speak frankly, sometimes reopening old wounds as they discussed both positive and negative aspects of their family's lives. This is especially true of Kay Bryan Edwards and Joe Bryan Jr., as well as Bryan grandchildren Mary Price (Pricey) Taylor Harrison and Bryan, Howard, and John Taylor.

Regrettably, a few Bryan family members repeatedly declined the opportunity to discuss their parents or grandparents. Their perspective and viewpoints would have added to the understanding of the subject of the book. I am sorry they chose that course.

Hopefully this book will paint a portrait of Joseph M. Bryan Sr. that is complete, factual and fair. Most, but not all, is uplifting. Like everyone, he had his shortcomings.

But his actions and decisions in the world of broadcasting, shrewd investments and philanthropy have had a significant impact on the lives of thousands, and the foundation he created will continue the good works he started.

This book is intended to lay it all out. It is a story of a man who overcame significant odds and hardships as a child who, through due diligence, perseverance and a bit of help from a wife who stood faithfully by his side, helped build a corporate giant and create a legacy of good works that will long live on. It's a legacy of benevolence of which he would be proud and one that others would do well to follow.

Joe Bryan, as his old political friend Kerr Scott used to say, plowed to the end of the row, even into his 99th year. He may have left a few weeds in the furrows, but there has been many a bountiful harvest and many, young and old, have been and will be the beneficiaries. Hopefully, this book tells it like it is. I am grateful to the many that helped make it so.

TABLE OF CONTENTS

FOREWORD

The first time I paid a call on Joe Bryan, I was in the company of his longtime good friend, William D. Carmichael, Jr., Vice President of the University of North Carolina. We went to Bryan's office in the Jefferson Standard Building in downtown Greensboro to make a request for a gift to finance a project at the University. Mr. Carmichael and Mr. Bryan had a joyful hour of reminiscence. But we left with no money!

I was, however, impressed with those shaggy eyebrows and full mustache making Joe look formidable, and I said so in an interview soon thereafter. He read the interview and called me to extend his friendship. That was the beginning of a joyful relationship that spanned several decades.

Ned Cline tells the full and fascinating story of Joe Bryan's fruitful and full life and of his impact upon the commerce of our state and nation; his many benefactions to the academic community for the education of our youth and the health and well-being of us all. The generosity he manifested, along with his gracious and public-spirited wife, Kathleen, impacted the city of Greensboro as well as the state and its people in a dramatic way.

I knew him best working in public television. He and his great team from his commercial stations substantially aided University television getting on the air. The spacious University television center bears the family name.

Joe Bryan was in many ways an intensely private man. Yet, among his generation of leaders he most certainly made a huge difference in the culture of our state, in the strength and quality of its educational institutions, and in the quality of life we enjoy. His good works continue through the foundation that bears his name.

These pages tell of the most useful and productive life of a good man working to benefit humanity in a most noble way.

William C. Friday,
President Emeritus,
The University of North Carolina

1

BEATING THE ODDS

J oe Bryan and his wife Kathleen could never quite agree on exactly where they met. He said it was in a hallway at Madison Square Garden during a hockey game. She said it was during a North Carolina Society Dance in downtown Manhattan.

The specific circumstances of that first meeting in early 1927 became a standing joke with the Bryans and many of their long-time friends during their 50-plus years of marriage as the couple's influence and philanthropy continued to spread and grow across Piedmont North Carolina and beyond.

"I always thought the first meeting was at the hockey game," Bryan said with a smile hundreds of times through the years. "But a hockey game wasn't romantic enough for Kathleen. She felt it sounded much better to say we met at some society event, so she always said it was at the dance. That was fine with me."

Truth is, if Bryan met his future wife and 57-year companion at the hockey match, that initial encounter didn't make much of an impression on either one. Neither could recall any details of the game or who won. The dance, though, was something else. Those memories remained near and dear.

Society-enriched North Carolinians who lived and worked in New York City or those with ties to those who did gathered each spring in the 1920s for an engaging social event that far surpassed anything back home. It was a significant happening, the thing to do and the place to be for anyone that was anyone or wanted to be.

Kathleen Price and her mother, Ethel, daughter and wife of the dapper Julian Price, president of Jefferson Standard Life Insurance Company in Greensboro, were among those attending the high society event in April 1927. Bryan, who at the time had no connections to North Carolina except friendship with a few moneyed people from the state, who worked on or near Wall Street, was an invited guest.

The dance was the night after the hockey game, which both Bryan and Price attended. Kathleen Price and her mom, who was determined that her daughter meet and associate with society's upper crust at home and away, had no specific plans to meet a fellow named Joe Bryan, either at the sporting event or the high society dance. But they were there to be seen. In fact, Kathleen already had a date for the dance with a fellow from her hometown of Greensboro. Her prearranged evening escort was Ben Cone whose name and family connection was already well known in Greensboro and in New York through the family-owned Cone Mills.

What the Prices didn't know, of course, was that Bryan already was on the inside track with some of New York's society elite so he fit right in, even if they didn't realize it. He had become accustomed, as a member of the Cotton Exchange, to socializing with the best and brightest of Manhattan. Kathleen, in later years, would learn to appreciate and gain advantage of his connections, just as he did hers.

Bryan showed up for the dance as a stag guest of his friend Eli Springs, a stock exchange broker and member of the well-connected Carolina Springs Mills family of entrepreneurs. And whether Bryan remembered the outgoing and appealing Kathleen Price

2

from the previous evening's hockey game or whether it was the mood of the dance, it didn't take long for him to make a move once the music started. He was smitten right away.

"I gave her what I thought was a big rush," Bryan would later explain. "I danced with her a number of times. But she let me know rather quickly that in the South, a rush wasn't a couple of dances. It was dozens of dances. I was just a slow Yankee who needed to learn about Southern ways."

That was the first of many lessons Joe Bryan would come to learn about the South during the ensuing years. Not all were to his liking.

But that dance was the start of something big, really big for both Joe Bryan and Kathleen Price. For the young society-conscious Southern belle who was swept off her feet by the charming Yankee on the dance floor, even if he was not nearly as debonair as he thought, Ben Cone was romantic history after that night.

There are, in fact, those back home in Greensboro who say that Bryan and Cone, who had numerous business and social encounters during the decades they lived and worked in Greensboro, never did really get along or have a close friendship. If so, it may have been the dance that did it.

That eventful evening in New York began what in the late 1920s was as close to a whirlwind romance as one could get. Joe Bryan and Kathleen Price were married in less than a year. The marriage not only affected the lives and futures of the couple, but it has had a continuing direct impact on the lives of hundreds, and indirect impact on thousands, of people in Greensboro, the state of North Carolina and beyond.

Kathleen Price's hometown and state, and Joe Bryan's adopted home in the South, are better off because the two did meet and marry. The resulting benevolence is part of the region's history. Regardless of the specific circumstances of their initial meeting, the fact that they did has been and continues to be a significant occurrence.

Millions of philanthropic dollars have poured over people, places, and things in Greensboro and North Carolina and other locations along the eastern Seaboard as a result of the Bryan marriage. Their generosity not only continues, but also continues to grow. Joe and Kathleen Price Bryan had increasing means to contribute to those with fewer resources and they did so generously throughout much of their adult lives. Through trusts and foundations they created, their good works remain as ongoing endeavors long after their deaths. They set an example with their giving, hoping that others would follow and expand their own benevolence.

Their wish already has become reality. The desire for benevolence has spread among their family members and friends who hold the couple up as models for doing good works.

The goal of trustees of the Joseph M. Bryan Foundation, in fact, is that their successors and their colleagues on other charitable boards will use the Bryans even more as role models for giving where resources can provide the most good for the most people.

"Mr. Bryan was quite creative in his philanthropy," commented Foundation president Jim Melvin. "We (current trustees) had the privilege of knowing him very well. Those who will follow us won't have that opportunity. We can look at how he would have done it. He gave us a feel for the kinds of things he had an interest in moving forward. What we are about is causing his spirit to live on through the kind of giving that he would have done and that he wanted to be continued."

Melvin's fellow trustee and long-time Joe Bryan lawyer and confidant Carole Bruce echoed that view. "That's our primary motivation for wanting his story out," she emphasized. "We want future generations on this foundation to have a source for understanding the person who created it. That's of critical importance, that going forward people will have the ability to understand the thinking of the person who has made these (Bryan's) gifts possible."

Lest anyone get the feeling that Joe Bryan's life was all a bed of

4

roses and charitable benevolence, however, it must be said that's not the case. Not even close.

In many ways, Joe Bryan and Kathleen Price were as different in their upbringing in the North and South as were their ancestors who fought on opposing sides in the Civil War to preserve their particular heritages. She had virtually all a young woman could ever need or want. Her parents adored her and her early life was in most ways always a charm. His early years were almost the opposite. He had barely essentials of need and hardly anything to fill wants for many years of his early life. His early family life was anything but steady or predictable, as hers was. His affluence would come only in time through sheer determination as well as help from Kathleen's family.

While Kathleen had the opportunity for the best schools, finest clothes and most sophisticated social life, Joe was for a time for all practical purposes homeless. Home for awhile was anywhere he could find a bed. He was able to attend a prestigious school only one year on borrowed money. He endured a family lifestyle that was, in many ways, bordering on dysfunction.

Kathleen's father was a primary leader in the family's hometown of Greensboro, a man of renown and highly respected as a pillar of society. Joe's father was a man whose grasp never extended to his reach. Young Joe's hometown was wherever his father could find a job, most of which didn't last long or pay enough to support a growing family that was ultimately abandoned and was subsequently split up after the youngest daughter died as an infant and the mother was shunted off to an institution for the mentally insane. In a more modern vernacular, young Joe Bryan could well have been declared a welfare child.

That, in effect, is the way his mother started out long before she met her husband filled with wanderlust. She was left without parents in her preteen years after her saloonkeeper father and mother both died before she was 10. She was sent to live with different relatives in various places, including one family in Mexico where she met her future husband who frequently referred to her as that "orphan brought up in an asylum in New York".

As an escape and in search of stability, she married while still in her teens. Rather than finding the stable home life she desired, however, she encountered a rocky marriage with an unpredictable husband, frequent bouts of loneliness and increasing emotional problems even as she produced six children in the first nine years of marriage.

As a young mother, she was bounced across the East Coast of the United States and parts of Mexico from one of her wayward husband's relatives to the next. Ultimately, following the death of her sixth child as an infant, she suffered an emotional breakdown and tragically became an inmate in an institution for the mentally insane and a ward of the state of New Jersey for more than 50 years.

That's the kind of life into which Joe Bryan was born and endured in his early years.

While Kathleen's parents cared for and protected her as a precious crown jewel, Joe's father scattered his growing brood across three states and parts of Canada before eventually leaving his sick wife at the institution for mentally impaired and dumping the couple's five surviving children with two of his spinster sisters in New Jersey. He then deserted the family and dropped out of sight for 32 years before eventually asking for forgiveness—by letter rather than face to face. By that time he was living with another woman in Florida whom he identified as his wife, although there is no known record among family members of his divorce from his mentally ill first wife and the mother of all his children.

During those traumatic times, young Joe's youngest brother was handed over — literally given away — to a non-family acquaintance because the two aunts said they couldn't handle so many children so young. From that day forward, Joe Bryan neither saw nor even knew the status of his kid brother for more than 50 years. Bryan, in fact, didn't even learn of the brother's death until 20 years after the fact. A well-to-do, but eccentric, woman raised the brother, but didn't legally adopt him until he was a young adult. While the brother's life was in some ways more normal than his other siblings who were bounced among relatives, he was later plagued with bouts of alcoholism and job changes. He was constantly troubled by what he referred to as his divided family.

Joe Bryan did have one uncle, his father's brother, who was a man of means and was highly regarded as a physician and chief of staff of Staten Island Hospital in the 1920s. That uncle, Dr. William Simon Bryan, financed one year of education for young Joe at a prep school in Massachusetts and for two years provided Joe with a temporary home on Staten Island when he had no other place to live. The uncle also later loaned Joe funds to buy a seat on the New York Cotton Exchange but required monthly installment payments plus interest of 4.5 percent. When the uncle died, Joe's inheritance of $5,000 was reduced by the amount of the debt still owed.

As a young man, Bryan lived at intervals with his uncle, his two aunts, in a boarding house with a janitor who paid him 10 cents an hour to do menial jobs and in an orphanage which he later described as disgustingly vile. The uncle and aunts had social connections in and around New York City and they worked to introduce their nephew to what they considered the right crowd, following his orphanage and boarding house stays, as one way of offsetting his earlier experiences. Bryan learned quickly and easily how to mingle with the affluent people of the city, a trait he never forgot.

The aunts had friends among some of the city's most influential citizens and there were other members of Bryan's earlier family who ranked above average in social standing. His physician uncle was considered one of Staten Island's more influential citizens, despite the fact he penny-pinched young Joe's schooling and job debts.

Possible embarrassment and trauma over his early background, however, may have been what prompted Bryan at his marriage to the prim and proper Kathleen in late 1927 to perpetuate a lie with which he lived the remainder of his life. In the Bryan's marriage announcement, Joe listed both his parents as deceased. He did that despite the fact his mother was alive, albeit unable to function in the mental institution, where she would live another 27 years. His vagabond father, although his place of residence was unknown to the family on the wedding day, lived until 1939.

No living Bryan family member knows if Kathleen's parents were aware when the couple was married that Joe's parents were both alive, despite his public denials. Kathleen knew of her husband's parental situation when the couple was wed, but she instructed Joe's siblings not to tell her own three children when they were young that the grandparents were still alive. It is only conjecture whether Bryan asked that his early family life be kept private from his children and friends or if Kathleen is the one who made that decision. Bryan, however, was well aware in his latter life that archivists he hired were digging into his history and leaving it as part of his official family and business records that he donated to the special sections division of Jackson Library at the University of North Carolina at Greensboro.

Neither Joe nor Kathleen Bryan ever discussed or explained to their children or long time friends and business associates the deception they maintained over Joe's early family status. Mental illness and family desertion in the early days of the Bryan marriage were not topics that were openly discussed. It was a family secret best left in the closet.

Only once in his adult life did Joe Bryan make a private trip to New Jersey to visit his mother —whom he had not seen since he was eight — in the mental institution. It was a traumatic and disturbing visit. He would later say his mother didn't recognize him and was unable to comprehend he was her son. He never returned to the institution and did not attend her funeral in 1954. Bryan and his brother split the $650 cost of their mother's burial. Bryan and his wife also once during their early marriage visited with his father whom they discovered was at the time living in Florida. That was the only time Bryan saw his father after the family was split up more than 30 years earlier and Bryan did not attend his dad's funeral in 1939.

The Bryans eldest daughter Kay Edwards didn't learn her grandmother was alive until seeing the grandmother's name listed on a family tree chart given to her as a Christmas gift by her father in the early 1950s. "I was shocked and horrified to see that," Edwards said later. "That's the first time I realized she was still alive. I asked my mother why she never told us about my grandmother and she said it was just something she had been told by my father not to discuss." Her father, Edwards said, never mentioned the topic; he just gave her the chart with his mother's name listed as being alive without a word of explanation. Edwards said she was asked by her mother never to mention the subject to her father, and she never did.

Because of the multiple problems in young Joe's upbringing, he had only one year of formal schooling beyond the grammar lever, at prestigious Mount Hermon School in Northfield, Massachusetts, paid for by his physician uncle. He never completed high school and never attended college, but that was never something he tried to hide. On the contrary, he discussed his lack of formal education frequently as he later worked to help others avoid the educational shortcomings he had encountered. His lack of structured schooling also didn't stop him from learning on his own. He became a voracious reader from the classics to sporting magazines and his knowledge of history and the language were impressive to his friends. He regularly good-naturedly in his retirement years chided friends for their lack of knowledge of history or language use.

So far as is known, Bryan never once discussed his early life or upbringing with friends in Greensboro or with his business associates in the insurance or broadcasting industry during his more than 30 years as a corporate executive. In the latter years of his life, Bryan did talk about his family history, but only with a small circle of close friends. His foundation trustees never knew the circumstances of his early life until research for this book was begun. His former fishing and shooting partners expressed surprise about his early family once they were told during this research project; he had never mentioned it to them. All had assumed his parents were long since dead as he had said in 1927.

The two people with whom he most often or most intimately discussed his traumatic childhood were his dedicated administrative assistant Ann Rambeaut and his big-hearted and caring friend Greta Medlin, a former journalist who developed a warm and lasting friendship with Bryan after interviewing him for a newspaper profile. Those conversations with Rambeaut and Medlin took place when Bryan was in his 80s. He kept his early life secret until then.

It's strictly a matter of conjecture what role Bryan's early hardships and heartaches played in his later life of dogged determination to improve his status and to contribute so many of his huge resources to help others. "But I think this helps explain why he did a lot of what he did," his legal counsel Carole Bruce said. "I think his early life explains a lot about his thinking in later life."

Minus any formal education himself, Bryan has donated millions to educational causes in both public schools and on college and university campuses.

Living with the trauma of his mother's mental illness seems to have placed a heavy burden on his heart when his wife Kathleen fell victim to the indignities of Alzheimer's disease during the 1970s and first half of the 1980s. He was not there to watch his mother's gradual demise of brain deterioration, but he was ever present during Kathleen's lingering illness. He agreed to medical shock therapy for his wife as one means of treatment, only to later realize that

10

such treatments only made her condition worse. He refused to allow Kathleen to enter a nursing home, perhaps from recollections of the scene when he visited his invalid mother. He insisted on keeping Kathleen at home with around the clock medical care until her death more than a decade after she became ill and slowly deteriorated into a nonverbal stage of life near the end.

Bryan donated millions to medical and Alzheimer's research at Duke University in search of a cure. The cure he so strongly desired was a long way away at the time of his own death, but Bryan's generosity toward Duke has allowed physicians and medical researchers at that facility to move to the forefront of nationwide Alzheimer's research. At the beginning of the 21st Century, progress at Duke Medical Center was pronounced, due in large part to resources provided by Bryan, on a drug that won't prevent but can postpone the dreaded brain decay of Alzheimer's patients.

Bryan gave away millions, and his foundation continues that practice, to develop parks and open space for recreational purposes for young people and adults. The 1,500-acre park at the northeast edge of Greensboro, named for Joe and Kathleen Bryan, was one of his greatest loves because it has provided so much to so many for so long.

Bryan so loved the park that he asked that half his cremated ashes be buried there with the other half buried at the family burial plot in a Greensboro cemetery. Buried beside Bryan's ashes at the park are the ashes of his beloved English Spaniel, Jason.

In addition to medical research and recreation, Bryan's millions have gone toward enhancement of educational programs, both at the public school and university levels.

Between those early years of hard times and his ability to generate millions to beneficial causes, Bryan led a life that was always interesting, sometimes dangerous and, to say the least, different.

He stepped forward to volunteer for the military in World War I, following his grandfather who fought for the Union during the Civil

War. He was never in actual combat, but served in the medical corps and saw up close and personal what the ravages of war could do as he treated wounded soldiers.

He secured his first real occupation the day he was released from the Army, getting the job literally as he walked — still in uniform — from the military ship to his uncle's home on Staten Island. He worked for awhile in the early 1920s in battle-scarred and governmentally corrupt Haiti where he regularly brandished a handgun for self-protection and witnessed the governmental turmoil that left him wondering if the country could or would survive.

He became in 1923 the youngest person ever to be selected as a member of the New York Cotton Exchange. He did well financially until the economic crash of 1929 when there was little demand for cotton or any other product to market.

The Wall Street crash came two years after his marriage to Kathleen whose father had still not become convinced his daughter had married well enough. In fact, before Julian Price would agree to the marriage, he carefully checked Bryan out through New York business contacts, including Bryan's financial status and personal character. Bryan obviously passed the test.

Price demurred so long, however, on agreeing to the marriage that Bryan grew impatient enough to insist on a response "or else" as he put it in a letter to his future father-in-law. Price, several months after the marriage proposal, responded to Bryan by letter that "you win, so come on down".

Between the Bryan marriage in 1927 and the couple's return to Greensboro in 1931, Kathleen's parents subsidized the Bryans Manhattan lifestyle by $200 a month. Young cotton broker Bryan was making a comfortable living in New York, but not up to the standard that Kathleen had been accustomed back home in Greensboro, thus the Price monthly subsidy.

The subsidy was something the Prices sent on their own. It was not something Bryan asked for or wanted. Rather, he accepted it to make his wife and her parents happy. He did a lot of that through the years, in fact.

Bryan would later say he came to Greensboro because Manhattan was no place to raise a family. He and Kathleen produced two daughters in the first three years of their marriage. While there may have been some truth in Bryan's statement about the hazards of bringing up children in downtown New York, it seems rather clearcut that Julian and Ethel Price decided it was time for their daughter to come home, regardless of what husband Joe might have preferred.

Joe and Kathleen Bryan came to Greensboro in the spring of 1931 when Julian Price promised a job to his son-in-law.

Bryan held a series of jobs during the next 30 years with Jefferson before his retirement in the early 1960s. His job titles were impressive: chairman of Pilot Life, first vice president of Jefferson, president of Jefferson Broadcasting, finance and executive committee member. Many of his titles, however, didn't carry much responsibility and he never reached the elusive job status of president of the company that his wife coveted for him and that he also hoped would come.

Bryan conceded his life inside Jefferson was not always easy or genteel. He constantly fought against the perception that he was there only because he had married the daughter of the boss. He constantly struggled to adapt his sometimes-gruff exterior Irish Yankee background to the more polite and gentlemanly ways of a southern corporation.

He was the one, however, who led the way in launching the profitable broadcasting side of the company that over time became one of the more visible parts of the corporate structure through highly respected radio and television stations and the growing broadcast popularity of Atlantic Coast Conference athletic events.

Bryan also in many respects deserves the honorary title of father of university television in North Carolina. He was the first private contributor to public TV in this state. He willingly gave up a commercial license that Jefferson Broadcasting had sought in order for UNC to begin its television operations. Without Bryan's generosity and commitment, public television in this state in all likelihood would have not started as early as it did and may well not have maintained the quality it has during the last decades of the 1900s.

In addition to his official duties at Jefferson, Bryan also became the unofficial social chairman for annual company conventions and entertainment. In that role, he had no equal inside the corporation. Other corporate executives marveled at his ability to arrange social functions inside the company. Among his friends who appeared at company conventions were cowboy star and singer Gene Autry and syndicated newspaper advice columnist Ann Landers.

Bryan's social connections also extended far beyond the Jefferson headquarters. He cultivated friendships with many of the best-known and most influential corporate executives in the country. He was a member of some of the country's most exclusive sporting clubs and regularly socialized with the country's rich and famous as he fished for salmon in Canada, shot pheasants and grouse in England and Spain and vacationed in the Bahamas. He never owned but one home, but he rented residences in exclusive territories in this country and elsewhere. He was one of the earliest and most recognized members at Augusta National Golf Course where he annually partied with golf course founders Cliff Roberts and Bobby Jones as well as Augusta regular Dwight Eisenhower.

Despite his many triumphs in overcoming his early upbringing to foster a successful career and his well known role as a major philanthropist and benefactor in North Carolina, Bryan— by his own admission with full agreement from his friends and associates — went to his grave with one major obstacle unresolved. That was the lingering estrangement within his immediate family. Bryan carefully chose to create his philanthropic foundation to exclude his children and grandchildren, saying they already had adequate financial resources from his wife and her mother. The bitterness created by that action prompted a lawsuit against trustees of his trust and resulted in public airings of the family divisions and feelings toward Bryan and, in some cases, among family members themselves.

The family feuding became so intense in 1999 that the original Bryan Family Fund was dissolved and its millions in assets were redistributed to eliminate involvement and philanthropic decisions by the Bryan grandchildren. The words most often used by Joe and Kathleen Bryan's friends in discussing the family situation are "sad" and "unfortunate" and "tragic". It was certainly a source of discomfort for Bryan.

Through it all, however, the Bryan name has remained strong in the field of benevolence. And there is every reason to believe that such will continue for decades to come. That's because Bryan, against what at times were seemingly insurmountable odds, made it so through a dogged determination to succeed and spread good works.

It is a legacy that would make this proud man even more proud. It is a legacy that many seek, but few achieve.

2

VAGABOND BEGINNING

J oe Bryan Sr. was born in Elyria, Ohio. But that was just the luck of the draw. More specifically, at that time it was the most convenient domicile of the most convenient relative of his father. The father had a fondness for impregnating his wife every 18 months or so and farming her out with a family member for childbirth and initial child-rearing until it was time to either show up for awhile and then, as was his habit, moving on again.

Joe's older brother Bart was born in Johnstown, Pa., in the spring of 1894 at the home of his paternal grandparents. His father sent his pregnant wife there for the birth of their first child while he remained in Mexico where the couple lived temporarily after their marriage nine months earlier, in September 1893, in Eagle Pass, Texas.

Joe was born 21 months later, on Feb. 11, 1896, in Elyria, again in the home of his father's relatives, after being conceived in Mexico where his mother returned within the first year after the first son was born. Her early correspondence shows she strongly despised living in Mexico, calling the natives "great thieves," but felt she had an obligation to be near her husband who was working in the mines there.

Next came daughter Anne, born 18 months later in August 1897, presumably also in Johnstown in either the home of another relative or a family friend. Records on the specific location of Anne's birth do not exist. Her birth and death certificates are both missing the city of her birth, simply listing Pennsylvania as the state, but records do show the family was living in rented housing in Johnstown a month before Anne was born.

Twenty-one months later, in the spring of 1899, a third son William was born in Lorain, Ohio. That's where the family had moved and lived for a short while — all under the same roof for a change — in several different boarding houses as the father obtained and left a series of jobs.

Within a year of the birth of the third son and fourth child, the Bryan family moved to Sydney, Nova Scotia, where the father found work, thanks to contacts through his two spinster sisters who repeatedly helped their brother find work as well as helped raise his children. The family remained in Nova Scotia for little more than two years, producing two more children in 23 months. Son Theodore was born in the spring of 1901 and daughter Dora was born in the spring of 1903.

Family historical records show the Bryans were for all practical purpose nomads during the nine years the six children were born. Letters among family members list four different mailing addresses in Mexico during one 24-month period, and five different addresses in Johnstown, Pa., in roughly the same time period. After the approximately two years in Nova Scotia, the mother was institutionalized, the children were split up among relatives, or in the case of youngest son Theodore given to another family, and the father dropped out of sight and contact for almost 30 years.

The Bryan children, despite the frequent moves and inability of the father to hold a steady job, seemed reasonably happy and functional during the earliest years of frequent childbearing. They were, of course, too young at the time to know about or attempt to understand the difficulties of their parents. But family records and correspondence show a steady pattern of the father's indifference to family responsibilities and the mother's slow but sure decline into a fantasy world of mental illness. Youngest daughter Dora died at seven months of age in Canada, shortly before the mother's institutionalization. It may, in fact, have been the death that drove her over the edge of mental illness, according to family correspondence.

The siblings were able to overcome their family problems and all managed to mature into productive adults. None, of course, found the financial or corporate success of Joe. Theodore had the most struggles with the family instability, but managed to overcome most of his difficulties even though alcohol and job changes plagued him through life.

A mixture of family heritage, personal friendships and politics played a role in the naming of the children. Eldest son Bart Ebert Bryan was named for the father Bartholomew with the middle name chosen from the maiden name of his mother, Caroline (Carrie) Ebert.

The small town of Elyria, Ohio, in Lorain County was a hotbed of partisan politics when Joe was born there while his father temporarily held onto a job in a bicycle factory. The town was renowned for what newspapers at the time called "good people, good schools and a large number of Republicans." It also had an intriguing history. The first permanent settlers arrived almost 100 years before Joe's birth in 1896, but as far back as 1787, attempts were made by Moravian missionaries and Christian Indians to establish a city. They were driven away by Delaware Indians who had previously settled there and it wasn't until 1807 that the first white citizens permanently located in the community.

Joe Bryan was named for two people: his paternal grandfather Joseph and the best known Republican at the time, President William McKinley. Grandfather Joseph Bryan fought for the U.S. Calvary in the Civil War against the southerners that his grandson would later join as a family member.

The Bryan family was made up of rock-ribbed Republicans who expressed ridicule and condemnation that the Democrats were foolish enough to nominate William Jennings Bryan as their choice for president. Fearing that someone in Elyria might think the family was even distantly connected to the Democratic nominee, Joe's parents chose McKinley for his middle name. That was a sure sign there were no ties to Bryan Democrats.

The irony in that is that Joe Bryan later became a staunch southern Democrat, both nationally and in his adopted state of North Carolina, at least until his former son-in-law Lauch Faircloth became a Republican and was elected a U. S. Senator in the early 1990s. Bryan was a delegate to several National Democratic Conventions where he became friendly with the Kennedys and other big-time party regulars, but he refused to attend any conventions after 1964, saying they were nothing but television productions with little value.

Son William was given a middle name of Haight in honor of a doctor friend in Mexico with whom Bartholomew and Caroline Bryan lived and worked as housekeepers before their first son was born.

Daughter Anne was named for her father's maiden sister who helped care for the child as an infant. Son Theodore was named for another Republican, Theodore Roosevelt. Dora, who died as an infant, was named for another spinster aunt who also helped raise the surviving children, both as infants and later after the mother's mental breakdown and the father's desertion.

Bartholomew Bryan, the father of the six children, was born in New York City in July 1869 to Joseph and Anne Henthorn Bryan, not long after his father completed his military service on behalf of the Union Army against the Confederates. Bartholomew was one of seven children fathered by Joseph, three by Jane Henthorn who died in her middle 30s and four by her sister Anne who became his second wife.

Grandfather Joseph Bryan, following his service in the military during the Civil War, had a career as an artist for the U. S. Treasury. He was also an amateur poet. Joseph Bryan and two of his brothers came to the United States by way of Liverpool, England from Dublin, Ireland prior to the Civil War. The family in Ireland had a wine and liquor import-export business. Not long after coming to his country, Joseph Bryan's two brothers drowned in a boating accident off the coast of Long Island. Shortly after the fatal accident that took the lives of his two brothers and unable to find work, Joseph volunteered for military service, as did his first son Lawrence. The father and son fought together for the Union cause.

Two daughters born to Joseph and Jane Bryan became Catholic nuns. The parents were devout Catholics and the mother raised her children in that faith in their native Ireland before coming to the United States. Joseph maintained that faith during his marriage to Jane. After her death, however, he left the Catholic faith in order to marry his late wife's younger sister Anne after he came to America in 1857. The Catholic Church in those days did not permit marriages to relatives of deceased spouses, so Joseph abandoned his Catholic beliefs, as did his second wife who raised their children as Protestants.

Three of the four children born to Joseph and Anne Bryan became successful, if not affluent. It was only Joe Bryan's father Bartholomew who was never able to settle down, as did his siblings. Son William Simon Bryan became a well known and highly respected physician who served as chief of staff at Staten Island Hospital and two daughters Anne and Dora became known as devoted church women and dedicated clerical workers with close ties to New York's society set. They repeatedly helped Bartholomew find work even as they constantly chided him to be a better provider for his children and ridiculed him when he didn't meet their expectations.

Bartholomew Bryan seemed to be a man of great vision, but he was never able to put down roots or establish himself in any profession for long periods of time, even when he was providing for his family before deserting them after his wife's mental illness. He worked for years for prosperous families at the Lorain Wheel Company in Ohio, which successfully manufactured bicycles and failed in an attempt to produce a line of automobiles. He was considered ingenious and creative although most of his ideas never came to fruition.

Bartholomew Bryan also had a penchant for stretching the truth about his successes and his personal background.

He repeatedly claimed, for example, that he was a graduate of the class of 1890 from Columbia University, a point that was included in his obituary notice 50 years later. According to records at Columbia, however, not only was he not a graduate of that class, he was not a graduate of any class from the university and never attended classes there.

It's unclear precisely why Bartholomew took his young bride Caroline to Mexico from Texas where he was working when they were married. Possibly it was because he was looking for a steady job that would provide security for his new family although, just as both before and after, that was not to be. His many jobs included mining, bicycle building, accounting, auto mechanics and steel industry construction.

It is clear, however, that his new bride wasn't happy in Mexico even though she was very much in love with her husband despite his vagabond ways. After being sent to Johnstown, Pa., to deliver her first born in May 1894, Carrie remained with her in-laws for the summer. But in a letter in September of that year to her husband's sister Annie, Carrie said she had advised her husband that she "could not consent to be separated from him another month" and she returned to live among what she called the "great thieves" of Mexican natives. By Joe's birth 18 months later in Ohio, Carrie wrote that she badly wanted to induce her husband to leave Mexico for good.

The family did return to the United States and settled in Johnstown for at least a short while when Bartholomew worked for a motor company. But the couple had no permanent address and lived in two different boarding houses while leaving their two sons back in Elyria with relatives.

As the family bounced among relatives and moved in and out of boarding houses for several years, Bartholomew continued his dreams of success in a series of jobs, none of which lasted. Young Joe, however, recalled those days with some sense of enjoyment in reminiscent interviews near the end of his own life. He recalled his father's limited security in bicycle manufacturing in Lorain, Ohio, his work as a accountant and his on-again, off-again jobs with the well-connected A.J. Moxham industrial family where Bartholomew's two spinster sisters worked in clerical jobs. It was the sisters' reputation for a good work ethic that got Bartholomew a paying job with the Moxhams. It was that that same connection that took the growing clan to Canada for two years before the ultimate collapse of the family unit with the mother's mental illness and the father's desertion.

"I was always my father's favorite," Bryan would later say of those earliest years in his memory. "He would often take long train trips and would take me along because he liked my companionship. Young Joe was considered the mascot for his father. On those trips, though, the elder Bryan and his buddies had a fondness for passing the bottle among them, a fact that young Joe watched and thought was worth discussing back home. He told his mother and his father's sisters of the drinking bouts of his dad on those trips.

"My dad boxed my ears for that," Joe recalled. "I didn't know my aunts were members of the Women's Christian Temperance Society and they didn't take to the drinking." He never told tales on his father after that.

It was young Joe's grandmother Anne Bryan who was the first disciplinarian in the Bryan household. Bartholomew seemed not to be overly interested in keeping the children in line, although he often complained that his wife wouldn't do it. "My grandmother Anne was the matriarch of the family," Bryan said in recalling his early years. "What she said was the law. When you were told what she felt and wanted, that was it." But the frequent relocation of the family and grandmother Anne's death in 1905 when Joe was 9 meant that she wasn't available for much discipline for long.

Joe Bryan grew up to become a distinguished and handsome gentleman with his custom-made clothes, white hair and British-looking mustache. But things were quite different as a child when he wore long curls and dresses, which were the order of the day for young boys of modest means, and he endured more than a little peer teasing for his appearance. "I was called names like Jo-Jo the dog faced boy," he recalled. "That got my rile up and I had a lot of fights. Unfortunately for me, I also had a lot of bloody noses because most of the boys were bigger and better fighters than I was. But I fought them anyway."

Life for the Bryans in Nova Scotia was tolerable, at least for the children, for the first year or so. But the father's tendency for flamboyancy and unrealistic dreams continued unabated even as the mother's emotional demise progressed. Bartholomew held a steady job with the Moxham family's steel mill and helped the Moxham's build a huge home — called the castle — but he couldn't resist the good life of showmanship. Even as the family struggled financially, Bartholomew spent his money on luxuries, first a small yacht called the "Schoboo" and then a schooner that brought the wrath of Carrie who criticized the purchases as overly expensive. Joe Bryan late in life recalled the fun trips on those two watercrafts, even as he admitted a deep fear of the dangers after witnessing an accident where several men lost their lives when their boat capsized. "My father always put me in the middle of the boat to help balance it," he said. "My mother said we couldn't afford boats, but my father bought them anyway. I didn't know what afford meant. But I just knew we didn't have much money."

The building of the Moxham castle was the highlight of Bartholomew Bryan's tenure with the steel industry job in Canada. The steel company job itself went well for awhile, but for Bartholomew it wasn't to last, partly he claimed at the time because of the mental condition of his wife. As a matter of fact, it is debatable whether Carrie's emotional state caused problems for her husband or if his inability to stick to regular work and his indifference to raising a family helped bring on her mental problems.

Bryan said in an interview late in his life that he never really understood his mother's mental illness, but was told by his father that having so many children in such a short time caused the problem.

The Moxham castle, however, was the talk of the town for most of the time the Bryans lived there. Arthur J. Moxham was highly regarded in Pennsylvania, Ohio and Alabama for his expertise in steel manufacturing in the latter half of the 1800s. Born in South Wales in 1854, he came to this country at age 15 and worked at an iron plant in Louisville, starting as a receiving clerk. At age 24, he designed, built and organized rolling mills in Birmingham, Ala.

He moved to Johnstown, Pa., in the 1870s and developed a new type of rail to be used for tramways and streetcars. When the devastating Johnstown Flood hit the community in 1889, it was Moxham who took charge and helped rescue survivors and restore order to the stricken city. He later moved to Lorain, Ohio in 1894 and opened another steel plant, the Lorain Steel Company. He had become prosperous enough to retire at age 45 in 1899. It was first in Johnstown and later in Lorain that Bartholomew Bryan's two spinster sisters Anne and Dora worked for Moxham and helped secure Bartholomew his first job in the steel factories.

Moxham, in retirement, sailed around the world in his yacht before stopping in New York where he was persuaded to move to Sydney, Nova Scotia by Henry Melville Whitney, a friend who was previously president of the Boston West End Electric Railway system. There was money to be made in steel in Nova Scotia, Whitney convinced Moxham. The two became partners in a new steel manufacturing plant there.

Moxham, his wife, two sons and two daughters moved to Sydney, but only over the strenuous objections of Mrs. Moxham who was not happy to leave behind her enormous house that reportedly cost her husband $350,000 to build in Lorain in 1893.

To pacify his unhappy spouse, Moxham agreed to duplicate the mansion in Sydney in a project that became known as the Moxham "castle" with Bartholomew Bryan as a member of the construction crew as well as a worker in the steel plant.

The Bryans moved to Sydney in 1900, closely following the Moxham family there, and lived in a rented farmhouse.

The Moxham house in Lorain was a replica of a Scottish clan castle. It had four floors, a swimming pool in the basement, an auditorium and stage on the top floor, ebony and mahogany woodwork and Italian marble interior trimming. The reception hall had a 45-foot ceiling, flanked by a circular staircase with a balcony on each floor.

When Mrs. Moxham lamented that she couldn't bear to leave the Lorain home behind, her husband said not to worry, they'd just take the house to Sydney. In effect, that's what they did. Only the shell of the home was left behind. All interior decorations, paneling, furnishings and amenities were removed, shipped to Sydney and reinstalled in a stone shell duplicating the Ohio home.

Things didn't go well for long with the Sydney steel plant, however, and Bartholomew Bryan made it known to his spinster sisters, who had by then moved to New Jersey, that his job as well as his family situation was not secure. After the plant's failure in the early 1900s, the Moxham family had to vacate the castle that stood vacant for years and was later used by the U.S. Army as a military hospital in World War II. After the war, the home fell into disrepair before the Cape Breton Arts Council began a failed effort to restore it to its original grandeur. The home was destroyed by fire in 1966.

While Bartholomew Bryan worked in the Moxham steel factory and on the castle, young Joe enjoyed a life of fun and games, but not always safe ones. He learned lacrosse and played with the native Indians who lived nearby. He was warned not to cross the railway tracks to where the Indians lived, but that didn't deter him. He played contact sports without a helmet and often wound up battered and bloody from the contests.

He also picked up diseases from the native Indians and transmitted both measles and scarlet fever to his siblings. Smallpox also was common in the area where they lived. "We were always told to stay away from homes with red flags in the windows, because that meant families living there carried the smallpox virus," Bryan said in a 1992 interview about his early life.

As a youngster, Bryan was not the docile child his parents might have preferred. He was, in fact, something of a problem for his parents, based on his father's letters to sisters Anne and Dora. Shortly after moving the family to Nova Scotia, Bartholomew wrote that Joe was becoming overly wild, even as a four-year-old. "I wish Ebert (the oldest son) would swat Joe a good one when that young tyrant become so domineering." In some respects, those early signs of aggressiveness were a trait Joe Bryan carried through his business life.

Two years later, in December 1902, Bryan's dad expressed even more concerns about his son, then six years old, whom he called overly troublesome. "I am very much worried about Joe," Bartholomew wrote his sisters. "He is on the street all the time and is getting pretty rough. Carrie has no control over him and doesn't seem to care. He goes to school when it suits him and does about as he pleases. He is not intentionally bad, but has all together too much run for a child his age." There was nothing in the letter to indicate that the father had attempted to reign in the lad.

Disciplining young Joe, however, was among the least of the

Joseph M. Bryan, at age 5, in 1901.

in dad's worries at the turn of the century. Following the birth of son Theodore and daughter Dora in Sydney, the family's situation turned sour rather quickly. Dora was ill almost from the day of her birth and died after a seven-month struggle, leaving the parents with five children, little hope for continued employment and Carrie's slow but sure slippage into despondency from which she would never recover.

Bartholomew wrote his sisters anguished letters outlining the dismal plight of the family situation.

Within six months of young Dora's death, a letter from Bartholomew to his sisters lamented Carrie's deteriorating mental state. "Carrie is very bad and I cannot say what the result will be," he wrote. "I'd like to find a suitable sanitarium (for her) and then we could study calmly the best disposition of the children. A sanitarium in the United States is the only hope unless I put her in an asylum here."

A week later, he wrote that things were even worse because his job was evaporating. "I have made up my mind to leave Nova Scotia because the company can't hold out much longer," he wrote. "The newspapers say times are not very prosperous in the United States and I am somewhat anxious about the future. But I can sell newspapers if the worst comes or I just might go to sea." Then he dropped a hint of needing financial help from his sisters. "I won't draw on your money unless it is absolutely necessary."

The family left Canada on Nov. 16, 1903 and lived for awhile at the home of the two sisters at Avon-by-the-Sea, NJ. The family's troubles continued to multiply.

Back in the United States, Bartholomew Bryan quickly gave up on finding any medical cure for his wife and placed her in Greystone Park Hospital, a state-run institution for the mentally in Parsippany-Troy, NJ, just outside Newark. She would remain there as a ward of the state for more than half a century until her death on May 1, 1954. There is no record that her husband ever visited her the mental hospital. Death was listed as chronic degeneration of the myocardium with an aggravating circumstance increasing dementia of the hebephrenic (child-like delusions and hallucinations) type. She is buried in a nearby cemetery.

Mrs. Bryan's mental condition and her hospitalization brought shame and embarrassment to Bartholomew's sisters. They blamed her illness on a character flaw. The illness was a fact the sisters tried to keep secret when Bryan the children were small and one they didn't openly discuss later in life. That may have been one reason Bryan never discussed the topic. He may have been following the lead of his aunts, either thinking they were right or merely honoring their request for silence.

Once Mrs. Bryan was confined to the mental hospital and the five surviving children were dropped with the two spinster sisters Anne and Dora Bryan, Bartholomew hit the road again, leaving his entire family behind. He said he was going to Chicago to find work and wouldn't be able to offer any care for his children.

Family records show that Bartholomew returned to his sisters for brief visits periodically over the next several years, but never to stay and seldom offered any financial support for his children and none for his wife. His two sisters repeatedly hounded him about that seeming indifference, but to no avail. "They tried to get him to assume his responsibilities of raising the children," Joe Bryan said during a June 1992 interview about the family circumstances at the time. During one brief foray to his sisters, Bartholomew took young Joe to live in a boarding house and would infrequently take his other children, one at a time, to live with him. But none of the stays with the father lasted long. "He always favored me," Bryan said of his dad, "But things never worked out. He deserted me several times."

Young Joe's aunts couldn't handle five youngsters in their home. Joe was once sent to live in an orphanage that he later said was "a terrible place" because of the squalor and abuse by those who ran the facility. Another time he was sent by his aunts to live in another boarding house with a stranger, a janitor who paid the lad 10 cents an hour to help sweep floors and empty trash cans. It was not a pleasant existence.

Bryan's sister Anne Bryan Stoute explained the family's early plight in an undated letter to Ted Bryan Ely Sr.'s wife after Anne married and moved to Barbados. "My mother lived in a sanitarium in New Jersey in a beautiful imaginary world, hopelessly insane. She first exhibited signs of her disorder right after Ted was born. We were taken in by the Moxhams for several weeks (after Ted was born), but when we returned our mother was different and during the next year things got into a dreadful state. Dad changed from a devoted father into a tyrannical stranger whom mother seemed to fear.

"She became more difficult after the next child (Dora) was born and when the baby died she went completely to pieces. Dad quit his job and brought us all to the sisters in New Jersey. They were most unsympathetic. Dad quarreled with them and left in a rage. We (children) were parceled out to relatives and were never allowed to forget that we were poor relations.

"Meanwhile, dad secretly remarried and dropped out of sight to escape our unkind aunts. Bart (brother) and I went to see mother about 12 years ago. She knew us but was not interested in us as grown-ups. She had no interest in reality. Mrs. Ely (who took the young Bryan sibling into her own home) was confused (about our backgrounds) because the aunts probably never told her much. Their attitude about mother was that the symptoms of her disease were defects of character. There is nothing in Ted's background to be worried about. We are all respectable citizens. Ted had always been on our minds as the little lost brother whom we love. For years, the aunts never told us where he was."

While the times away from the aunts for young Joe and his siblings were temporary as well as disquieting, the trauma of his kid brother Theodore was permanent. The aunts handed over Theodore, at age four, to a childless woman acquaintance who had been recommended by the Moxham family from Nova Scotia. The woman, Mrs. John Ely, was the eccentric widow of a doctor who had earlier been killed on a horseback riding accident. Mrs. Ely had heard the two aunts were having trouble with handling so many children, told the aunts she felt Theodore was the cutest of the bunch and offered to take him because she had always wanted a little boy. Mrs. Ely, well to do by standards of the time, raised Theodore in her home with nannies, but did not legally adopt him until he was 22 years old when she changed his name from Bryan to Ely.

From the time Theodore was turned over to Mrs. Ely in 1903 until the middle 1980s, Joe Bryan had no knowledge of the status or location of his younger brother who died of a heart attack on October 18, 1968. Bryan learned of his brother's death only after discovering with the assistance of a professional researcher in 1986 that Theodore had a son. Bryan and the son, Ted Ely Jr., would later meet, in February 1987 in Bryan's office in a scheduled formal appointment, eight years before Bryan's death.

Bryan became interested in his own family background in 1982 and hired a graduate student genealogist and archivist to trace his family's roots. That's how he learned about his brother's death and the existence of his brother's son and made contact through the archivist.

"My dad did not often talk about his Bryan heritage," Ted Ely Jr. said of his father in a 1986 letter to Bryan archivist Gary Parks and his Uncle Joe after he received a letter from Parks and first learned that he had an uncle in Greensboro. "I am anxious to learn more about our family and my uncle," Ely Jr. wrote. "My father was a wonderful person, but in his adult life he was bedeviled by his two-family background."

Ely Jr. said in a 1999 interview his father was never quite able to

31

overcome the family split, but that there was little talk of it at home. "He never talked about his feelings much," Ely Jr. said. "After my mother died in 1946, there was no more correspondence at our house from anyone on the Bryan side of the family. My dad just said we should enjoy life as a family because it was a life he never had growing up. He always resented the fact that he was the one (in the family) who was split off from the other children. It always haunted him that he was the one given away. About all I knew of his background (until the middle 1980s) was that his original name was Bryan and that he had a lonely childhood.

"He was a good man, but he had a lot of similarities with his own father in difficulties holding down jobs and fighting alcoholism. But I was delighted to meet my Uncle Joe and learn more about my early family. Uncle Joe had a striking resemblance to my father. He talked with me about his humble beginnings and the troubles within the family. He talked about living in Canada and the tough times and his father leaving the family. He said his father had great visions, but could never stick with anything long. But never talked about his mother, never. Maybe he was embarrassed over his mother's condition, but he never mentioned her to me. Coming into the Price family as he did, he was reluctant to talk about his own early family life although I think he was proud for having overcome it. Kay (Bryan's daughter) has told me she was curious of the circumstances of his family, but he was never a great communicator with his own children and didn't talk about his early life with them. He was proud to have succeeded because he had the determination to do it. He always tried to look at the positives and not the negatives of his life. He told me that once he got to North Carolina, he was careful what he said about his past."

Ely Jr. has continued a friendship with Bryan's daughter Kay Edwards since Bryan's death. He visits Edwards each year.

Once Bartholomew Bryan confined his ill wife to the mental hospital, family records show she was no longer considered a viable

Theodore Bryan Ely Sr., Joseph M. Bryan's younger brother, who was given away by his spinster aunts after Bryan's father deserted the family. Ted was raised by widow Mrs. John Ely, who took him in because she said she always wanted a little boy and he was the cutest of the Bryan siblings.

part of the family. Seldom was she even discussed among relatives, and only then within the immediate family, based on detailed family correspondence. Joe's father evidently gave up on both his wife and family following his infrequent trips to see the children in the months after returning from Nova Scotia, and he left for good. There is nothing in family records to indicate that he ever helped on any regular basis with financial support for either his wife or children after he deserted the family. Family records do, however, show that aunts Dora and Annie constantly berated Bartholomew for not showing care and support for his family. They also blamed him for his wife's mental illness, suggesting that it was his fault for marrying someone of less status who allowed herself to become ill because of her own family heritage. In effect, the aunts said, Bartholomew had married beneath himself and he was to blame for the family's instability.

It was not until 1937, more than 30 years after deserting his family that Joe Bryan's father sought any form of forgiveness for his actions, but then in writing through only one of his children. On December 18, 1937, the father wrote a letter to his son Ted who was then married and in his late 30s. So far as is known, the father never sought to make amends or explain his actions to his other children.

"This is hard for me to do after so many years of seeming neglect," Bartholomew wrote to Ted. "For that neglect, I humbly ask that you will forgive me, even though I do not appear to deserve it. There is nothing to be gained by rehashing the cause of my apparent desertion of you but I want you to think of me as kindly as you can because my time on this earth is drawing to a close. I would like very much to be at peace with my family before leaving for the Promised Land."

That letter was written after the father had suffered a stroke that left him partly paralyzed. "You were a lovely little boy and as cute as could be and all these years you have been on my mind," the father wrote his son. Then, perhaps out of guilt from his own more than 30 years of indifference and lack of concern, Bartholomew Bryan offered some ironic advice to his long-lost son. "Stick to your relatives and your family. Write to them as often as you can and don't let anything come between you and your family. I regret I won't be able to give you anything for Christmas but a card, but with this letter I want to send you my love that you have been cheated out of for all these years."

Ted Ely replied to his father's letter with a telegram, but the contents of that reply no longer exist. The father and son had no further correspondence, according to family records. Bartholomew died 22 months later, October 16, 1939.

It was not until 1914 that young Joe received his first structured form of education — for one year — beyond his somewhat sporadic attendance at grammar schools and high school during the years of the family's frequent moves and his parents' instability.

At one point as a child, he was sent to reside with a family in Framingham, Massachusetts where he attended grammar and high school. He received a diploma from Franklin Grammar School in Framingham in the spring of 1910, one of 131 students to complete grammar courses from four schools in the city. He also attended high school for two years while living in Framingham and earning his own support by performing custodial chores. At age 16, he dropped out of high school to begin full-time work as his soul means of support. He never received a high school diploma.

After two years of struggling to find jobs to buy food and clothes, Joe returned to the homes his aunts in New Jersey and his physician uncle in New York City and sought their help in securing more schooling. The relatives agreed to support him for one year at a private boarding school in exchange for a promise to dedicate himself to serious studies.

In requesting that Bryan be allowed to attend the private school, his aunt wrote the school that he had the desire to improve himself, but needed help because of a shortage of funds. "He had two years of high school, but then had to go to work," his Aunt Annie wrote the school. "His father, my brother, is not in a position to help his son, I'm sorry to say, and his mother is in a sanitarium. My nephew has got to make it on his own in the world, but he is anxious to go on with his education if you can help."

Bryan also wrote the school pleading for acceptance. "My purpose in life is to use my education to the best of my ability and in the right way so that I can become worthwhile in some occupation."

At age 18, a determined Joe Bryan enrolled at prestigious Mount Hermon School in Northfield, Ma. He did well there, was content with his progress and planned to remain to complete the required courses. But it wasn't to be in what was yet another disappointment for the young man who so much wanted to put his heartbreaking past behind. After one year, his aunts and uncle declined to make further payments. Joe Bryan's formal education was over.

Bryan's correspondence with his aunts concerning his opportunity to attend Mount Hermon shows he was elated, but that he had a constant struggle to pay his bills once he got there. "You asked if I would like to go there," Bryan wrote from Framingham where he was working as a laborer. "I would like to go any place where I could improve my education. I'm very glad to get the chance." He enrolled at Mount Hermon in the spring of 1914.

At the school, Bryan tolerated what he called "a lazy" roommate and a long list of boring sermons along with his financial problems. In November 1914, Bryan wrote his aunts that he needed money. "Even though my hospital bill was only 50 cents, I found myself unprepared to pay it," he wrote." Also, my last chemistry bill which is only $2 has not been paid." A month later, he wrote that he would eventually need another pair of shoes. "I have only the heavy ones you sent, but I don't need a second pair right away. The one pair I have will do for awhile."

Caroline (Carrie) Ebert Bryan, mother of Joseph M. Bryan, who lived 52 years in a mental institution in New Jersey after Bryan's father deserted his family.

Despite his lack of formal schooling — or perhaps because of it — education would become one of his prime interests in later life. Thousands of students from elementary school through university levels have and continue to benefit from his generosity in the area of academic excellence.

Bryan's generosity toward and his interest in higher education during his corporate years and after retirement resulted in his being awarded six honorary doctorate degrees from college and university campuses.

Bryan never talked about his lack of formal educational training or the turmoil within his family until the last decades of his own long life. It was one of his many secrets for a long time, but one he overcame through sheer determination to succeed. One reason he never talked about his early childhood and teenage burdens, according to a few select friends in whom he confided late in life, was that he didn't want anyone feeling sorry for him. "He didn't want people saying 'Oh, poor Joe' and he didn't want sympathy," his friend Greta Medlin offered as a way of explanation. "He just wanted to get things done, to help people accomplish things, through his giving, for themselves based on their own talents and merits just as he had done."

For Joe Bryan, obviously that strategy worked. And quite well, too.

Bartholomew Bryan, father of Joseph M. Bryan, in 1936, three years before his death in Florida, where he lived after deserting his family more than 30 years earlier.

3

BREAKING THE CHAINS

Being accepted at Mount Hermon Preparatory School in Massachusetts in the spring of 1914 was for Joe Bryan the first of many positive turning points in a life that was so overburdened as a teenager. With his father's visions and promises of caring for his children far surpassing even anything close to reality and his mother's mental illness diagnosed as incurable, Bryan initially had little hope as a young man of becoming successful.

But he didn't seek self-pity or blame anyone. Rather, he showed his true grit by proving the worth of self-determination and just plain gut instinct to make something of himself

Given the family circumstances, Bryan could easily have drifted into an unproductive life, or worse. He could have found plenty of excuses. But that wasn't his style. He dedicated himself to succeed, to make the best of what little he had and to prove to those who doubted his ability that ingenuity and courage could win out over temporary hardships and shortage of immediate resources.

"I realized I didn't have a very good education," Bryan said in a late-life interview of his teenage years of constant moves across the northeastern part of the United States and Canada and his early indifference to attending classes. He dedicated himself to self-improvement.

In April 1914, Bryan enrolled at Mount Hermon in Northfield, Mass., to begin what was his first real break from the entanglements of his family life. While he would continue to maintain familial ties in later life, this was his first chance to prove he could compete on his own. It was, he would later say, a wonderful lesson in self-discipline and self-esteem.

The cost of tuition for the year was $70, payable in four installments. It included classroom costs, food and lodging, laundry and gym classes. On the application from his two aunts was the hope that the school would provide him a purpose in life. He appeared, the application specified, to be anxious to grow up and become a good and useful person and had shown ample energy, self-reliance and courage to succeed. Among his "bad habits" was listed his use of tobacco, but his paperwork showed he had promised to refrain from smoking once he enrolled. That's a promise he did not keep once he left the school. While never a heavy smoker, he was a regular user of Winston cigarettes even into his early retirement years before giving up the habit late in life.

His Aunt Annie wrote on his Mount Hermon application along with the first payment from his uncle that finding tuition was no easy task because of his absentee father. "But we expect him to turn out well," she wrote.

Young Joe was accepted along with his initial tuition payment on the recommendation of a family friend who taught there, but a bureaucratic glitch almost caused his rejection. The aunts forgot to send the required $5 enrollment fee, a fact that the stern school principal duly noted and insisted be sent promptly.

"I felt happy there," Bryan would later say of his experiences at the school where most of the students were significantly more financially stable than he. But he proved in one semester that he had what it took to compete both inside and outside the classroom.

Academically, he excelled rather quickly. The lack of discipline and instability within the family in his earlier years didn't seem a hindrance. Indeed, that may have given him increased determination. His highest grade was in Bible studies where he scored an E for excellent. He received a G for good in geometry and French, an M for medium in English and chemistry, a P for passing in history and was graded satisfactory in personal conduct.

He had hopes of joining the Mount Hermon football team, but he tipped the scales at only 132 pounds and was far outweighed by virtually every other team member. "The coach quite properly said that I was not rough or tough enough to compete at football, so he advised me to switch to the track team," Bryan explained in a 1992 interview. He succeeded in that endeavor and became a long distance runner on the track team.

As a student, Bryan kept his aunts informed of his progress and needs, in addition to his academic grades, with regular "Dear Aunties" letters. Initially, he just signed his letters with "your nephew," but switched to "affectionately yours" after they sent him some money when he notified them he was out of funds and may have to return home even though he had offered to work on campus for tuition.

But finances continued to be a problem, as were, in his view, some of the meals and the required, overly long Sunday night religious services. While his grades in Bible studies remained high, his interest in the sermonizing of vespers speakers didn't last. "We had a fairly poor sermon today," Bryan wrote his aunts on August 30, 1914. "The preacher gave the usual sermon on being good, which took about two hours." He frequently wrote his aunts about ministers talking "overtime".

The lack of interest in regular church attendance and sermons remained with Bryan through his life. He was never a regular worshipper at any church. Lack of dorm heat at Mount Hermon was an inconvenience, too, and in one correspondence Bryan asked his aunts to please send an extra suit of long underwear. "Please don't forget to sens the underwear," he pleaded in one letter. The aunts sent the underwear, along with a Bible. He responded that he was "proud" of owning both, but the underwear apparently offered more immediate warmth to the body than the biblical words did to the soul.

Bryan liked the Saturday night chicken dinners, but never learned to appreciate the Sunday night regular fare of baked beans. "Feast before famine," he wrote of the menu of chicken before beans.

Bryan occasionally went to Boston to see the Red Sox play at Fenway Park when he could scrape up enough cash, which wasn't often. He later said he made that trip only when he could save enough change for the train ride, game ticket and hot dog. Once when he became ill at Mount Hermon, he had to borrow 50 cents from a classmate to cover his medical bill until his aunts sent reimbursement.

Good times and good grades aside, however, Bryan was forced to leave Mount Hermon after his first year. There was no money for another term. His aunts said they didn't have tuition and his uncle, the doctor, concluded that one-year of formal education there was enough. Instead of more tuition, Dr. Bryan offered his nephew a place in his home on Staten Island. Bryan lived there for almost two years, watching his uncle perform surgery, driving his uncle to treat patients in their homes and dreaming of one day becoming a doctor himself, despite his lack of former education or medical training.

He had earlier given passing thought to becoming a journalist because he had both enjoyed and done well in English courses at Mount Hermon and in earlier grammar school. "I had thought of becoming an editorial writer," Bryan told a friend. "That meant I could have pontificated all I wanted." As a student of history during his two years of high school, Bryan researched and wrote an essay on the need to change the form of city government in one Massachusetts town. The local newspaper printed his essay and the city leaders accepted his ideas on streamlining the government.

Bryan abandoned his plans for journalism when he moved in with his uncle. "I thought being a doctor would be a good profession," Bryan later explained. But that would have required far more educational training than he could afford or that his uncle was willing to finance.

Bryan also worked one summer following his year at Mount Hermon as a farm laborer for $20 a month and free lodging. But that manual labor and repeatedly watching his uncle perform surgery wasn't satisfying enough for someone as filled with the ambition and desire to improve himself as the just turned 20-year-old Bryan was. He wanted more freedom, more challenges and more chances to prove his mettle.

In the spring of 1917, Bryan volunteered for the Naval Reserves, but was rejected for what naval officers said was a physical disability that was never explained. Bryan didn't let that rejection deter him. He then volunteered for the U. S. Army Infantry Officers Reserve Corps, fibbing on his application by saying he had completed four years of high school and two years at Mount Hermon and listing his occupation as a clerk for an insurance company. The Army obviously wasn't as particular about his background or his physical condition as the Navy and on June 19, 1917 Bryan became a private in the medical section of the U. S. Army Expeditionary Forces.

After his initial World War I training, Bryan was shipped to France and promptly promoted to the rank of sergeant. "I asked them why I was given that rank," he later explained with a touch of good humor, "and they told me it was because I had a loud voice." Whether for that reason or another, Bryan took on the duties of a medical staff sergeant. He was never an active participant in direct combat, but the Army took advantage of his superficial knowledge of an operating room from working with his physician uncle. He

44

spent most of the next 18 months seeing the ravages of war while helping treat wounded soldiers brought in from battle. "I was never personally involved in the killings or agonizing gas attacks, but I was involved in seeing the effects on soldiers who had been exposed to the nerve gas," he would later explain. "A lot of them died, including replacement draftees."

Bryan came home from the war in May 1919 and was discharged at Camp Dixon on Long Island. The Mount Hermon disciplinary training and the military experience, he felt, had made him a man, ready to plunge headlong into life and a career. He started his foray into the business on the very day he was released from the military before he ever reached the home of his uncle the doctor on Staten Island.

That was the end of his military career, but not the end of his involvement with what many would call further wars, first in business and later regrettably within his own family at home.

On his way to his uncle's home on the day of his release from the Army, Bryan was hired by George H. McFadden Brothers, a New York cotton and coffee brokerage company at a starting salary of $12.50 week. He used the friendship of his physician uncle with one of the McFadden officers as leverage to secure the job interview and was hired on the spot. As paltry as that beginning pay may was, it was more money that he had ever made on a regular basis.

The young broker obviously worked hard, learned quickly and convinced his supervisors that he was ready for greater responsibilities. Six months into the job of commodity trading, Bryan was asked to accept an assignment that was both financially significant for the company and also fraught with significant personal danger.

At the end of 1919, McFadden transferred Bryan from the relatively comfortable confines of a New York office to the hazardous streets of Haiti, an unstable country engaged in a bloody civil war and where routine human slaughter was accepted as the price of running the government.

The excitement of a new company responsibility outweighed the risk of personal harm for Bryan who was determined to prove his worth in Haiti just as in New York. "I was willing to travel anywhere and have the chance to accomplish something good," Bryan said in a 1992 interview about his move to Haiti. "The company had clients with barrels of money and they needed somebody to find out what was happening down there." One of his tasks was to roll bundles of $20,000 in McFadden customer funds to leave with factors to buy and sell commodities and to ensure the money was handled properly amid the corruption and bloodshed among government officials and warring factions of the citizenry. He was constantly armed and often in danger.

Bryan lived among the violence in Haiti for two years, residing in Port-au-Prince where he shared a house with two other bachelors, one a British accountant and the other a man who regularly had trouble securing work because he was suffering from malaria. Bryan carried a handgun for self-protection against thugs and robbers during his stay in the country. The government was in constant upheaval throughout his time there and during one four-week period the country passed through four different presidents, one who was decapitated and his head hung on a spike for public display.

Bryan's letters from Haiti to his two aunts paint vivid pictures of the deplorable and often dangerous conditions in the country. "The average native here is a poor, shiftless, ragged, barefooted and starved individual who has little to recommend him for employment or anything else that is worthwhile," he wrote in December 1919. "They have a hand to mouth existence. They even have to be compelled under penalty of confinement to observe even the simplest rules of hygiene.

"The natives are Negroes who have been brought over from Africa by the French. They have revolted and the country has been at the mercy of petty graft, revolution, disease and all that goes with it. One president after another has been shot. The country is over-

Joseph M. Bryan at age 25 in Haiti, while working as a commodities broker in 1919 following military service in World War I. Note the firearm, which he wore for protection against bandits, on his right side.

run by bandits who prey on and steal from the natives. When the bandits are not stealing, they are shooting and burning or doing all three."

Amidst all that, Bryan was a risk-taker while living in Haiti. On one occasion he bucked the advice of friends and trudged up the side of a mountain where bandits made their homes. It was dangerous, he later conceded, but he wanted to prove he could do it safely and thought he would be the first man to reach the top. When he reached the peak, he found cigarette butts and wrapping, proving he was not the first person there. "That just proved to me that no matter how far out front of everybody you think you are, or how much better you think you are, there is usually someone else ahead of you," Bryan told a friend late in life. It is a lesson, he said, that he never forgot.

Twenty-four months in Haiti were enough for Bryan who saw little job security in continuing to work in a country so divided and so corrupt. In 1921 at his request, he returned to New York to continue his duties for another two years with the McFadden brokerage house.

But he still wasn't satisfied and was growing increasingly anxious for more financial security and a more challenging job. Using his training and knowledge of commodities trading from the McFadden Company, Bryan applied to become the youngest member ever chosen for a seat on the New York Cotton Exchange, the commodities equivalent of the better-known stock exchange. He had help there, too, and used the recommendation of a friend of his physician uncle to secure the application. The only problem was that the seat on the exchange required up-front money because cotton exchange members had to purchase slots for an opportunity to sell. And Bryan had no money to buy the seat.

Once more, he turned to his uncle, the doctor, for help, just as he had done a decade earlier when he needed financial assistance to enroll at Mount Hermon School. Dr. Bryan was willing to help, but not to offer any handouts. He agreed to provide the necessary

$27,000 as a loan at 6 per cent interest — a staggering amount of debt for the would-be broker — but only on condition that his nephew agree to make monthly payments to repay the debt principal plus interest. "He wanted to make sure that other members of the family didn't think I was getting special treatment," Bryan said of the loan. Bryan made regular payments, but missed a few over the ensuing years during slow selling periods following the economic collapse in 1929 and still owed part of the debt when he married, resigned from the exchange and moved South eight years after the debt was incurred.

When Dr. Bryan died in 1932, the year after Bryan moved from New York, he left $5,000 in his will for each of his nieces and nephews, but stipulated that if any of his nephew's original loan was still unpaid, that amount should be deducted from his inheritance. And that was done.

It was in late 1923, at age 29, that Bryan became a member of the Cotton Exchange, the youngest person ever selected. It was a tough assignment, requiring diligence and determination to compete for sales commissions against more seasoned and more experienced brokers, some with cutthroat attitudes. Competition was stiff and colleagues or competitors cut Bryan no slack. In one day of furious trading, he was accidentally — at least he always assumed it was an accident — jabbed in the hand with a sharp pencil by another trader. He didn't take the time to get the wound treated for fear of losing some trading income. The lack of medical care left him with the stab mark on his right hand that he carried to his grave.

In some trading transactions, the bidding was so close and furious that brokers determined winners and losers with a flip of a coin. Throughout his tenure as an exchange broker, Bryan used what he called his lucky silver dollar to determine winning bidders when a coin toss was needed. The coin was minted in San Francisco in 1923, the year he joined the commodity exchange. He carried that coin, constantly rubbing it in his pocket, for the remainder of his life; it was worn thin at his death in 1995 after more than 70 years of use.

While working in the fast-paced cotton brokerage trading and joining the social scene in Manhattan during the roaring middle 1920s, Bryan met two native North Carolinians who would become lifetime friends who would have impacts on his future in ways far beyond what he anticipated at the time. Without the first of those two meetings, Bryan might never have come to Greensboro. Without the other, broadcast journalism in this state would be considerably different.

One acquaintance was Eli Springs, a member of a prominent Carolina family, who was first a Bryan colleague on the cotton exchange and later became a member of the New York Stock Exchange. It was Springs who arranged the meeting of Bryan and his future wife Kathleen Price.

The other was William C. (Billy) Carmichael, a native of Durham who had moved to New York in the early 1920s to open his own investment company. Carmichael would later become a top official at his alma mater, UNC-Chapel Hill. It was Bryan and Carmichael who, with able assistance from the public relations skills of renowned band leader Kaye Kyser, led the way to creation of public television in North Carolina.

As a cotton broker, Bryan was readily successful, at least until the Crash of 1929. Compared to his modest upbringing, he felt he was quite prosperous and began to mesh with the society clientele of the city. Long before he met his future wife with her high interests in the New York social scene, dinners, parties and society gatherings became routine for Bryan as he met increasing numbers of influential people, both on and off the cotton exchange floor.

That's how he became a guest in the spring of 1927 at the North Carolina Society dinner and dance when the striking Kathleen Price of Greensboro arrived with her mother Ethel and her hometown date Ben Cone. He went to the dance with his friend Eli Springs, but Billy Carmichael was also there.

Springs, who was at the time was participating in his own long distance romance with a bright and energetic young woman named Katherine Wooten in Charlotte, asked his pal Bryan to attend the society dance in hopes he would make some new friends among the Tar Heels there. Little did either of them know just how fortuitous that invitation would become or the lasting significance it would have on the history of North Carolina in general and Greensboro in particular.

That arguably may well have been the most meaningful North Carolina Society dance ever. It surely was for Joe Bryan and Kathleen Price.

4

THE SOUTHERN SHIFT

The spring of 1927 brought with it the impending signs of economic trouble both on Wall Street and across the country. But the truly rich didn't seem overly worried. They could afford a dip or two because they were riding along so comfortably and things were going so smoothly following the temporary perils of World War I. Worry, the rich felt, could always come later, if needed.

After all, Herbert C. Hoover, a millionaire Republican businessman who had succeeded in the corporate world as well as earlier in public service, was in the White House. His credentials were impeccable compared to his predecessor Warren G. Harding and the world of high finance in New York was eminently more satisfied with Hoover at the helm than what was perceived as his dreaded Democratic Catholic opponent Alfred E. Smith.

Manhattan brokers Joseph McKinley Bryan and Eli Springs certainly felt few immediate worries, political or economic, because business was good. Springs never changed his mind about the merits of Republicans and, in fact, split politically from his friend Bryan following the administration of Franklin D. Roosevelt. Bryan would later become a Roosevelt-style Democrat at least through the John Kennedy-Lyndon Johnson years. But in early 1927, politics and potential economic doomsday were not uppermost on Bryan's mind. Love was. The same was true for Springs.

Bryan and Springs each worked hard for their respective brokerage exchanges, and divided their free time initially among the golf courses of New York and then increasingly in the golf-rich area of Southern Pines, North Carolina. That gave them excuses to make desired trips to Greensboro and Charlotte to see the women whom they had grown to love and who in the fall of that year, only three weeks apart, would become their wives for life. Bryan and Springs were groomsmen in each other's wedding.

The Bryans were married on November 19, 1927 and the Springs on December 10. The Bryans, in fact, cut short their honeymoon at the Homestead Resort in Hot Springs, Va. in order to be a part of the Springs gala event, bringing along a case of quality champagne to add to the celebration. Both weddings were society events that would be long remembered for their elegance and style.

The Bryan wedding was an evening gala in the King Cotton Hotel in downtown Greensboro. Because Bryan was not Catholic as was his bride, the couple could not be married in a Catholic Church, but the Right Rev. Vincent Taylor of Belmont Abbey officiated. The newspaper story of the wedding gushed with praise of the elegance of the occasion, running on for more than a column and half of narrative plus a two-column photograph. The bride's father owned the newspaper at the time. The story of the wedding called the event one of interest throughout the south and east.

The bride was characterized as a "striking brunette, beautiful in her wedding gown, an imported model of ivory transparent velvet over gold lame cloth, fashioned surplice style. Her veil was of ivory tulle with a close fitting cap of rose point lace, cascading down to the shoulders, entwined with gold threads over a panel of the lace. She wore ivory moire slippers with gold kid trimmings."

53

The wedding story called the bride "one of the most popular members of society in this city — whose charming manner and pleasant personality have won her many friends throughout the south and east" who would miss her once she moved to New York with her new husband.

Not only was the Bryan wedding big news in Greensboro, they made the newspapers in Virginia on their honeymoon. *The Homestead News* described the couple in detail as they moved along the walking trails and sipped tea in the Great Hall at the resort in the afternoons.

The bride was described as a direct descendent of the "illustrious French family, Marquis Picot de Boisfieullet, as well as the noted families of Chief Justice Marshall and Henry Clay" and as an alumnus of Notre Dame College in Baltimore and Converse College in South Carolina. She did attend both those schools, but never graduated from either, although both later awarded her honorary degrees. Mrs. Bryan's family history shows her ancestor Henry Clay was, in fact, not the famous governmental leader and orator, but a different person of the same name.

During their whirlwind romance of 1927, the Bryan and Springs couples were in frequent company of each other, sometimes when the beaus were visiting their girlfriends in North Carolina and other times when the women would visit New York. "We would get together when we could," Springs' widow Katherine said of the early meetings. "We all became very fond of each other. I always thought Joe was a remarkable young man and Kathleen had a lot of class. Joe was always the life of every party."

The closeness of the two couples was reason enough for the Bryans to cut short their honeymoon to participate in the Springs wedding in Charlotte where it is clear that good times and partying were both frequent and heavy. It was a touch of too much partying for Bryan that caused a temporary embarrassment at the Springs wedding, and later became a laughable and long-lasting memory.

Kathleen Price Bryan on her wedding day, November 19, 1927.

An hour before the announced time of the Springs wedding, the beaming bridegroom Eli realized his best man was in what has since euphemistically become known as "poor condition" because of over indulgence in strong drink. In other words, he was intoxicated. Springs poured his wedding attendant into his car, drove him to the country club for a cold shower and helped him get dressed.

Returning to the church, Springs was chagrined to notice dozens of friends gathering outside with no sign of ushers to lead them into the sanctuary. Dropping off his best man, who was by then somewhat sober and able to stand alone, Springs rushed to his parents' home to find the other groomsmen upstairs, dressed only in underwear, sipping champagne, while their wives or other female friends were downstairs in a snip over their actions. Springs ordered the men hurriedly dressed and to the church, albeit by then not on time.

The scheduled plan at the church was for groomsman Bryan to signal the organist that the bride was ready to start down the aisle by placing a handkerchief over his mouth. "Joe was feeling a little bit, if not tipsy, overly happy from the champagne," Mrs. Springs explained with a hearty laugh. "He decided on his own he didn't want to give the signal, so he was showing another groomsman what the signal was by demonstrating the handkerchief routine. The organist didn't know it was a demonstration, not the real thing, so when she saw the handkerchief on Joe's mouth she launched into the wedding march. That act caused a great deal of confusion because I was nowhere near ready to go down the aisle. But the organist just sort of let the wedding music trail off and went back to playing some other tune. Eventually, I was ready, the signal was given by the other groomsman for the wedding march to begin and everything worked out fine. We all took Joe's sudden change of plans in good humor, but we never let him forget it. "

The Springs and Bryans remained close friends both in New York following their weddings and later when both couples relocated to North Carolina, the Bryans in Greensboro and the Springs just south of Charlotte.

Eli Springs, early in the friendship, regularly teased Bryan about his northern habits and seeming inability to adapt to the southern way of life, in Springs' view, the proper way. But he changed his mind once Bryan moved to Greensboro, saying that his pal had become so southern that he was even comfortable not wearing an undershirt.

Shortly after their marriages, the two couples vacationed together, once on a ski trip to Montreal when Kathleen was pregnant — but didn't know it at the time — with the couple's first child. It was the new Mrs. Bryan's initial attempt at skiing and she spent most of her time sprawled in the snow, unable to move without help getting up.

Her doctor wasn't happy about the trip, which he learned about only after the fact. "We later marveled that Kay (the first Bryan daughter) arrived without any mishaps following that trip," Mrs. Springs said.

Katherine Springs was at her friend Kathleen Bryan's bedside when baby girl Kay (formally Kathleen, named for her mother) was born September 10, 1928 at Miss Lippincott's Sanatorium on Madison Avenue, a private hospital where all the society-encrusted New York children were born. The sanatorium was something of a social coming out scene for new mothers, the type of place where parents would bring silk blanket covers, family photographs for display and where routine stays were two to three weeks while the new moms worked off excess weight.

The only real difficulty with Kay Bryan's birth was the anxiety of her father. For a macho guy like he normally was, he turned into a bundle of nerves. "Joe was quite worried and upset," Mrs. Springs recalled with her typical warm smile. "He didn't know how to act with a new baby coming. But we got him calmed down and we all came through it just fine." Katherine Springs was also present at

Miss Lippincott's when the second Bryan daughter, Nancy, was born two years later on October 15, 1930.

The newlywed Bryan couple began their married life in New York in cramped quarters on the 13th floor in a large apartment complex on upper 5th Avenue. Rental space was scarce at the time and Bryan later said they found their place only because it was on the 13th floor and was shunned by people who were superstitious about living there.

The family resided there until Nancy was born, then moved to a larger apartment out of necessity. Bryan was no more ready for the second child than the first. "I hadn't anticipated another child so soon," Bryan later explained. "We had to find a larger place." The second residence was on 93rd Street.

The Bryans lived comfortably, some might even say elegantly, in those early years of marriage. They had nannies to care for both daughters, as was the custom among the more affluent residents of the city.

Kathleen Bryan, however, was unable to sustain her previous Greensboro lifestyle without some financial help even though her husband was doing well as a cotton broker. His income wasn't enough to satisfy the family wants along with the needs or to sustain the social life they desired. Kathleen got direct financial help from home. Bryan accepted the family subsidy, because it helped him sustain the lifestyle his wife had grown to love and that her parents preferred, but his pride suffered. Between the Bryans November 1927 marriage and their return to Greensboro in 1931, the couple received a minimum $200 monthly check from Kathleen's parents, Julian and Ethel Price, to cover the cost of maid service and child-care after the daughters were born. This allowed the Bryans to use their own resources for other things, including an active Manhattan social life.

Raising two children in New York was not always easy for the Bryans even though they had full-time help with childcare thanks to the Price subsidy. The two daughters, their father said, were entirely different. Daughter Kay was by all accounts a quiet and happy child while Nancy was something else. "Nancy cried all the time," her father said. "I thought that was strange, but fortunately we had a nurse to help handle that." The Bryans also had kitchen help. Bryan had decided early in the marriage after sampling some of his wife's meals that cooking was not her strength. The practice of hiring cooks for the family continued throughout their marriage.

The longer the family maintained their New York lifestyle, the more anxious they became about the future. While the daughters were too young to remember what it was like while living there, it seems clear that both parents were concerned as the decade of the 1920s concluded that things would not likely continue as in the first few years of their marriage.

By the end of the decade, it was obvious that the Herbert Hoover economic plan wasn't working. Bryan was living on sagging commissions, plus the subsidy from his Greensboro in-laws, from his brokerage sales and by 1929 the demand and price of cotton had all but evaporated. Cotton was selling for a nickel a pound, if you could find a buyer. Bryan's income had dropped along with cotton prices and the family subsidy was more needed than ever.

Because of that loss of income, the economic crash of 1929 cast a heavy pall over the Bryan family income situation. "Things pretty much changed overnight when the crash came," explained Mrs. Springs whose husband also felt the economic pinch in his job at the stock exchange.

By the spring of 1931, the Bryans and Kathleen's father had had enough of Manhattan and the world of cotton brokerage. They agreed to a move South, to Kathleen's hometown where Joe had been promised a job with his father-in-law.

Bryan always said he left New York of his own choosing because he and his wife had concluded that the city was not the place to raise a family. "There were pathetic gas fumes even in Central Park,"

Bryan said in a 1992 interview about his move to the South. " I just thought it was no place to raise children."

While that may have been true, there was one other solid reason for the move. Julian Price had decided it was time for his daughter to come home. He offered his son-in-law a job as an inducement to bring about the move. Bryan agreed to the move, he later said, but not to a job working with his father-in-law. But it turned out that was not a call he made; Julian Price made it for him.

Katherine Springs learned from her friend Kathleen Bryan that Julian Price had made the decision after the crash of 1929 that it was time for a change. "Kathleen and I never discussed exact circumstances," Mrs. Springs recalled. "But I just knew that Mr. Price was anxious for Kathleen to come home and he had the interest of his daughter in mind. He felt they would have a much finer life if Joe would become a part of the family business. Joe agreed, but he was a very proud man and a very independent man. I don't doubt that it was a little bit hard for him to have his wife's father insist that he come in the business with him."

Bryan later said as much.

"I always said I would not work for my father-in-law," Bryan said in an interview. "I had agreed to the move but thought I was coming to Greensboro to work for Pilot Life Insurance where Jefferson Standard owned most of the stock. But things got twisted around and when I found out the facts of life (about what Julian Price wanted) things were entirely different from what I expected." Bryan's first office was just down the hall in the downtown Jefferson building from that of his father-in-law who kept a close watch on his son-in-law's job performance.

Bryan was so sure he would work for Pilot, in fact, that he went for an interview with Charles Gold, son of one of the company's founders, at Pilot Life on his first weekend back in Greensboro and was anticipating starting to work the following Monday. During that same weekend, however, Gold died of a shotgun blast. Speculation was that the death was a suicide although for public consumption the company put out the word that he died in a hunting accident.

Bryan offered a bit of dark humor over Gold's death. "Some people said the man killed himself because he was afraid he was going to have to work with me," he said with a bit of the self-deprecating humor that he was fond of using among social friends through his adult life.

Price, despite his determination to get his daughter home from New York, was aware that bringing Bryan into the company would not be a smooth transition and might cause some friction among executives. Being the direct person that he was, Price informed company officials in early 1931 that he was planning to hire his son-in-law and if there were any objections they should speak up then or not at all. If he heard any carping about the new hire later, Price told his corporate executives, that was grounds for dismissal. Nobody offered any objections, at least not in earshot of Price.

Bryan's initial job responsibilities with Jefferson were inauspicious, as was his starting pay. The first job assignment was overseeing the company tearoom, the Jefferson restaurant on the top floor of the building, and the starting salary was $65 a month. That was just $15 a month more than his first job as a broker in New York almost a decade earlier. Julian Price was known for low salaries and he made no exception for his son-in-law. Price did, however, keep the private subsidy to his daughter going to cover cost of childcare and domestic help at the Bryan household.

"I did all the dirty jobs at Jefferson that nobody else wanted to do or had any interest in," Bryan would later say of his first assignment. "I was made a vice president but I was put in charge of all the dirty work. I guess I was a natural to do that because the Army had trained me to look after things. The first challenge of managing the tea room was to stop the thefts. The hired help was stealing their heads off," he said. "They were stuffing whole chickens inside garbage bags and carrying then out. I had to do all those things because Ralph (Price) couldn't do it." Ralph Price was Kathleen Bryan's sole sibling whose life within Jefferson Standard was always molded around what others wanted regardless of his own intelligence and ability. Early clashes between Ralph Price and Joe Bryan were just the first of many differences between the son and son-in-law of the company president.

Bryan's duties within Jefferson slowly but surely expanded far beyond the initial tearoom food theft responsibilities although he was never able to assume the job his wife coveted for him and he would have readily accepted: company president.

He was a senior vice president at Jefferson, chairman of the board at Pilot Life and president of Jefferson Broadcasting. But neither he nor his wife was ever able to muster either stockholder or company director support to make him president of the entire company. Bryan was never accepted as enough of an insider to win the presidency. He was a Yankee in a southern company and he was not a Price even if he was married to one.

While there is no doubt Bryan would have moved into the presidency of Jefferson if given a chance, he later told at least one close friend that he had no regrets about being passed over. "I'm not sure I would have made a good president," he said. "I was a better behind the scenes person. I don't know if I would have been a good leader." But there is no reason to believe he would have turned down the job if he had been given a chance to accept it.

Bryan's responsibilities within the insurance side of the company, in fact, were never especially significant even with the titles he carried. At board meetings he most often sat near the back of the room, not with the top officials at the front. His insurance role was more of a questioner about investments than about policy or administrative decisions although he was a frequent inquisitor of how things were done even if his role was essentially peripheral.

Bryan's greatest influence by far with Jefferson was in the broadcast side where he was responsible for decisions that had a tremendous impact on the company's future and growth from the middle 1930s through the 1960s inside the company and also on the outside through his support for public television.

As his influence and presence continued to grow, however, Bryan was never far from the eye or dominance of his father-in-law. From his arrival in 1931 until Price died in an auto accident in 1946, other Jefferson executives continuously linked Bryan to Price even though the two were never considered especially close. There was never any doubt who was in charge. It was Price who was the boss.

Price was without question the dominant figure in the company during the decades from the early 1920s through the fall of 1946 when he was killed. He gave up his title of president in 1945, because his wife had earlier insisted on it, and turned that designation over to his son Ralph. But even then, no one doubted who was still in charge. Bryan and his wife had privately hoped for him to receive the presidency title, but his mother-in-law for years had been determined that the job was to go to her son instead. Mrs. Price died in 1943, but her husband respected her desires enough to two years later name his son chairman, as she had wanted.

There were those within the company at the time who felt that Kathleen could have assumed the presidency. She was described by close friends as both intelligent and outgoing enough to do the job, although members of her own family disagree on whether she could have run the company. She was, however, a lot like her father in that she was direct and serious in wanting things done her way. Her dad regularly took Kathleen, clearly the apple of his eye, instead of his son to company meetings while she was growing up. Ralph, on the other hand, was the clear favorite of his mother even though he was extremely introverted, lacked basic management skills and was, in fact, more interested in world peace and international law than in running an insurance company. He accepted the company presidency because it was expected, not because he really wanted the job.

63

Women, of course, didn't assume leadership roles in those days even if they had the ability so when Julian Price assumed the title of board chairman the presidency stayed in the family and went to son Ralph. Clearly it was not a job that Ralph Price desired or was ready for. He quickly proved a failure in trying to handle the responsibilities.

Bryan at the time was beginning to cultivate his image and reputation within the company as a person who was interested in conventions and outside leadership roles as well as a person who could be difficult to work with on a day-to-day basis. He was made board chairman at Pilot Life in order to allow him to seek the top leadership role in the American Life Convention, an insurance lobbying group. The head of that group was required to be the head of an insurance company, so Bryan assumed the title of Pilot chairman before seeking the lobbying association title which Price had earlier held. He also became the lead Jefferson person when it came to lobbying for legislation in Congress. His engaging personality fit those roles and he was considered successful at those endeavors.

Inside the company headquarters, Bryan became the champion of planning company conventions and securing engaging speakers and interesting parties. At one New York convention, he rented an entire theatre so those Jefferson convention participants could all attend a Mary Martin production. "He was the best at that of anyone I've ever seen or known," commented Seth Macon, a long-time Jefferson executive and unofficial company historian.

Bryan later became friends with syndicated columnist Ann Landers and arranged for her to speak at company conventions. He also was friends with cowboy star Gene Autry as a result of some Jefferson loans to Autry for business ventures and brought Autry to Greensboro for company and family socials. Bryan and Autry were personal friends and business associates for more than 40 years. "I have never known anyone that I had more respect for than Joe," Autry wrote in early 1986 in a letter to help Bryan celebrate his

Kathleen Price Bryan, at age 6, in 1905.

90th birthday. "There is no one I would rather be with than Joe."

Bryan was well liked by the rank and file Jefferson employees who would speak of his generosity and kindness, but he was not well known by most who worked there.

"He could sometime be a little aloof," said veteran Jefferson employee Cecil Martin, "and nobody got to know him very well. But he was nice to workers in a quiet way and was always concerned about the welfare of the people, far more than Ralph Price was."

Among Bryan's company interests were the Jefferson Club, a private club for employees started by Julian Price. Club employees cleared the land for the clubhouse and were encouraged to use the facilities on New Garden Road for family fun and relaxation. Dues were initially $1 a month for most employees and $1.25 a month for those making more than $5,000 a year.

One clerical worker said she was told by a company executive H. P. Leak not to ask for any more pay raises. She mentioned to Bryan that secretaries were underpaid, and he authorized a salary increase of $15 a month. "He was very thoughtful," said Clara Mae Hines. "I always respected him for that. He was kind to us."

Bryan also befriended the best known of the company secretaries who never allowed a severe handicap interrupt her job performance. Mary Taylor, for years the trusted secretary of Julian Price even after she lost her eyesight following improper medical treatment, remained with the company after Price's death. Totally blind, after an oculist put the wrong drops in her eyes during a routine eye examination, she continued to produce the company newsletter and perform regular duties, and do whatever else Price asked as president.

Mrs. Price called her husband and Miss Taylor the "pick and shovel team" because they worked long hours and full weeks..

After Price's death, Bryan began caring for Miss Taylor outside the office, cashing her paychecks and helping with many of her personal responsibilities. A Catholic and sister of the priest who married the Bryans, Miss Taylor showed her appreciation for Bryan's kindness by giving him a St. Christopher's medal that he carried until his death.

Miss Taylor was highly regarded by company executives who admired her work ethic despite her blindness and what at times could be her intransigent ways. Once when she was invited to attend a company convention out of the country, she refused to give her age required for a passport. She agreed to list her age as more than 21. She went to the convention. Miss Taylor was also one of only two people in Jefferson history who was allowed to continue working for a regular salary beyond her 65th birthday. The other one was President Roger Soles. Although Miss Taylor was never paid a high salary, she lived frugally as a spinster and at her death held Jefferson stock valued at approximately $800,000.

Even with his kindness to Miss Taylor and many of the rank and file employees, Bryan was not known for gentility among Jefferson executives in the early days of his tenure. He was, company retirees say, hard to deal with and uncompromising in making decisions. He was direct and unbending like Price, but he had the additional disadvantage of sounding overly gruff because, he readily acknowledged, he was a Yankee.

It is conjecture how many of his unpopular actions were of Bryan's own choosing or how many were on direct orders from Julian Price. There is general acceptance among Jefferson executives from the 1930s and 40s that Bryan was often as not carrying out Price's directives. Bryan was regarded by many as Price's "hatchet man" who was doing things that Price wanted done but didn't want blame for doing.

Bryan conceded he was often given the task of doing Julian Price's bidding, regardless of the lack of pleasantries. Bryan said he had standing orders from Price to maintain a roving assignment to "move and act wherever there was a vacuum."

Bryan said he and Price had private signals on how to handle certain matters that might be unpleasant and unpopular. "I knew certain things he wanted done," Bryan said of his father-in-law. "Sometimes he would bring people to me and say "Look, Joe, I've been listening to Mr. So and So's proposition but I've told him to talk to you about it.' I knew that was his signal to me. I was to turn it down. If the idea had been any good, he'd have said yes. He brought things to me that he wanted to reject. I was his hatchet man."

Bryan's office remained nearby his father-in-law on the 14th floor at the Jefferson Building until Price's death in the fall of 1946. While Bryan's influence with Price was growing, they seldom socialized together outside family events. Price once told his fellow members of the social M&M (Merchants and Manufacturers) Club in downtown Greensboro that while his son-in-law was not one of his best pals, he wanted him in the club because Bryan was married to his daughter. Bryan was immediately voted in as a member where only the elite were allowed to join. The M&M Club, long since disbanded, was the private, men-only organization where Greensboro's corporate executives would regularly go to relax, play poker and imbibe in alcoholic beverages away from spouses and employees. The club met in the basement of the O. Henry Hotel in a room off limits to the general public.

Even as Bryan's responsibilities and stature at Jefferson continued to grow, however, he was still regarded for years as Kathleen's husband and the company president's son-in-law rather than a respected leader among company insiders. "The folklore at the Jefferson was that Mr. Price had bought a husband for his daughter," commented Mrs. Marjorie Warren who worked as a Jefferson bookkeeper and was married to Jefferson executive Karl Ljung. "Joe was not a popular person at the time. He was gruff at first, but he mellowed later in life." The early perceptions of Bryan, Mrs. Warren and others agreed, were unfair.

Bryan conceded that his life at work was anything but smooth in the early days at Jefferson, but he also agreed he might have been kinder and gentler at times. "I had to live down being the son-in-law," Bryan said. "I say live it down. I don't know that I ever did. It was tough going, particularly being a damned Yankee. But I could take it. And I usually threw it back as fast as they could send it to me."

Bryan eventually outgrew the perception of living in the shadow of his wife and father-in-law. But the problem was not something he took lightly nor was it something he was willing to let hang over his head forever. He was determined to establish himself as his own man and as a man who could make positive and profitable decisions for the company. He got his first chance in 1934, but it was not in insurance. It was in radio. He was, of course, still years away from overcoming the reputation of being beholden to the Price family, but it was a virtually bankrupt radio station that started him on the road to business and financial success.

That radio station investment also helped convince Julian Price that his son-in-law could be a shrewd business dealer. It was an investment that has generated millions of profits for "the Jefferson", as the company was called by long-time employees, and one that established the company and Joe Bryan as among the pioneer leaders in the field of broadcasting.

5

MISSION ACCOMPLISHED

Joe Bryan figured he had little to lose and a lot to gain when he went to Julian Price in the spring of 1934 with a business proposition. Bryan, not a man of great patience and itching to establish himself with both his father-in-law and other Jefferson Standard officials, was weary. After three years with the company, of carrying out Price's specific orders or handling duties that nobody else wanted, he was willing to take a gamble, especially one he felt would pay dividends for the company and make points with the boss. Bryan wanted, indeed he needed, something to call his own in order to prove he was more than just the Yankee son-in-law who had been given a job with few significant responsibilities.

Jefferson was doing quite well under the leadership of Price who had become president 15 years earlier. But it was apparent that Price wanted to enhance both his own power and control at the top and to expand the influence of the company beyond the then existing boundaries. Price, shortly after becoming Jefferson president, had extended his investments beyond the insurance field by buying Greensboro's afternoon newspaper, *The Record*, and selecting his daughter Kathleen as society editor. In fact, Price put the newspaper ownership in his daughter's name although he made the business decisions. She had the ownership title, but he had the clout just as he did at the insurance company up the street. Price sold his interest in the paper in 1930, three years after Kathleen married Bryan and moved to New York.

Knowing his father-in-law's interest in other businesses and wanting to break out of the routine of little more than busy work at the Jefferson, Bryan made his move in 1934. If Price wanted to be involved in business expansion, Bryan was determined to be an integral part.

Operating out of rental space in a small room of the Jefferson Building at the time was a fledgling A.M. radio station with a weak signal and an even weaker financial base. When a windstorm knocked over the station's flimsy transmitting tower atop the building, there was not enough cash in the bank account of the station's owners to repair it. The station, also facing the threat of shut-down by the Federal Communications Commission because of an unreliable signal, had little hope of ever returning without an infusion of capital.

The station, with call letters WBIG (We Believe In Greensboro), was actually the second one for the city, but like its predecessor, seemed doomed to failure. R. Odell Holland started the first station, WQAZ, in 1921 with a license paid for by the *Greensboro Daily News*. It was, at best, a makeshift operation that obtained its electrical power from the wires of the downtown trolley lines. Eighteen months after its first broadcast, a fire in the studio put it out of business. Holland was out of money and the newspaper owners refused to invest any more.

The city had no radio station for four years until WNRC (Wayne Nelson Radio Company) began broadcasting in 1926 on 10 watts of power from the eighth floor of the Jefferson Building. Nelson owned the equipment and was paid by the local Chamber of Commerce to broadcast "as often as possible" positive stories to help promote the city and the chamber's interests. Four years later struggling entrepreneur Edney Ridge, who would become a U.S. Marshall, took over management of Nelson's station and changed the name to WBIG. As the station's call letters implied, without shame or apology, the station became a full-time city booster.

Constantly operating on the verge of bankruptcy, WBIG was ready to fold in 1934 after the tower collapsed. Legend has it that the only asset owned by the station at the time was a studio grand piano with a lien on it, which a music company repossessed, and that Jefferson Standard took the station license in lieu of past due rent. The piano part of the legend is true, but not the license control. Jefferson didn't "take" the license. But Bryan stepped in to save it.

What actually happened was that Edney Ridge approached Bryan with an offer to personally buy the station for $10,000. Ridge said the station must either be sold or close. "I was interested, but I didn't personally have $10,000 lying around," Bryan later explained. "I had a lot of other places to put what little money I had at the time." While Bryan's pay had risen some from his original $65 a month starting salary four years earlier, his bank account wasn't anywhere close to fat enough to find that amount of money to buy the station.

But Bryan said he felt the station ought to remain on the air and believed that with good management it could even show a profit. "I wasn't convinced it would immediately be a good investment, but felt it could eventually be," Bryan said, "I also felt it ought to remain a part of the community. After some preliminary discussions, the manager (Ridge) came to me one morning and said if he couldn't find a buyer by noon that day, the station would close."

That's where Price entered the picture. Bryan took the offer to buy the station to his father-in-law who initially was reluctant to become involved. It wasn't that Price did not feel the deal would be a good one, but he didn't want to become involved with Ridge whom he didn't respect because of some unpleasant earlier business associations. Bryan convinced Price to invest with the promise that he (Bryan) and not Ridge would assume the management and turn a losing venture into a profitable one.

Price authorized Jefferson to put up the $10,000 purchase price and add another $12,000 for equipment to make the station viable and reliable. With Bryan making the management decisions, WBIG turned a profit of the $22,000 investment after one year, giving Jefferson its total investment back. "I personally took great pride in seeing that happen because I was largely responsible for it happening," Bryan said later of the station's turnaround. Price was clearly pleased with the radio station investment and the performance of his son-in-law. The station continued to show a profit and remained a booster of the city until Jefferson closed it and it went off the air on November 20, 1986.

That relatively small investment on the heels of the Great Depression was a major turning point for both the Jefferson and for Bryan. Broadcasting became a significant part of the company's strategy and has through the years brought in huge profits. Clearly, broadcasting gave Bryan his first opportunity to show his savvy investment strengths even though his ultimate success in future decades may have surprised even him.

The broadcast side of the company also gave Julian Price a way out of what was becoming a growing dilemma within his family and the corporate structure. His son Ralph and son-in-law Bryan seemed headed for a board room collision, each expecting to become president with Price's retirement. "Mr. Price wanted me to succeed in broadcasting, to see it happen because he felt I was in competition with Ralph for chief executive of the Jefferson Standard," Bryan later said. The competition, according to retired Jefferson executives, was more imaginary than real, but Bryan's initial success with the bankrupt radio station was the chance Price needed to separate the duties and lessen the corporate contact between his two family members.

From that humble beginning and the $22,000 investment in WBIG sprang the development of WBT radio in Charlotte, Jefferson's second venture into commercial radio, and later a series of profitable television and newspaper enterprises.

Jefferson bought the fledgling WBT from CBS in September 1945. WBT was making money when Price authorized its purchase at Bryan's suggestion, but it had not yet become a dominant Charlotte voice. It would, however, become the premier station in the Carolinas with the infusion of Jefferson dollars and the hiring of capable station administrators and a stable of talented broadcasters.

Jefferson Standard, however, turned down an offer in 1957 to purchase radio station WPTF in Raleigh, that city's premier broadcast outlet, for $750,000. Bryan felt the price was too high. Jefferson also rejected a chance to purchase station WTOB in Washington, D.C. during the same time period.

The next step in the company's broadcast growth was creating what would become the state's best known television station, WBTV in Charlotte, the first commercial television station in North Carolina. WFMY in Greensboro brags that it was the first commercial station in North Carolina to broadcast live programming, which is true, but WBTV was the first TV station in the state to go on the air.

Then came Jefferson ownership of television stations in Florence, S.C., and Richmond, Va. The success of Jefferson's commercial television enterprises led, with Bryan's support and assistance, to the formation of North Carolina's public broadcasting network under the auspices of the University of North Carolina in Chapel Hill. Bryan was one of the earliest supporters of university television. Without him, it is not an overstatement to say, public television in North Carolina would not have been started as early or achieved its present reputation for high quality. His early and passionate support for university television, in fact, may be one of his greatest achievements even though it is one of the lesser known ones. That, though, is a story in itself, separate from his other successes at Jefferson.

While it was Joe Bryan, with the very able help and assistance of radio and television pioneer Charles Crutchfield, who put the Jefferson's broadcasting division on the right track, it was Julian Price who built the solid foundation for the entire company. If any one person deserves credit for the early success of Jefferson, it is Price. Ironically, however, it was not until the summer of 1999 that Price's name was put on public display anywhere in Greensboro as one of the early leaders of the community when a public park was named in memory of Price and his wife Ethel. That recognition was made possible through the generosity of Price's granddaughter Kay Bryan Taylor Edwards, Bryan's oldest daughter, and her children. Mrs. Edwards donated $2 million and her children gave another $1.5 million for the purchase price of land for the park provided it was named for her grandparents.

The irony of that $3.5 million donation for a passive public park on New Garden Road in Greensboro is that the land, owned by Jefferson Pilot, is the same property where Price started a company clubhouse and recreational area for Jefferson employees. So, in effect, Price's granddaughter and great grandchildren bought land Price once owned and donated it for park use. Jefferson, meanwhile, is developing the remaining company-owned land around the park for upscale residential and retail use.

The original Jefferson Standard Life Insurance Company, now Jefferson Pilot Corporation, has been a mainstay in and bedrock of Greensboro since 1912 and has grown cautiously yet steadily under strong leadership of several presidents. Never as flamboyant as some other insurance companies or as well known, Jefferson has nevertheless earned a deserved reputation for solid investment strategies and steady growth throughout its history. Greensboro is known as much for its landmark Jefferson Building downtown as for any other single event, save perhaps the lunch counter sit-ins during the early civil rights days of the 1960s.

Despite public perception, however, the company was not founded in Guilford County. Jefferson is an eastern North Carolina company, founded in Raleigh in 1907 by a small group of motivated and creative men, and moved to Greensboro five years later as part of a merger of several companies. Jefferson's headquarters came to Greensboro as much for convenience as for business reasons, although the economy played a part in the relocation. But history has proved the move was the right one and the decision some years later to hire a young Virginia former telegraph operator named Julian Price as a sales agent would prove to be equally rewarding. It was Price who, after advancing rapidly to become president and gain control, moved Jefferson from essentially a hometown company toward becoming a regional and national financial service enterprise.

Brothers P.D. and Charles Gold, members of a Wilson, N.C., newspaper family were the first to conceive the idea of forming Jefferson Standard. They had come to believe the admonition of Atlanta newspaper editor Henry W. Grady who said the South had vast potential for economic growth and prosperity beyond what existed at the time from agriculture. But it was more than just Grady's challenge that prompted the Gold brothers to act. They were concerned that northern institutions, particularly insurance companies, were siphoning off valuable Southern assets.

Shortly after the turn of the century, these same outside insurance companies were caught up in congressional hearings involving business irregularities. The Golds grabbed onto the tainted public reputation of non-Southern companies as their time to act. They merged their vision and the investments of two dozen affluent, mostly eastern North Carolina businessmen to create Jefferson in 1907, starting with $500,000 in capital stock in August of that year.

Among the original investors were Josephus Daniels, the well-known Raleigh newspaper publisher, and George Holderness of Tarboro. Holderness started out as a farmer, but became a highly successful businessman. He developed the first milk pasteurization plant in eastern North Carolina and then became one of the founders of the telephone company serving communities in his part of the state. Holderness' son, Howard (Chick) Holderness, would 43 years later become Jefferson president, marking the second time Joe Bryan was passed over for the top job. That action proved to Bryan and his wife Kathleen yet again that there were those still within the company who didn't want or desire their leadership abilities in the president's office.

Jefferson Standard opened its doors on a hot, sultry day in early August in a suite of offices in downtown Raleigh costing $55 a month. There were three paid staff members at a total starting salary of $300 a month. *The News & Observer* of Raleigh was effusive in its editorial praise for the new company, proclaiming the feat as a major economic boost to the region and representing at the time the largest corporation ever formed in North Carolina. The newspaper's praise omitted the fact that its publisher and owner Daniels was an original investor who was anticipating making money off the deal.

Daniels would later go on to become Woodrow Wilson's Secretary of the Navy where he would carry out a moral crusade, banning alcohol at officers' mess aboard military ships and working to clean up red light districts in cities with high numbers of prostitutes and sailors. Daniels would later boast that his actions had given America the "soberest, cleanest and healthiest fighting men the world had ever known." Daniels would also attempt to simplify Navy recruit training by abandoning the terms port and starboard for left and right and to force sailors to wear pajamas, but he gave up on both those efforts in the face of strong opposition.

The company name of Jefferson was chosen because P. D. Gold had a fondness for Thomas Jefferson and he wanted the company to symbolically represent what he called the high standards of the former president. The company's original logo was created by

Gold, based on a Capitol Rotunda painting he liked, depicting the nation's founding fathers delivering the Declaration of Independence to the Constitutional Congress. A replica of that logo stands today in the foyer of the Jefferson Pilot offices in downtown Greensboro.

The company founders also used the Jefferson theme in its original marketing strategies. The initial marketing slogan was: "A Jefferson Standard Policy is a Declaration of Independence for the family." It obviously worked. Life insurance policy sales grew rapidly, some say too rapidly in those early years.

Joseph G. Brown of Raleigh was elected the first Jefferson president and bought the first life insurance policy. Despite the initial successes in insurance sales, the early days showed signs of management friction and future problems. Barely a month into the company's operations, corporate secretary H.G. Chatfield resigned in protest of an executive committee decision to write deferred dividend policies. Co-founder Charles Gold quietly took his place. Twenty-five years later at Pilot Life Insurance Company in Greensboro, it was Gold's son Charles who first interviewed Joe Bryan for what Bryan mistakenly thought was to be a job at Pilot. It was the younger Gold who died of a self-inflicted gunshot wound before Bryan's non-existent job was to start.

Six years before the Gold brothers and their investors started Jefferson Life in downtown Raleigh, a dozen prominent Greensboro men organized their own mutual life insurance company in their hometown under the name of Security Life and Annuity Company. One of the founders and the first president of Security was George A. Grimsley who had initially moved to Greensboro in 1890 as the city school superintendent. Grimsley High School in the city is named for him. He is also credited as being the catalyst for starting the first public library in downtown Greensboro.

In 1903, two years after the formation of Security Life in Greensboro, another group of local businessmen organized Greensboro

Life Insurance Company and hired a young Virginia railroad telegraph operator with no finance training but high energy and ambition as a sales agent. That man was Julian Price.

The two Greensboro insurance companies were quickly successful even in competition. Meanwhile, back in Raleigh the success of Jefferson was beginning to show a downside. The company was making huge profits but stockholders were clamoring for dividends to, in some cases, help pay off bank debts incurred in making their investments in the company.

In 1912, Jefferson Life in Raleigh and Security and Greensboro Life began merger talks, hoping to pool resources of the three for leverage in branching out to other states for sales. The merger negotiations were led by Jefferson's Gold and Greensboro Life's Price. Security was the largest of the three companies, but the Raleigh-based Jefferson had what could be called weighted clout and power among its influential founders, particularly the Golds, Daniels and Holderness. Jefferson officials agreed to move their headquarters to Greensboro in exchange for keeping that company name. Security and Greensboro Life officials agreed to give up their corporate names in exchange for maintaining company headquarters in Greensboro and for being allowed to choose the top corporate officers.

George Grimsley was picked as president of the merged companies. Julian Price, who already had risen rapidly to become head of Greensboro Life, was chosen vice president. The year after the successful merger, the Jefferson began paying a dividend. It hasn't missed an annual dividend since.

Grimsley, credited with building a solid school system before switching to the corporate world, may well have been a worthy school administrator and educator and a competent insurance executive. But he was no match for the hard-charging and visionary Price. The period of discontent between the two grew steadily and in 1919, directors of the merged company removed Grimsley as president, shoving him aside and giving him the title of board chairman with little or no duties and naming Price president with duties and responsibilities to match the title.

The rest, as they say, is history, although Price wasn't satisfied with just the top administrative title. He wanted ultimate control, something he could get only after a bitter inner office battle more than 15 years later. Even without full control in his earliest years as president, however, Price took the company onward and upward on a steady course over the next 25 years. He was determined to expand and increase profits. His achievements surely would have been even greater except for two factors. First, his plan to install his meek, mild-mannered son Ralph as company president backfired and resulted in a public feud and coup within the corporate family that lingered for decades. Second, Price was tragically killed in an auto accident before he had a chance to accomplish all he had set out to do.

Grimsley, meanwhile, didn't suffer silently for long after being pushed aside in favor of Price. In 1920, less than a year after being booted to board chairman of Jefferson and the same year women gained the right to vote, Grimsley resigned and formed another insurance company with a name almost identical to his original one at Security Life. Grimsley chose the new corporate name of Security Life and Trust Company and began to compete with his former employer. But he saw greater potential out from under the shadow of Jefferson Standard and Price. Grimsley moved the company headquarters from Greensboro to Winston-Salem in 1924 and soon began a series of successful corporate mergers. What started in 1920 as tiny Security Life and Trust over the next half century ultimately became part of mammoth Integon Insurance Company.

Price, as was his custom, didn't wait long to put his mark on the Jefferson once Grimsley was out of the picture. When he took over as president, the company was located in the downtown Dixie Building at the corner of South Elm and Sycamore Street.

Sycamore later was renamed February One Place in honor of the civil rights lunch counter sit-ins at the Woolworth's Store across the street at the same intersection.

Prior to opening up in the Dixie Building, Jefferson's first headquarters was in the Fisher Building in downtown Greensboro at the intersection of Elm and Market streets, directly across the street from where the Jefferson Building now stands. The two-story Fisher Building, which later housed a bank that closed in the Crash of 1929 and never reopened, was later demolished to make room for what is now the Southeastern Building.

Nothing about either of those early office buildings was good enough for Price whose dominant personality and desire to excel as company president drove him to unparalleled heights. Price, confidant in his own ability, brooked no continence with those around him who didn't do their best. He demanded of others what he demanded of himself.

The Price stories are legend, but the descriptions vary with the teller.

Price could be genteel and benevolent, like the time a man walked into his office and begged for money to buy a new pair of shoes. Price claimed at that moment that he had no cash in his pocket — although in truth he wasn't sure the money would go for shoes anyway. Instead of giving the beggar money, Price removed his own shoes and gave them to the man who walked out with Price's shoes on his feet. Price later walked down the street shoeless and purchased a new pair for himself.

He could also be cantankerous and hard to please, like the time he bawled out a subordinate who lamented his mistake and feared loss of his job. "Well, I guess you are just going to fire me," Jefferson officer Karl Ljung responded when Price finished his verbal thrashing. "Hell, Karl, if I was going to fire you, I wouldn't be standing here cussing you out," Price retorted. Ljung not only kept his job, but also moved steadily higher on the corporate ladder and retired as a respected company vice president.

He could be hospitable toward strangers, especially homesick soldiers stationed at the Greensboro military base just prior to World War II who were in need of a bit of recreational liquid. Several soldiers pulled into Price's driveway one weekend evening thinking they were at the home of a well-known peddler of illegal liquor with the same name. They looked up the address in the phone book and drove to the home of the Jefferson president, not realizing he wasn't the fellow they were seeking.

According to Price's version of the story that he enjoyed telling, a soldier rang the doorbell and said he had heard that this was the place to get drink. Price said it sure was and obliged on the spot. Then the G.I. asked if he could get a full bottle. Price obliged that, too. Don't bother with payment, Price told the startled stranger; just enjoy it with your buddies. The soldier thanked his generous donor, but never returned, presumably eventually figuring out he had the wrong Julian Price.

And then there was the day Price grew impatient and agitated while waiting for an elevator in the Jefferson Building. Black male Jefferson employees manually operated the building elevators at the time. "You know, I own this building and I still can't get a damn elevator when I want one," Price grumbled to himself, but loud enough for bystanders to hear. "And I'm going to do something about it, too." A month later, the Jefferson Building elevators were converted to automation.

"Mr. Price could be impetuous," said Horace Kornegay, a former North Carolina congressman who as a young lawyer with offices in the Jefferson Building overhead Price's elevator comment. "He got his elevators fixed so he could get one quicker, but he didn't fire the former elevator operators. He just gave them new duties as unofficial ambassadors for the company," which meant they retained their salaries with virtually nothing to do. Kornegay, as a congressman in the 1960s, would help break through years of bureaucratic logjams to get federal parkland along the Blue Ridge Parkway in western North Carolina named for Price.

Price was also a bit devious, but in a good-hearted way, when he wanted to accomplish his mission without inflicting a heavy hand. Legend has it that he once used sly trickery to shame leaders at Greensboro's affluent and prestigious First Presbyterian Church to pay their debt when they temporarily reneged.

Jefferson Standard, with Price's blessing, had loaned the church a significant sum of money for repairs and expansion of the sanctuary shortly before the country's economic collapse of 1929. Church members stopped payments on the loan after the crash, claiming there was no money.

Price realized he had a potential serious public relations problem as well as a realistic financial one. He wanted the debt repaid, but he surely didn't want to foreclose on a church, particularly not one where many of his affluent friends were members. He devised a plan. On a Saturday morning when he knew church staff and leaders would be in the building, Price prearranged with a Catholic priest friend to join him on a visit to First Presbyterian. Price and the priest walked through the facility, discussing aloud what changes might be needed to convert the place to a Catholic house of worship. The church staff witnessed the exchange and overheard the conversation between Price and the priest. Shortly thereafter, payments on the debt were resumed. Price, so far as is known, never admitted his act was a sham. But he got his company money back.

Price was raised a conservative Baptist in Virginia, but he broke with that faith during the 1928 election campaign after becoming a supporter of Catholic presidential candidate Al Smith. One unpleasant event — a bigoted sermon — during that campaign convinced the sometimes-stubborn Price that the Baptist church was not for him. Price's wife Ethel was a devout Catholic, having converted to that faith during her student years at the College of Notre Dame in Baltimore before becoming the first graduate of the

Watts Hospital nursing school in Durham. Although Price never personally accepted the Catholic faith, he devotedly supported his wife's rights to her beliefs and, in fact, later paid to build a Catholic Church in her memory.

Price's last day as a Baptist was in the summer of 1928, the day he listened to the Rev. J. Clyde Turner at First Baptist Church, where Price was then a member, lament the evils of presidential candidate Smith and the fact that a Catholic was running for president. There are differing versions of exactly what Price did — he either stood at the time to express his displeasure or later spoke privately and not very pleasantly to Turner — but he made known he was offended by what he felt was the discriminatory sermon. His wife, Price told the Rev. Turner, was a devoted Catholic and she and a lot of his friends were good, Christian people who ought not to be ridiculed for their religious beliefs. To condemn Smith for being Catholic was to condemn all Catholics, Price said. He pledged that very day "never to darken the door" of First Baptist Church again. And he never did.

From that day forth, Price never attended church anywhere for Sunday services. He kept his faith private. Each Sunday morning he would go to his office in the Jefferson Building and listen to radio sermons by his friend the Rev. Charles Myers, pastor at First Presbyterian. Price maintained a friendship with Myers, and once bought Myers a new car, even though he didn't personally attend Myers's church. Price's funeral was conducted at First Presbyterian, as was Joe Bryan's a half-century later, although neither man was a member of that denomination.

Price's agitation with Baptists didn't end with the Al Smith campaign either. In the mid 1940s, after he pledged funds to build a new Catholic Church in memory of his late wife Ethel, a mountain Baptist minister criticized Price for supporting Catholic causes. Price fired back with a vengeance.

The Rev. J.C. Canipe of Boone's First Baptist Church wrote

Price of his disappointment that Jefferson Standard money would go to Catholic causes. "Couldn't you have made a gift to some orphanage?" Canipe asked. "God pity America when (Catholics) get control."

Price was outraged and didn't allow that criticism to go unchallenged. "I am disappointed in this enlightened age to find one, especially a minister of the Gospel, so intolerant as you," Price immediately replied to Canipe by letter. "You have probably heard I am building a large dam in Watauga County. When the dam is completed and the lake is full of water, I would like to arrange for you to come over to get your second immersion, hoping this amount of water will wash all of your sins away, but I do not guarantee it."

Price steadfastly held to his direct approach throughout his life, whether cutting business deals or cutting up bigoted Baptists. The marks he made on Greensboro are pronounced. It all started with that tall building in the center of town. But that was only the beginning.

6

SKYSCRAPER ON A FARM

Julian Price had Jefferson Standard Life Insurance well on the road to success when Joe Bryan came upon the corporate scene in 1931 after three-plus years of marriage to Price's daughter Kathleen.

While Price and Bryan were never overly fond of each other because their personalities and backgrounds were so different, they were each astute enough to know they and the company could prosper better if they played to each other's strengths and sought to ignore their conflicts whenever possible. That plan worked.

Once Bryan had shown he could make a profit out of a bankrupt radio station, Price gave him more freedom and responsibility to branch out into company ownership television stations and significant newspaper loans. Both were profitable for the men and the company. Bryan became the lead company negotiator on many of the company's non-insurance investments during the decades of the 1940s and 1950s, before and after Price's death. He became a shrewd investor for the company and for himself.

Jefferson's subsequent ownership of profitable newspapers and cable television franchises would come later under the leadership of

President Roger Soles. Soles was a dedicated no-nonsense investment strategist, and a highly respected one, despite what was perceived among associates as a sandpaper personality. But he kept the company on solid financial ground when other insurance companies were struggling. It was Bryan, however, who got the non-insurance phase of the company started through the broadcasting operations before Soles took charge.

Bryan saw his father-in-law take the lead in different activities and fell in line to follow in the same steps, both inside and outside the corporate offices. Price once served as chairman of the American Life Convention, an insurance lobbying association. Bryan later held the same honorary post. Price became active and was elected to top offices in the Shrine organization. Bryan later did the same thing. They joined the same social clubs, always with Price in the lead.

Bryan also learned quickly from his father-in-law how to make a dollar independently of the insurance company. Price was a master of knowing how to pick business deals for maximum advantage. He personally secured properties from North Carolina to Florida from the late 1920s and early 1930s when prices were deflated and then selling them off for profits once the economy recovered. That's the way, for example, that Price wound up owning both the King Cotton Hotel in Greensboro and the Carolina Hotel in Raleigh. He also held deeds to apartment buildings and a hotel in Tampa. Price left ownership in the King Cotton to his son Ralph and ownership of the Carolina Hotel to his daughter Kathleen.

"Julian Price was outstanding in his ability to get things done," commented Seth Macon, a long-time Jefferson executive who as a new company employee became friendly with Price in the early 1940s. Macon started with Jefferson just prior to World War II when his first duties were running errands for Price. After military service, Macon rejoined the company and earned a reputation as a respected corporate executive and unofficial Jefferson historian as well as a major supporter and benefactor to Guilford College.

Bryan also had a knack for investing and made huge amounts of money after retiring from Jefferson when he became savvy at putting small amounts of cash into oil drilling operations in the deep South and drawing out large profits. He also made profits for his wife by investing her money in oil wells, despite the fact she was not overly keen on what she felt were risky endeavors. No one will ever know with certainty, of course, but speculation among Bryan's friends is that Bryan's wealth grew as much from oil speculation in his retirement as from profits at Jefferson while he was working, maybe more so. He transferred his oil profits into additional Jefferson stock that produced still more profits.

Bryan's initial investments after moving to Greensboro came from watching Price cut deals on land and other property. The actions by Price were those that Bryan appreciated, despite the personal differences of the two men, and he later talked admiringly about his father-in-law's self-confidence and financial finesse.

"He had a single desire to make Jefferson Standard number one in the United States," Bryan said in a 1982 interview, 36 years after Price's death. "He lived through some tough times. It was difficult going in the 1930s and even before. But he always kept his head up, always had confidence and enthusiasm and he would inspire other people. That was one of his great fortes, inspiring other people to work to the best of their abilities. To my mind, he was fantastic, a genius in finances. He never followed orthodox thinking, but he had great imagination."

That was a Price trait that Bryan adopted. Bryan's leadership and primary financial support for maintaining Bryan Park in Greensboro, the UNCG School of Business, the Duke University Alzheimer's Research Center are among the better known significant enterprises that Bryan's own vision and resources helped provide.

It was the construction of the downtown Jefferson Building in the early 1920s that removed all doubt, if there ever was any, that Price was a man of vision who would not accept no if he felt the answer should be yes. He dismissed as shortsighted those who said he was moving too far too fast, including raconteur Will Rogers. Rogers came to Greensboro for a performance shortly after Price had finished the 17-story downtown skyscraper and laughed out loud along with his audience at what Price had done.

It was his first time, Rogers said with his usual wit smothered with more than a little dripping sarcasm directed at both the towering Jefferson Building as well as a dinky downtown, of seeing a skyscraper put up in the middle of a farm.

Price never even blinked at ordering the construction of the new Jefferson headquarters. He knew what he wanted and knew how to get it. He put building plans in place six months after becoming company president.

Jefferson had outgrown its original Fisher Building headquarters when it moved one block south on Elm Street to the Dixie Building in 1914. By the time Price became president in 1919, the company was spilling out into other seven other office buildings in downtown Greensboro. Price said enough of that, calling the scattered offices inefficient and costly. He wanted corporate headquarters all under one roof and he wanted a showplace.

He got both and downtown Greensboro was transformed forever.

Land acquisition for the new skyscraper actually began five years earlier, before Price took over the presidency although nobody at that time had the visions of Price for what was to be put on the property. Jefferson's lawyers in 1914 put in a bid of $151,000 for the county-owned site at Elm and Market where the county courthouse then stood. That was a handsome profit for the property on which original records show the initial purchase price to the county was $150.

Guilford County's government had outgrown the courthouse facility and when Jefferson offered its bid, the deal appeared closed until some neighboring business owners objected to the sale with a claim that the property should be set aside for a downtown park. The site was embroiled in controversy for three years before Jefferson finally won the right to buy the land in 1917 for $171,000, an increase of $20,000 more than their bid three years earlier.

When Price became Jefferson president two years after the land was purchased, he moved with dispatch to put up new headquarters unmatched by anything the city had seen — or would see for decades. Jefferson directors on January 12, 1920 authorized Price to proceed with plans for a new building "suitable to the company's needs". Price apparently saw enormous needs. He asked for a twin-towered 17-story building with 313,410 square feet, marbled floors in the corridor and offices far more opulent than anything in town.

When the building was completed, it was at the time the tallest building between Washington and Atlanta. It made Julian Price and all of Greensboro proud, except for those few neighboring merchants who didn't want anything shadowing their own stores. Price, in effect, told those merchants to go to hell. The building was a showcase and a regular topic of conversation with its marble floors, terra cotta granite clad tower richly ornamented with exuberant neo-classical, gothic, Romanesque and art deco design.

The new skyscraper cost $2.5 million. But Price had managed the construction costs well and when the facility opened in October 1923, he made sure it was debt free. Price didn't believe in heavy debts.

When the Jefferson tower was doubled in size and opened in August 1990, the price tag for the new wing of the building was in excess of $35 million. That figure was high enough that even Price might have gulped if he were still around.

Price insisted that the front of the original building on the east should be made appealing to the public. But keeping in mind the earlier objections of the neighboring stores on the West Side of the property to the original sale of the land to Jefferson, he left the rear of the building on the west bland. He concluded that if the merchants facing that side of the building didn't want him there, he would just leave their view plain looking. Furthermore, he surmised that other buildings likely would go up and block the view of his building from the west, so there was no need to put money into making that side attractive.

The Greensboro Record reported eloquently on the new Jefferson building, calling it "immaculate guarding Greater Greensboro by night and by day — a milestone of progress marking a new and greater era in the history of this metropolis." Price, of course, owned the newspaper when that story was written.

Price may have been destined for leadership because of his childhood. If so, however, he took his time finding his niche although once he started there was no holding him back. Unlike his son-in-law Joe Bryan whose upbringing was anything but normal, Price had what could be described as the perfect childhood in a decidedly Southern, God-fearing family of Virginia Baptists and community leaders. While Bryan's father drifted from one job and one town to the next, Price's dad was a steady anchor in the community of Meherrin, Va., a railroad crossing halfway between Danville and Richmond.

Meherrin was a quaint working class village when Julian Price was growing up there. Residents were hard workers, toiling daily in a wire factory, tomato cannery, brick manufacturing plant and soft drink bottling plant and wood-carving mill. There were only half a dozen stores, but citizens could get anything they wanted: groceries to glasses and clothes to caskets. One major store in the city was a dispensary owned and run by Joseph Jones Price and his wife Margaret Hill Price. Julian Price was one of eight children in the family.

In addition to the dispensary, Joseph Price ran the village's largest mercantile store where merchandise for sale included liquor. He also ran the only hotel and served as postmaster and town notary public. He was also an entrepreneur, developing a market for sassafras root, bones and sumac that he sold out of a warehouse he built and starting what was described as a large bartering business. His motto was a single word, but a clear one: "Push". His son Julian adopted that slogan as his own. Joe Bryan would modify that slogan slightly, but use it often. Bryan's words were "do it now."

Mrs. Price was considered a stern aristocrat who believed in strict discipline for her children. She was also a pillar in her Baptist church, never missing Sunday services with her children in tow. She never seemed to be bothered by the fact that her husband sold liquor in his store even as she railed against strong drink in her church meetings.

Julian Price maintained his mother's weekly Sunday service schedule until he split with his Baptist minister in Greensboro over the Al Smith Catholic issue. But he did not follow his mother's practices when it came to alcohol consumption or her abhorrence to profanity because he indulged in both. He did, however, look with disdain at women who drank or cursed.

Mrs. Price also was an early advocate of a good and strict education. She was graduated from Hollins College. She and her husband started their own private school, mostly for the benefit of their own children, but they accepted other children in the community from more affluent families.

Joseph Price died in 1887 and his wife continued his successful businesses until shortly before her death in 1922. The Prices felt family members should be together, even in death. Julian Price's ancestors purchased land for a family cemetery in Meharrin and all early family members and spouses are buried there except Julian who is interred in his own mausoleum in Greensboro's Green Hill Cemetery.

Julian Price chose not to follow his father in the mercantile business. Instead, he chose railroading after becoming fascinated with the telegraph machines that clicked constantly in the rail depot in his hometown while he was growing up. He bypassed college, over his mother's objections, and secured his first job as a railroad telegraph operator at age 17 in 1884 at a $1 a day in Meharrin. He transferred to other small Virginia cities for the railroad, ultimately moving to Richmond as a dispatcher for Southern Railway at $60 a month, $5 a month less than he would later pay his son-in-law Bryan for his first job at Jefferson. Before Price started his telegraph work, he labored as a part-time woodcutter for the railroad to help supply fuel for wood-burning engines.

He quit the telegraph business in 1903, disgusted, he told friends, that the railroads were owned by westerners that didn't show much concern for southern employees. He spent the next two years as a salesman for American Snuff Company, but tired of the buggy rides over desolate back roads of rural Virginia peddling the powdery tobacco product. At the urging of a physician friend who advised him to both stop selling and using tobacco, Price joined Greensboro Life Insurance Company, the forerunner of Jefferson Standard in 1905. When he was hired at the insurance company, he bought 10 shares of stock, paying $250 down and signing a bank note for $1,000. He paid off that debt quickly because of his aversion to owing people money.

Price had a slow beginning in insurance, but it was apparent before long that he had found his calling. On one of his first sales attempts in Greensboro, an impatient prospective client asked Price how many policies his company had in place. "Damned if I know," Price replied with a confident grin, "but when I get yours they'll sure as hell have at least one." He made the sell.

Price was easily recognized as the nattily dressed man on the streets of Greensboro, with his ever-present walking cane and hat that was part of his daily attire, inside his office as well as outside. He started his habit of wearing a hat while working as the railroad telegraph operator, a job which kept him running among unheated railroad shacks on winter evenings. He also kept his hat on, he once said, because when he was ready to go, he didn't need to waste time looking for it. With it on his head, he always knew where it was. People often joked about Price and his hat, but never within his earshot. One hat story depicting Price's seriousness with wearing it was connected to Karl Ljung at Jefferson, the man who once thought Price was going to fire him. At a Jefferson directors meeting, Ljung discreetly asked Price's son Ralph to quietly suggest to his father that he remove his hat when the meeting started. Ralph delivered the whispered message. His father retorted without a whisper: "Tell Karl to go to hell." The hat stayed on Price's head throughout that meeting and many to follow.

Price was once a regular poker player, using his gambling winnings as a regular source of needed income, but stopped once he became head of Jefferson and began earning a higher salary. "I nearly always played with folks who had more money than I did. I couldn't have lived in the early days on my salary of $90 a month as a married man," he told a newspaper reporter of his early days on the job. He gave up poker once his salary was enough to support him, he said, and because he had a "good wife" who was not happy with his gambling.

Price clearly adored his wife Ethel Clay whom he met in Durham where she was a nurse in Watts Hospital after becoming the first graduate of the school of nursing there. The couple married in Ivy, Va., in an Episcopal ceremony even though she had become a Catholic years earlier while studying at the church-affiliated College of Notre Dame in Baltimore. Ethel Clay graduated from the Baltimore school in 1892 with a degree in English literature before enrolling in nursing school. Her daughter Kathleen later received an honorary degree from the College of Notre Dame after she and her brother Ralph made a substantial donation to start the Ethel Clay Continuing Education Center in December 1973 in memory of their mother.

There is nothing in the family's historical documents explaining why the Prices chose an Episcopal wedding, with her being Catholic even though the Catholic Church frowned on such marriages at the time. Her church accepted the marriage as a civil ceremony, not a religious one, but Mrs. Price never let that Episcopal wedding deter her continued devotion to her Catholic faith.

When asked why the Catholic Church didn't object to her grand-mother's Episcopal wedding vows, Kay Bryan Edwards attributed it to economics. "Affluent Catholics were just allowed to do certain things that poor Catholics could not," she said.

The Prices and their children were quite generous to Catholic causes following the Price marriage, including virtual total payment for the construction of Our Lady of Grace Church in Greensboro. Julian Price originally contributed $400,000 in Jefferson Standard stock to start that church and his daughter Kathleen and son Ralph later added another $300,000 to finish the project.

The Prices doted on their two children, he on daughter Kathleen and she on son Ralph. Kathleen's personality was more like her father's and Ralph's was more like his mother's. Ethel Clay Price, who frequently described herself as a descendant of the famous orator Henry Clay, was content to remain a homebody while her husband made the news as a powerbroker and successful insurance executive. She was known as an expert cook and seamstress, talents that her daughter Kathleen never acquired. Mrs. Price made a lot of clothes for her children and for Joe and Kathleen Bryan's young children even though the family could afford to buy the finest clothes available.

Mrs. Price's father was Henry Clay, but he was not the famous Kentucky Senator and Secretary of State under President John Quincy Adams. Her father was Col. Henry DeBoisfeuillet Clay from Ohio, a Captain in the 14th Regiment Infantry of the Union Army in the Civil War. He was twice wounded in battle and later requested a government pension by listing on his application his wounds and what he said was a sun stroke suffered on the battlefield that made him unable to work. Col. Clay's son Ralph A. Clay, Ethel's younger brother, was a veteran of the Spanish American War and died during the war in his early 20s although family records are unclear if he died in battle or of other complications.

While Ethel Clay Price's father fought for the Union forces in the

Civil War, as did Joe Bryan's grandfather, Julian Price's ancestors were devoted Virginia southerners who were strongly on the side of the Confederacy. Price family military records are sketchy or missing because Union soldiers burned and destroyed property and files as they pillaged through the Virginia countryside, including the neighborhood where Julian Price's ancestors lived. "The Prices were devastated by what happened during the war," said Ms. Elise Franklin of Greensboro, a descendant of the Prices of Meherrin.

While Ethel Clay Price was a devoted mother and wife, the same cannot be said for her parents. Her mother, Hattie "Daisy" Field Clay, divorced her husband the colonel — who later married his housekeeper — following the Civil War and moved to England and then to France, where she married a Frenchman named Kellogg and lived there until her death in the 1930s. After moving to France, Hattie Clay cut all ties to her family in the United States. On one occasion, in fact, she refused to come to her front door to see her own daughter, claiming she had no children. That occasion was when her daughter Ethel, who with her husband Julian, had made a trip to Paris in an attempt to make contact with her mother. Ethel later told friends of her personal hurt at being rejected by her mother, but she nevertheless kept a portrait of her mother hanging in her home.

Despite that rebuff in Paris, Kathleen Bryan and her brother Ralph Price also held an affection for their grandmother and supplied money for the upkeep of her grave in France until their own ill health and deaths. After Mrs. Kellogg died, her furniture was brought from France back to Greensboro where Ethel Price kept it in her home until her death in 1943. The family then loaned several large pieces to the Greensboro Historical Museum where it was housed in the Dolly Madison Room for several years before being returned to the family and divided among various relatives. For awhile after the furniture was split up, rumblings were prevalent among the Price and Clay sides of the families over who received what, but the issue faded with time.

The Clay/Kellogg furniture brought from Paris to Greensboro filled two boxcars. Julian Price agreed to pick up the tab for shipping because his wife asked him to, but he later complained that he could have bought three times the amount of the same furniture in this country for what he paid in tariffs to bring the family pieces to America.

The Clays were obviously proud of their heritage and accomplishments of family members who came to this country as early as 1770 and settled in Georgia. Several family members served with distinction in the Revolutionary War and subsequent conflicts and several became public officials and diplomats. The first ancestor of Ethel Clay known to come to America was Ralph Clay of Yorkshire, England. It's unclear exactly what the family connection, if any, was to the famous Henry Clay of Kentucky. That Henry Clay was born in Virginia in 1777, seven years after Ethel Clay's ancestors settled in Georgia. His early ancestors were from Wales. Accurate or not, however, Ethel Clay's family documents through the years continued to list the famous Henry Clay among the ancestors.

There is also some question on the place of birth for Ethel Clay Price. She was born in October 1874 while her soldier father was on assignment with the United States military in Europe. One copy of her death certificate lists her place of birth as New York and another lists her birth in Jamestown, VA.

There was lingering jealousy between the Clay/Price side of the family and the Bryan side after Joe Bryan married Kathleen Price over which family had the most aristocratic background. In the minds of Clay family members, Bryan's Yankee family heritage was never considered as important or significant as the Southern Clays and Prices, according to family records. Bryan, in spite of his immediate family problems as a young man, also had some aristocracy, along with a few paupers, in his lineage if family historical documents are correct.

Either in an effort to settle the family feuding over aristocratic lin-

Ethel Clay Price, at age 24, in 1898.

eage or out of personal interest or both, Bryan in 1982 began an earnest quest following some earlier attempts to unwrap his family history by hiring a series of people to trace his ancestors. He found good and bad news from that experience, but he also had made frequent attempts much earlier to learn about his family tree.

Bryan wrote to a man he believed to be a distant cousin in Atlanta in late December 1946 in search of some family history, some of which he conceded might not be what he wanted to find. In his letter to Shepard Bryan, a state court judge, Bryan said he was simply curious about his ancestors. "Maybe there is some family skeleton lying around that shouldn't be dug up," he wrote. "That wouldn't surprise me a bit and wouldn't disappoint me. But I would hope there wouldn't be more than six or seven.

"As you know, our family all were dumped on the shores of the northeast section of the country, to be exact in New York. Our end of the Bryans seems to be petering out. I would like to get something finally assembled to pass on to the children. That which isn't suitable, of course, we would ignore." That letter brought Bryan no new information.

"I really think at the time he had something of an inferiority complex," commented Gary Parks, who in the early 1980s was a UNCG graduate student who was hired by Bryan at $10 an hour to look into the Bryan family history. "He wasn't sure about circumstances of his family of Irish Catholics who first came to this country in the 1840s about the time of the massive Potato Famine in Ireland. He had heard so much talk about his wife's family heritage of being descended from the famous Henry Clay and such. And he had certainly had a sad upbringing here because of his parents."

After some success with Parks' work that lasted four years, in which Bryan learned of the death of his long-lost brother and the existence of his brother's son, Bryan then hired the respected DeBritt research organization in London to do further family exploration. The DeBritt research staff was known for working with roy-

Julian and Ethel Clay Price in the early 1940s.

alty. What the DeBritt group found, after much prodding and push-ing by Bryan, was that while Bryan had some important and influ-ential people in his past generations, one of his grandfathers was so poor he was considered a pauper.

"He wasn't happy with that report," Parks said. "He didn't find what he wanted. He said that for $3,000 you'd have thought they could have found something other than that his grandfather was too poor to own anything and was a pauper. I think he always wanted a more illustrious background to match his later rise in the corporate world and his social status. He was obviously proud of his own accomplishments and successes."

Bryan later hired Kevin von der Lippe of Greensboro, a serious-minded history major at N.C. State University, who diligently worked for more than six years researching and organizing the Bryan family history and records. It was von der Lippe who uncov-ered much of the family history that is now part of the official archives at UNCG.

Both Parks and von der Lippe had praise and respect for Bryan and his generosity toward his adopted community as well as for his interest in learning of his family history and recording it accurately.

"I feel blessed for having spent six and a half years with him," von der Lippe said. "He genuinely cared for people and had a pres-ence that few have. He was a powerful voice in this community."

"Joe Bryan did so much good for so many people and I respected him greatly," Parks said. "I admired him for his strength and dedi-cation. I learned a lot from him."

As Jefferson Standard continued to expand under Price's leader-ship in the 1920s and 30s, his influence on local affairs kept pace. Despite his dogged determination that his employees work hard and produce at high levels, he also wanted them to have time to relax in their hours off the job. He provided them opportunities for benefits while they were not working, perhaps to help offset his rep-utation for paying low salaries. The year the new Jefferson Building opened, Price approved a plan for group life insurance for employees. A year later, in 1924, Price bought the Frazier farm on historically significant New Garden Road for use as a company club and recreation area. New Garden Road was the scene of troop movement and battles during the Revolutionary War.

The Jefferson Club became one of Julian Price's favorite places along with the downtown skyscraper he built, perhaps even more so than his beloved property along the Blue Ridge Parkway in western North Carolina. Price spent many hours at the Jefferson Club; sometimes relaxing and sometimes cutting power deals with the local establishment. His son-in-law Joe Bryan would adopt the habit of Jefferson Club attendance as well, but his visits were far more social and more public than the Price forays there.

Bryan's Jefferson Club parties would become legend as he used them to enhance his reputation as one of Greensboro's most noteworthy social leaders. Mrs. Bryan was also an enthusiastic party giver. Her friends often joked that she never saw a party she didn't like. But it was the parties that Bryan personally arranged, some after his wife became ill and after she died, that people in Greensboro still rave about.

"Joe was forever chasing that bright elusive social butterfly," a family acquaintance said of Bryan more as a statement of fact rather than criticism. "He was interested in having parties and being at the right place at the right time. That was a major part of what pleased him."

The Bryan social life in Greensboro may have begun at the Jefferson Club under the influence of Julian Price, but it was Bryan himself who extended that social interest far beyond his home area. It became one of his trademarks.

If Julian Price began the social scene at Jefferson, Bryan just expanded and refined it to a science and became the city's best-known distributor.

7

CORPORATE CLEANSING

As the South struggled from the disquieting dilemma of the Great Depression into economic recovery just prior to and after World War II, Jefferson Standard Life Insurance Company and the City of Greensboro moved in tandem on a steady course of progress. Jefferson is due more credit for helping the city to advance than the other way around, but the two were inextricably connected. One man played a significant role in both. That man was Julian Price. It was his son-in-law Joe Bryan who attempted to follow that lead, albeit through a significantly different methodology.

Price's corporate dominance as president of Jefferson was plain for everyone to see. His deal making on behalf of the city was far less visible, but in many respects no less important for the local citizenry.

And as Price's power and influence grew, the same could be said for his son-in-law Bryan. While Bryan was unable to completely escape the shadow or influence of his domineering father-in-law, he made a series of corporate steps that helped him shake off at least some perceptions of indifference and lack of respect among colleagues from his earliest years with the company.

Bryan maintained a steady march up the corporate ladder without ever reaching the pinnacle. He said late in life that he realized he would never become president because he was never comfortable with becoming part of the office politics that would have been required to get the job. He wasn't a glad hander and he didn't suffer fools gladly. Furthermore, the corporate hierarchy had always considered him as outsider because of his background. But he never looked back on what might have been.

"I don't indulge in the luxury of bemoaning what I have failed to do or did wrong," he told an interviewer in 1982. "That's all gone and past. What happens today and in the future are the important things." Indeed, he was looking to the future until the very end of his 99 years. That may have been solely because of his vision for making things better or it may have been because so much of the past was too depressing.

Despite some heavy odds on both the corporate and family sides, Bryan obviously still did quite well. There's no argument that his first job with Jefferson in 1931 was a make-shift one created by his corporate president father-in-law who was determined to get his daughter back home from New York even it meant providing a job for her husband. But rather than whine, mope or seek sympathy, Bryan proved his durability.

From his first assignment as custodian of the company kitchen, Bryan became company secretary in 1933, vice president in 1936, first vice president in 1947 and senior vice president in 1956. He joined the company's board of directors in 1933 and the executive committee in 1943. He was instrumental in forming the company's finance committee in 1950, serving as its first chairman and continuously holding a seat on that investment group until his retirement in 1961.

Even with all those titles, however, Bryan was not an integral part of the day-to-day operations of the insurance division of the company. In fact, he was never all that personally interested in the insur-

Joseph and Kathleen Bryan with their personal friends and business associates Mr. and Mrs. Gene Autry. Bryan arranged Jefferson Standard loans to cowboy star Autry to purchase radio and television stations, making a lot of money for both.

Joseph M. Bryan Sr. on horseback while visiting a ranch owned by his friend, cowboy movie star and singer Gene Autry.

ance side of the company. He said to a friend outside the company that he found insurance somewhat boring, not nearly so intriguing as broadcasting. His greatest influence, by far, had to do with the company's non-insurance investments and broadcasting. He served as chairman of the company's broadcasting division from 1945 until his retirement in 1961 and was in a leadership role during the formative years of television as well as corporate investments outside insurance policy marketing.

"His primary role in the insurance company was to critique what someone was doing," one former associate said. "And he was pretty good at it, too. He had a good feel for economic trends and a nice feel for how a business should be run. He was able to help set some overall, long-time directions for the company."

He became a close personal friend of cowboy star Gene Autry after initiating some major business loans for Autry to invest in television stations, newspaper ownership and other business enterprises. Through Bryan's connections, Autry entertained Jefferson employees at social functions in Greensboro and at company conventions elsewhere. That friendship remained until Bryan's death even though Jefferson (after Bryan's retirement) declined a request to loan Autry money to buy a major league baseball team, the California Angels.

"I didn't want to get involved in any loans for a baseball team," former Jefferson President Roger Soles said of the Autry request for borrowing to buy the major league team. Bryan likely would have approved of the loans because his past business dealings with the cowboy star had been so successful, but at the time the baseball team loan was requested Bryan was no longer involved with the company except for maintaining his office in the headquarters building.

During his tenure with Jefferson, however, Bryan was designated by his father-in-law to make deals for millions in loans to some of the nation's largest newspapers, a move that later led to Jefferson owning dozens of newspaper properties across the country and making huge profits.

Soles said Jefferson never put more than $90,000 of its own money into newspaper properties and never had debt of more than $23 million. When Soles sold off the company's newspaper properties in the late 1980s, the company netted $147 million in profits.

Price had an interest in getting Jefferson into the business side of newspaper publishing from his past experience as owner of the Greensboro Record. "I then got interested in the same thing," Bryan said, "and Mr. Price permitted me to specialize in making newspaper loans." Jefferson Standard also became an investor in newspapers because banks were not interested in making such loans, according to Bryan. "No bank or self-respecting lending institution would make a loan to a newspaper in those days (the 1940s) because they couldn't find enough tangible assets to justify it," Bryan said in a 1980 interview. "Publishers always wanted to show lenders their brick and mortar, the printing side of the business. I didn't want to see all those things because they were all hot and dirty. I preferred to sit in the publisher's cool and comfortable offices and look at their bottom line figures. What interested me was the earning capacity and there was some fantastic earnings at some of the newspapers where we made loans."

With Price's blessing, Bryan made Jefferson loans to newspapers in Tulsa, Louisville, Philadelphia, Denver, Phoenix, San Jose and Indianapolis. In Indianapolis, Bryan actually personally owned the Star newspaper — but only for half a day — without ever putting up a dime. The owner refused to sell to prospective buyer Eugene Pulliam — grandfather of future Republican Vice President Dan Quayle — and the only way to close the deal was for Bryan to personally agree to buy the company in the morning and then sell it that same afternoon to Pulliam. That's what he did without the seller ever knowing details of the arrangement until after the fact.

As the Jefferson executive handling the loans to the publishing industry, Bryan became both respected and praised by newspaper owners across the country and he became friends with some of the most influential publishers in the nation.

On one newspaper loan, Bryan had a nudge from U.S. Supreme Court Justice William O. Douglas. Douglas was a friend of the man who wanted a loan to purchase the Denver Post, but Bryan wasn't initially interested. "I got a phone call one morning from Justice Douglas whom I knew rather well," Bryan said. "He said he wanted me to do something for him. I asked what and he said he wanted me to make the loan to his friend." Bryan made the loan and Jefferson made money.

Bryan was also chairman of the board of Pilot Life Insurance Company after Jefferson bought the company but before it was merged with Jefferson into Jefferson-Pilot Corporation and a member of that company's executive committee. In that capacity, he had little to do with daily operations, but was a stickler for financial details in board meetings, usually asking questions he already knew answers to even if other executives didn't. He prided himself in keeping up with details, even while appearing detached, as a way of insuring that the corporate decision were the right ones to keep the company moving forward. His primary interests were in company investments, not insurance policies.

He did, however, offer regular suggestions in writing to both his father-in-law and subsequent presidents on ways to improve staff morale and profits. Some of his recommendations were adopted as company policy, but many were ignored, a point he found frustrating. On one occasion in May 1937 Bryan wrote a colleague an inner office note lamenting that "I am a poor salesman for (good) ideas as my lot seems to be championing lost causes. You need a new jockey for your race."

Bryan headed the company's Washington lobbying efforts on insurance and tax law issues during the 1940s and 1950s. In that role, Bryan became friends with North Carolina's somewhat eccentric U.S. Senator Robert Rice (Our Bob) Reynolds. Bryan's biggest complaint about their relationship was that Reynolds couldn't hear and was too vane to wear a hearing aid. Bryan, of course, also encountered hearing loss later in life, most likely from his many years of shotgun shooting without earplugs.

Reynolds, among other things, was a political maverick and champion of controversial causes. He founded the Vindicators and the American Nationalist Party, both opposed to United States entry into World War II. He was, however, the kind of personality that Bryan enjoyed. Before going to the Senate, Reynolds was a well-known raconteur, having been a professional wrestler, football coach, book salesman, war correspondent, ranch hand and criminal lawyer. Reynolds was five times married, the last time in 1941 at age 57 when he wed the 19-year-old daughter of Evelyn Walsh McLean who at the time owned the Hope Diamond. "He ran his Senate committees with an iron hand," Bryan said of his friend Reynolds. "But he just couldn't hear much that was said most of the time."

The Washington lobbying job, however, often frustrated the impatient Bryan who wanted more action much faster. He felt he had little to show for his efforts in terms of satisfaction from his colleagues. "I have put a lot of time and money in order to have an entré on the Washington level," Bryan wrote then company president Howard (Chick) Holderness in 1959. "Now I find some (in the company) were of the opinion all during this time that I was expendable as far as they were concerned, and they still feel that way. I wouldn't be human if I didn't feel (bothered). This also goes for Kathleen whose help and support on many occasions has been invaluable. Her willingness to forgo personal preferences for activities of a social, entertainment and traveling nature for the company is perhaps better recognized by the industry as a whole than the immediate Jefferson Standard family, including some of the directors."

Holderness replied that he felt Bryan was overreacting, maybe even a little paranoid. "I have always stated that in my opinion you were doing an outstanding job (as company lobbyist)," Holderness responded. "I can assure you that if others appraised it differently within the company, it was in spite of what I have said." Holderness added, however, that it might be time for someone else to assume those Washington duties.

That was one of many times that Bryan and his wife felt unappreciated by Jefferson executives and directors despite their vast stock holdings that came through their own purchases and inheritances. The most disturbing and emotional time was when Holderness was named president in 1950 in the midst of a period of public company turmoil and embarrassment. Bryan and his wife were personally anxious for him to have the job as president and both for a time thought they had votes within the board of directors to win. But it was not to be, thanks to some quiet deal making by Jefferson director J. Van (Jack) Lindley, a man who would become well known as the "gray fox" and backroom operative—and with good reason, too.

As Bryan quietly went about his duties within the corporation during the late 1930s and 1940s, his father-in-law Price was formulating a plan for the city government. Once Price was firmly in control at the company, he turned more of his attention to outside matters, particularly local government. He was elected to the Greensboro City Council in 1920, the year after becoming Jefferson president and served six years before sitting out one term and being elected two years later for one more term. His council tenure was focused on street paving, elimination of railroad grade crossings, and an expanded municipal water and sewer system. His key contribution, though, was helping to implement the city manager form of government.

Price's influence at city hall, however, stretched far beyond his own terms in office. He was a powerbroker behind the scenes for council candidates over parts of three decades. He essentially picked who would run and when they would do it. Price pretty much ran things everywhere, according to William Jones, a retired local brick company owner and son-in-law of one of Price's hand-picked council candidates, Orton Boren. Jones recalled his father-in-law saying Price told Boren in 1944 that it was his time to seek a council seat. Boren demurred, fearing it might cost him money in time away from his brick manufacturing plant. Price just told him to run and not worry about losing money because he (Price) would make up any company losses. Price also chose when Ben Cone, Huger King, Jack Lindley, Paul Lindley, and C. M. Vanstory would seek public office.

Bryan did not follow Price's lead in immersing himself as a power broker in local politics, publicly or privately. While Bryan was financially supportive of various state and national candidates, he never sought office himself nor played any direct role on behalf of others in campaigns for elective or appointive office with two notable exceptions, both involving Republicans although Bryan was a Democrat. Bryan worked privately — but diligently — to help ensure the appointment of his friend Greensboro lawyer N. Carlton "Woody" Tilley to a lifetime federal judgeship in the early 1990s and he expended considerable sums to help elect his former son-in-law D. M. (Lauch) Faircloth to the U.S. Senate in 1992. He was successful in both attempts.

In all his years in the corporate world and later as a major philanthropist, Bryan said the Tilley appointment is the only time he ever personally asked any politician for any favors. In that case, however, Bryan enlisted the aid of North Carolina senators Terry Sanford and Jesse Helms as well as South Carolina Sen. Strom Thurmond.

Both Price and Bryan also became involved in governmental appointments outside the local arena, but not of their own choosing. Price served during the administration of Gov. Angus McLean

111

in the late 1920s as head of the state Salary and Wage Commission and also served as president of the Federal Home Loan Bank in Winston-Salem that was later located in Greensboro for several decades before moving to Atlanta. Bryan, albeit reluctantly, also accepted one honorary position as chairman of the State Elections Board from Gov. Luther Hodges in the late 1950s. When Hodges asked Bryan to take that post, he initially declined, saying it would be too controversial.

"That's really more than I can do," Bryan told the governor.

"No it isn't," Hodges replied. "Besides you don't have any choice. I've already had the election ballots printed with your name listed as chairman." Bryan served through the next election in that post.

In 1936 Price was promoted as a Democratic candidate for North Carolina governor among his friends and business associates. He received considerable support within the corporate community across the state where he was well known and respected. He toyed with the idea of running, but only briefly as the term of Gov. J.C.B. Ehringhaus neared an end.

While most of the public response to his potential candidacy was positive, Price received some private correspondence suggesting that all the campaign talk was just a sham to get further recognition and more business for Jefferson. Such talk clearly irritated him. Price ruled out a statewide campaign, he said, because he was offended that anyone would think he was using politics for personal advantage and because he didn't want to put his Catholic family through anything akin to the bigoted 1928 presidential race when the religious prejudice became an issue. Instead of Price, voters elected Clyde Hoey as governor.

The face of downtown Greensboro began changing in 1918, the year before Price became president of Jefferson Standard. But that was just the beginning. During his first year as head of Jefferson, Price watched with pride as a new downtown hotel construction project was started under the direction of New York architect

Charles Hartmann. The hotel, a long time landmark, was the O. Henry, named for the city's native son and writer William Sydney Porter whose pen name was O. Henry. Price so much liked what he saw in that building that he offered architect Hartmann a deal. Move from New York to Greensboro, Price asked Hartmann, and Price would hire him to draw plans for his dream of a new Jefferson Building.

Hartmann agreed and within four years the Jefferson Building was reality. That move by Price resulted in Hartmann's deft drawing board touch being put on the facades of Grimsley and Dudley high schools, the Guilford Building, King Cotton Hotel, administration building at N.C. A&T State University and L. Richardson Hospital. Hartmann also designed Country Club Apartments on North Elm Street, partly owned by Price, which would become important much later in Joe Bryan's philanthropy.

While Price was engaged in various building projects around Greensboro when Bryan joined Jefferson, Bryan had building plans of his own, although not nearly of the scope of his father-in-law. Bryan just wanted a home. And frugality was an important part of his plans.

Bryan and his family immediately entered a higher standard of home life — despite his paltry salary of $65 a month — once they came to Greensboro than they had been accustomed to in New York. From a cramped apartment in Manhattan, the family moved into a spacious rented home at 701 Sunset Drive in Greensboro in an area known at the time as "cough drop hill." That name came from the presence in the neighborhood of the Richardson family, founders of Vicks VapoRub, and the fact that a large number of doctors lived nearby. The Richardson family had created Vick Chemical Company 25 years earlier after inventing what was considered a magic formula for fighting colds known as Vick's Magic Croup Salve. It later was renamed VapoRub.

Price, who had each month subsidized the Bryan family in New

York, also assisted with family expenses in Greensboro after helping secure the rented home that was once home to Greensboro mayor Huger King, one of Julian Price's hand-picked mayors, among other prominent residents.

Bryan wanted his own home, but at the right price, and he wasn't reluctant to ask for favors in getting it. Pilot Life Insurance, by that time owned by Jefferson, operated a subsidiary construction division and Bryan went directly to the top to ask for home building help. What he wanted was to get a home constructed without any profit for the Pilot subsidiary, a perk he sought for working at the parent company.

Bryan wrote Pilot president Emry Green in the fall of 1934 and he would like company assistance with his home construction. "Personally I do not see why any money at all should be made by any of our subsidiaries for doing this job for me," Bryan wrote. "Can you help me out?" Bryan said he had spoken with some contractors who were insisting on building him "a mansion" that he couldn't afford. Green, either out of kindness or fear of offending the company president's son-in-law, offered immediate help. "Just talk (with the company contractor) and have him advise you just what the cost will be to erect your residence without adding any profit," Green responded within days after Bryan made his request.

Bryan purchased the lot for his new home at 711 Sunset Drive, just up the block from the house he rented, but not through a Realtor because he wanted to save money. He searched public records for land for sale as a result of foreclosures remaining from the Depression era a few years earlier, thinking he could get a better bargain. The lot he bought was obtained at a public auction on the downtown courthouse steps. Bryan put in his bid of $2,000 only to see it increased by local businessman Willie Holderness, brother of the man who would later get the job as Jefferson president that Bryan had sought. Holderness forced Bryan to pay $3,000, a 50 percent increase over what he had intended. Bryan later expressed

unhappiness at the higher land price forced upon him by Holderness, saying it caused him to cut out some frills in the home that he
and his wife wanted but could no longer afford. Mrs. Bryan wanted
a circular staircase from the front foyer to the second floor, but she
didn't get it. Bryan said the increased land cost forced him to eliminate the extra expense of that style staircase.

The purchase turned out to be a profitable one. The home cost
$31,000 to build in 1934. At Bryan's death in 1995, the home was
valued in excess of $800,000.

There were many land foreclosures and bankruptcies in the affluent Sunset Drive neighborhood around the time Bryan purchased
property. Julian Price apparently prevented at least one from taking
place, saving a life in the process.

Heavy-duty real estate developer Alfred Scales, father of Julius
Scales who later was scandalized for his Communist Party connections, had a major debt to pay to Price and Jefferson on a $1 million
life insurance policy. Scales went to Price's office seeking relief in
paying the premiums because of shortage of cash in the middle
1930s following the stock market crash.

Price said he couldn't defer payments and that Scales' only
choice was to pay up. Legend has it that Scales responded that, in
that case, Price's only choice was to pay off on a death claim. Scales
then calmly walked to Price's 14th floor office window, raised it and
threatened to jump. Price abruptly changed his mind and decided a
deferred premium payment could be arranged. It will never be
known if Scales actually would have jumped, but Price wasn't willing to take that gamble with a $1 million double indemnity payoff
staring him in the face.

While the actual truth of Scales threatened suicide may have been
embellished with time and telling, another Price rescue was more
significant to the city. It involved Wesley Long Hospital that went
through troubled times just as a lot of businesses and individuals in
the 1930s. Times were so tough at the hospital. Salaries were paid in

115

scrip when no cash was available. Hospital official Joe Henry Barrier went to Price for help.

"The horse is sick," Barrier said of the hospital, "but it just needs some good strong jockeys." Price jumped in the saddle when told of the need. He loaned, without public notice, the facility enough money to pay employees and purchase essential supplies. Barrier later said Price saved the hospital from shutting its doors.

In another little known act, Price also is credited with saving what is now Campbell University from bankruptcy and closing. The school, was a financially struggling small college during and immediately following the Crash of 1929. The school's founder James Archibald Campbell sought a Jefferson loan from Price to keep the school open and meet the faculty payroll. Price agreed, but was initially turned down by the company's board. Price wouldn't accept that decision.

"My understanding is that Mr. Price then held another private conversation with his directors and they turned around," Campbell President Norman Wiggins said in late 1999, recalling the school's history. "My information is that Julian Price saved this school."

In 1967, a Campbell official and descendant of the school's founder, Dr. Leslie Campbell, came to Greensboro to thank then company president Chick Holderness for the kindness shown by Price some 60 years earlier. "I thought he was coming to ask for money," said retired Jefferson executive Seth Macon. "But all he wanted was to say thank you. We didn't even know Mr. Price had done that. He never let anyone know. But he did that in order to keep that school open."

Jefferson Pilot in more recent years has established a scholarship program at Campbell and former Jefferson president Roger Soles has donated $300,000 to the school located east of Raleigh.

Campbell President Wiggins, a former law school professor at Wake Forest University with expertise in trusts and wills, also has benefited personally from an association with the Price/Bryan families. Wiggins serves as a trustee of several Bryan family trusts and has collected several hundred thousands of dollars trustee fees, according to court documents. That fact is a sore point with members of Bryan's family who say they've seen few if any real services rendered for the fees collected. Wiggins chose not to discuss his role as a trustee.

Price continued at the helm of Jefferson and in the heart of city affairs until the middle 1940s. His wife Ethel had been insisting for years that it was time for him to loosen the reins on both corporate and municipal affairs by the time he reached his 75th birthday in 1942 and turn more duties over to their reclusive son Ralph. While reluctant to do either, particularly with company matters, Price conceded he had begun to find more enjoyment in his second home, called The Rock House, on Highway 321 just outside Blowing Rock in western North Carolina. He also had big plans for his nearby mountain farm, a vast estate of 4,200 acres of rolling mountain landscape, along the Blue Ridge Parkway and slowly retreated from keeping his finger in so many governmental affairs in Greensboro.

In love with the beauty and serenity of his farm along the Parkway, Price decided he would build his wife a stately house on that property so they could live blissfully in retirement. That was a major step for him because he had once been reluctant even to buy his first home in Greensboro. Until midlife, Price had been a renter not a homeowner, arguing that it was cheaper to let others worry with taxes and maintenance. "Fools buy, smart people rent," he often repeated with relish when asked earlier in his career why he didn't own a home.

When he built his initial home, a Tutor palace by local standards, in Greensboro's historic Fisher Park, he called himself a fool for such expenditures. But that's what wife Ethel wanted.

With plans to ease off on work but convinced his wife would survive him, Price in the early 1940s converted many of his personal assets and much of his stock equity holdings to Ethel's name, leav-

Julian and Ethel Clay Price, center, with Kathleen and Joseph M. Bryan Sr. at the Price's 45th wedding anniversary in April 1942.

Kathleen Price Bryan and her brother Ralph Price with a portrait of their father Julian Price and a resolution commending the senior Price at the Jefferson Insurance Company's 50th anniversary celebration in August 1957.

ing himself with relatively few assets. For a man who did such careful planning in business and civic affairs, the asset transfer turned out to be extremely poor planning on his part.

On October 26, 1943, fate dealt Price an ugly hand. Suddenly and without warning Price's devoted wife suffered a fatal heart attack. The official cause of death was coronary thrombosis brought on by arteriosclerosis. But she had seemed perfectly healthy one day only to be dead the next. That left Price personally devastated and financially in a deep hole. Her death meant Price would retain only those assets the law allowed and most of his former vast holdings would ultimately pass to others as his wife's will specified. His dream mountain home for Ethel was never built. His Parkway farm would ultimately wind up in the hands of the federal government.

After Price's death three years later, Jefferson bought the Parkway property and donated it to the federal government for park purposes as one means of helping eliminate some of Price's tax liabilities because his personal assets were not enough to cover his tax debts. Jefferson officials also personally purchased some of Price's company stock shortly after his death and solicited buyers for other shares to help offset his government debts.

Price's personal preference likely would have been for his daughter Kathleen rather than his son Ralph to take his place as company president, because he was so devoted to her, but women didn't do things like that at the time. Mrs. Bryan, however, was later elected to the Jefferson board of directors in 1961, the first woman ever to hold a seat on that board. Her daughter Nancy would later hold the same seat.

Price couldn't bring himself to seriously consider son-in-law Bryan for the presidency even though Bryan had shown he could get things done, mostly at Price's bidding. Bryan was still not liked by many of the Jefferson executives who felt he had never become southern enough to fit their image of Jefferson's top executive.

Remembering his late wife's admonition to give son Ralph a

chance, Price asked directors to name Ralph president in 1945 at the time the senior Price assumed the title of board chairman. There was more than a little reluctance on the part of Jefferson directors to choose Ralph because he was considered extremely weak in leadership skills and had never shown any particular interest in running the company. But the senior Price asked that his son be given a chance. He got his wish, but it was one that most Jefferson executives would later regret and concede should never have been made. There was no doubt in anyone's mind, however, who would be running the show. Julian Price might not be called president any longer, but he was still in charge.

Fate and the shock of death struck again in little more than a year after Ralph Price became president. Julian Price, just one month shy of his 79th birthday, was killed in an auto accident on the way to his home in Blowing Rock on October 25, 1946. His death occurred on the eve of the third anniversary of his wife's death. Three others in the car when it crashed rounding a curve on Highway 421 several miles east of North Wilkesboro were injured, but none seriously. There was no autopsy performed, and the exact cause of death has never been determined. Law enforcement officers listed likely causes as either mechanical failure or Price's suffering a fatal attack and falling on the chauffeur driver, causing him to lose control and slam into an embankment.

Price's death brought an outpouring of sympathy from across the country, including nationally known high public officials and corporate insurance executives. But it also brought on more than a few financial problems for Price's family and business associates as well as a lingering and embarrassing dual management scenario within the company. In death, Price regrettably brought on a degree of public uncertainty and disarray that he would never have allowed during his life. Bryan was caught in the middle of it all. There would be dark days ahead. But there would also be golden opportunities. Bryan would accept his setbacks and still come out ahead.

8

BRYAN BRANCHES OUT

Julian Price's death brought dramatic changes to both Jefferson Standard Life Insurance Company and Joe Bryan's chance to excel inside the corporate boardroom where he had for so long been considered an outsider.

Bryan accepted without complaint or condemnation the fact that he lost out for the presidency of Jefferson to Ralph Price the year before Julian Price died in the car crash. He knew full well that no matter how badly he or his wife might have wanted the title and responsibilities, it wasn't his lot to get either— at least not then. "There was absolutely no way anyone other than a Price was going to get that job," a close watcher of Jefferson and a Bryan friend for decades commented. "Ethel Price was determined to make sure her son got it. Even after she died, Julian wasn't about to go back on his promise to her that Ralph would be picked."

Ralph Price and Joe Bryan were never close friends. They were, in fact, more distant from each other than Bryan and the senior Price because their personal makeup was so different. Bryan was a hard-charging, engaging investment person who loved to be out front and who was determined to make things bigger and better for him and the company. The younger Price was just the opposite. He couldn't or didn't want to lead, wasn't particularly interested in insurance sales or corporate investments and was much happier directing most of his energies to more esoteric issues like world government and international law.

It was pretty clear soon after the senior Price's death, if not before, that Ralph was not the person for the presidency, yet directors were reluctant to quickly overthrow the decision that Julian Price had made so shortly before he died. What was decided at the highest levels of the company was to just proceed with Ralph holding the title of president but others making most of the decisions.

One decision that Ralph Price abruptly made, however, was both significant and symbolic. Joe Bryan had held onto an office adjacent to his father-in law on the 14th floor of the Jefferson Building from the time he joined the company. Speculation was that the senior Price kept Bryan in a nearby office so he could keep close tabs on the son-in-law. Regardless of the reason for the office location, Bryan was near the seat of power, a point he enjoyed, even if he didn't hold much power not delegated by the senior Price.

Shortly after his father's death, Ralph Price abruptly altered the office makeup, shifting Bryan downstairs to the 11th floor. The move brought Bryan larger and more palatial office space, but it was a clear symbol that he would no longer be a part of the inner circle. The real power had been and would remain on the 14th floor where all presidents before and after had held fourth until the early 1990s when the president's office was shifted to the new tower. Bryan maintained that 11th floor office until his death in 1995. When Bryan retired in the early 1960s, his wife asked that part of his retirement package include retention of his office. Jefferson directors granted her request, although at the time they didn't realize it would be for another 30-plus years.

There were periodic discreet discussions several times in the ensuing decades inside the 14th floor offices about asking Bryan to vacate his office following his retirement, but nothing ever came of it.

When Howard Holderness turned the presidency over to Roger Soles in 1967, Holderness reminded Soles that the two "needed to do something about Joe" remaining in his office space.

"Oh, just leave him there," Soles said. "It isn't costing the company much and it would create a lot of hard feelings if we asked him to move out. It's not a problem with me. Let's just leave things alone." Holderness thanked him, saying he felt relieved Soles didn't want Bryan to move and, more importantly, didn't want Holderness to be the one to tell him.

But while Bryan was symbolically removed from the center of power in early 1947, it didn't slow his pace. He began to branch out both inside and outside the company corporate structure. Eighteen months earlier he had won Julian Price's approval to expand the company's broadcasting arm beyond Greensboro when Jefferson bought WBT radio in Charlotte from CBS. That was just the beginning. Ralph Price may have determined where Bryan's office would be located, but he didn't or couldn't determine the breadth and depth of the more aggressive Bryan's business dealings.

Ralph Price, even with the title of president, was unable to slow Bryan's rush to other enterprises. The Jefferson board saw potential for higher profits and more business from broadcasting, so Bryan was firmly entrenched in that non-insurance command post even though he was, to paraphrase George Bush a generation later, out of the loop of the 14th floor. Ralph Price held the presidency title, but he was merely an observer of all that was happening.

Bryan was fortunate enough when Jefferson bought WBT radio to inherit a dedicated and talented leader and radio personality named Charles Crutchfield who would later became an influential, nationally known and highly respected broadcast executive. It was Bryan and Crutchfield who together forged the foundation for what is today both public and private television in North Carolina.

Crutchfield and Bryan had several things in common in their

123

backgrounds, but neither knew it at the time they became business associates. Crutchfield's father was once a cotton broker just as Bryan was in his early adult life and both their fathers always seemed to be stretching beyond reality. Both fathers abandoned their families while their sons were young.

Bryan and Crutchfield also shared an abiding interest in education although neither man had a college degree. Crutchfield tried college and then dropped out while Bryan never attended college classes.

Crutchfield was born in Hope, Ark., a fact he seldom acknowledged after Hope native William Jefferson Clinton became United States president in 1992 because Crutchfield held disdain for Clinton's moral behavior as well as his politics. Crutchfield's family moved to Spartanburg, S.C. when he was eight.

"Since Clinton was elected, I just tell people I am from Spartanburg," Crutchfield said in an interview just weeks before his death in August of 1998 at age 86. Crutchfield's father once made a lot of money as a commodities broker, but he lost it after becoming an alcoholic and, his son said, a womanizer before dying broke of sclerosis of the liver.

Bryan and Crutchfield, with able marketing expertise from Tar Heel native and nationally known bandleader Kaye Kyser and University of North Carolina promoter par excellence Billy Carmichael, were also the pioneers for public television in this state as well as creators of the first commercial station in North Carolina. Without those four, university television would have had a much tougher birth, and likely not existed until much later. It was Joe Bryan, in many respects, who made the first really significant step toward formation of public television in North Carolina. He provided the resources when few existed. Supporters of public TV owe him a tremendous debt of gratitude. "Without you, it (public television) would not have happened," then UNC president Gordon Gray penned in a note to Bryan shortly after the first public television broadcast.

124

Once he became hooked on the merits of radio, Bryan determined that the next logical step was television. While on a Jefferson business trip to New York in the mid-1940s, he was intrigued with the new medium of video broadcasting after seeing people lining the streets of Manhattan gawking into store windows at the thing called television. He brought the idea for personal and corporate involvement back to Greensboro.

"That fascinated me," Bryan said of his trip to New York where he first witnessed a television screen. "I said I want that; we've got to have that. It's the coming thing. So I came home to Greensboro and we put in an application for a TV station license."

Crutchfield, however, was the man behind Jefferson's initial interest in WBT radio just as he was later crucial to the success of television. Crutchfield, a man whose melodious radio voice and shrewd management skills were a lot smoother than his occasional hot temper, joined WBT as an announcer in 1933 at a weekly salary of $20, roughly a decade after the station had gone on the air in 1922. The first broadcast signal was from the basement of a home of station founder Fred N. Laxton. The station receiver was located nearby in a garage which, according to legend, doubled as a chicken house.

The early days of WBT were not unlike those of WBIG in Greensboro, a hit and miss operation mostly for the benefit of the Chamber of Commerce. The station's owners came and went in those early years. One owner was a Charlotte Buick dealer who matched station call letters WBT to his own ad slogan, "Watch Buicks Travel" that led to unfounded rumors in later years that the station was named for an automobile. Subsequent owners increased the station's power from 100 watts in the beginning to 5,000 watts by 1928.

CBS bought the station in 1929 and increased the power to 25,000 watts and hired a country bumpkin, yet savvy announcer named Grady Cole who preceded Crutchfield by four years. Cole was so popular that he was named by Collier's magazine as "Mr. Dixie" among radio announcers and held a place of prominence in radio for a quarter century. It was Cole who over the next several decades would become the evangelist for farmers and housewives who hung onto his every word on topics ranging from the weather to the price of eggs and buttermilk. At one point, Cole held more than 70 percent of the Charlotte radio audience. And while Gov. Kerr Scott is credited with the state's massive road-building program of the early 1950s, it was Grady Cole who ginned up the popular slogan for Scott's "Get Farmers out of the Mud" campaign.

Cole and Crutchfield were the public anchors of the station with Cole doing weather and news reports and Crutchfield serving as disc jockey, salesman and entertaining raconteur. Crutchfield was the brains of the operation.

Among Crutchfield's first duties in addition to selling commercial time and spinning records was forming a country music — then called hillbilly — band under the name of the Briarhoppers when he learned a sponsor was willing to buy ad time if such a program would be started. Crutchfield said he was told a company was willing to buy an hour's broadcast time six days a week, more than he had ever sold to any one sponsor.

"I was asked if we had a hillbilly band and I said sure," he said. "We didn't have any such thing, of course. I wasn't even sure what a hillbilly band was. But I durn sure didn't want to miss out on the ad revenue so I made sure we got us a band in short order. And the show went on the air."

He formed the band that became increasingly popular even as he routinely ridiculed the two prime products he was advertising: Purina chicken feed and Colorback (a hair color restorer). Crutchfield seldom followed the written script of his commercials, instead simply made fun of the products.

"It says here in the ad copy that Colorback will keep your hair from turning gray," he daily intoned, sometimes chuckling aloud.

"It doesn't say if it will also take out your hair's roots, but I guess it won't or people wouldn't be buying so much of the stuff." The advertisers apparently didn't care what Crutchfield said about them so long as he mentioned their products by name on the air. WBT listeners bought tons of chicken feed and hair coloring based on Crutchfield's recommendation.

By 1945, CBS needed to sell the station because it wanted to buy other outlets with broadcast signals that overlapped with Charlotte. There were half a dozen immediate bidders, among the most serious the *Charlotte Observer*. But Crutchfield didn't want the town's newspaper to also own the radio station.

He devised a plan to discreetly find out what the *Observer's* bid would be. "I was talking with one of the directors at the newspaper and just casually mentioned that I understood the newspaper might be interested in buying the station," Crutchfield explained. "He said yes, they were interested. We sort of talked about what the price and the value might be. He just volunteered that the newspaper was willing to go as high as $1.5 million because they thought they could get it for that. I told him, yeah he probably could because that bid was higher than the others that I had heard about and that I doubted anyone would bid any more. I suggested he stick to that as his high bid. He seemed satisfied with my assessment." Then Crutchfield began scouting the bidder that he really wanted: Jefferson Standard.

He placed a call to Julian Price in Greensboro, explaining that he wanted Jefferson to have the station because of the company's reputation for quality and integrity. Price liked the sound of that praise. "I believe you can get the station if you will just add $5,000 to expected high bid from the newspaper of $1.5 million," Crutchfield told Price. Several bids, including the one from the *Observer*, came in on the nose at $1.5 million. Price put in a bid at $5,000 more. That's how Jefferson bought the station, by outbidding the competitors by $5,000 on the original $1.5 million bid price. The

Observer executives were chagrined, but they had lost out to the cunning of Crutchfield.

Price put up Jefferson's money and put son-in-law Bryan in charge of closing the deal. Bryan also had a personal friendship with CBS president Frank Stanton from his earlier days in New York, a fact that Bryan later would contend played a role in Jefferson getting the station. "Frank Stanton personally wanted me to have that station," Bryan said many years after the purchase. "And Mr. Price wanted me to do this because I was competing with his son for the CEO job at Jefferson." The specific impact of the Bryan/Stanton friendship on closing the deal will never be known, but it certainly didn't hurt. The competition with Ralph Price was more fiction than fact.

Bryan's initial visit to WBT after the purchase to review the financial statement and look at facilities was something short of auspicious. His first official act as WBT head was mistakenly killing the broadcast signal. That happened when Bryan insisted on seeing the station's transmitter. Crutchfield took him to the site where Bryan, without warning or permission, promptly yanked open the gate to the fence surrounding the high voltage wires, automatically knocking the station off the air. Crutchfield often joked about that with Bryan and others. Bryan enjoyed the fun of hearing the story told on him, sometimes telling it himself.

For legal and tax reasons Jefferson did not put WBIG and WBT under a single operating division. WBT was assigned to Jefferson's subsidiary, the Southeastern Realty Company in Greensboro whose name was changed to Southeastern Broadcasting Company when Jefferson bought the station. Bryan later said that was done strictly to save money on taxes. That name was changed to Jefferson Standard Broadcasting in 1947, became Jefferson-Pilot Broadcasting in 1972 and Jefferson-Pilot Communications in 1985.

Jefferson-Pilot Communications, of course, has become well known in the Carolinas for its popular and profitable telecasts of

Atlantic Coast Conference basketball and football contests.

When Jefferson purchased WBT, Bryan promised Charlotte listeners and those in other cities along the East Coast where the station had a vast audience that he would maintain high standards and be supportive of the community. "We will remain your station, be your voice and operate for the greatest good for the most people," he said in an early broadcast under Jefferson ownership. He kept his promise, particularly during World War II when the station regularly promoted the merits of buying war bonds and offering free time to the Red Cross and other war-related causes.

Bryan and Crutchfield eventually became good friends and business associates, but it took a while. "Joe was a great investment man," Crutchfield commented. "But he knew absolutely nothing about broadcasting even though he was technically in charge of WBIG in Greensboro when the company invested in Charlotte. He gave me pretty much of a free hand to run WBT. He also gave me a lot of trouble because of his background as a sergeant in the Army. For a time, he was on the phone all the time down here (Charlotte). Joe was an elusive type person, not easy to get to know. But once you got to know him, you loved the guy. It took me several years to get accustomed to him, to find out what he expected and insisted on. Once we had that understanding, he stayed out of the way, let me run the place and we got along just fine."

From that rocky beginning, Bryan and Crutchfield put together plans for the first North Carolina commercial television station, WBTV, which went on the air in July 1949. WFMY in Greensboro would be the first station some years later to telecast a live program, but WBTV was the first television station in the state to go on the air.

Bryan was determined to beat WFMY, to be run by the owners of the Greensboro newspapers that Julian Price had once owned, when he learned of their interest in starting a television station. "When I learned they were putting up a television tower here in

Greensboro," Bryan later said, "I said to the folks in Charlotte, let's get busy in a hurry. We did and we went on the air first."

While Bryan was initially sold on the business advantages of television, he wasn't able to turn a quick profit as he did with WBIG and he began to doubt his own wisdom. The Charlotte TV station lost approximately $50,000 a month in the early days and Bryan's loyalty to the medium was shaken because of mounting debts. He wrote his brother Bart, who was an advertising executive with the St. Petersburg, Florida, newspaper that he didn't know if TV would last. More importantly, he said, his directors were getting anxious for profits and getting tired of red ink. He wasn't sure what to do, but wasn't ready to give up. "We don't have any textbooks to follow on what we're doing right and wrong," Bryan wrote his brother.

That pressure from directors may have been a factor in Bryan's pinching of pennies in the early days of the 1950s. He was continuously stingy with corporate dollars, a fact Crutchfield found intolerable after years of what he felt was nitpicking by Bryan. Every year Crutchfield was required to travel to Greensboro to justify virtually every penny in his budget.

Crutchfield was not a man of great patience, just like Bryan. Their mutual lack of tolerance put them on a collision course over budgets, and one day they collided. Each December when Crutchfield came to Jefferson's corporate offices for salary reviews, the agitation intensified. Crutchfield wanted to give $5 a week raises for broadcast employees. Bryan would argue the employee was hardly worth half that and habitually argued in favor of pay raises of only $1 a week for some employees.

"One year I want over there and he was up to the same old thing, arguing over these little peanut pay raises," Crutchfield said. "I was bullheaded and had just had it with him. I was easy to get mad in those days and I decided I wasn't going to listen to any more of that kind of crap. I just stood up, threw my budget papers across his desk where he sat in that big swivel chair and told him he could take station and shove it. (In truth, Crutchfield's words dealing with the shoving were considerably more specific, but he asked that his concise language not be repeated in print). Joe's eyes flew open, but I just said to hell with it and walked out."

Other Jefferson executives in the room at the time anxiously ran down the hall to catch Crutchfield, urging him to come back and apologize. He refused and stormed out of the building. Crutchfield returned to Charlotte, cleaned out his office desk and went home, knowing he would be fired. It had happened before when he had lost his temper and ranted at other bosses. He had been fired from several radio stations in South Carolina and Georgia for challenging decisions of station owners. Crutchfield joked that he had been fired from more jobs than most people were ever hired for.

He was also well aware that Bryan was not known for allowing employees to push him around and that many Jefferson officials were intimidated by Bryan's gruff exterior. Some, in fact, would tiptoe past Bryan's office, hoping not to distract him. Others would ask his secretary about his mood, then decide whether to either approach him then or wait until another day.

Later in the day of Crutchfield's outburst in Greensboro, Bryan drove unannounced to Charlotte and rang Crutchfield's doorbell. "I saw him standing there and figured he had come to fire me, as I guess he should have. But I was as surprised to hear what he said about my temper outburst at him," Crutchfield explained. "He told me he realized I was right and he was wrong. That's when and how we really agreed on mutual respect and understanding. He just needed someone to react that way and I was the first one. I don't know if anyone else ever did. But we became great friends after that, working well together. He was a great person and I learned a lot from him. He wanted high quality. Once I got to know him, he was wonderful to work with. He was as fine a fellow as I never knew."

Crutchfield later did resign from WBTV, but changed his mind before actually leaving. He also took a two-year leave of absence to work for Radio Free Europe in Greece, a fact that Bryan agreed to but didn't appreciate. "Charlie was always looking for a government job," Bryan later said. "When we started that TV station it was Larry Walker (a station official as well as entertainer) and I who did the job. And it was a helluva job, too." Others give Crutchfield more credit than Bryan did in getting the television station going.

Bryan was considerably more generous in his praise of Crutchfield when the latter retired from Jefferson. "You are a definite leader," Bryan wrote. "I spotted that in you early on and you were my personal choice to take our investment and make it pay off. I was right in my judgment of you, and although you have given me an anxious moment or two through the years, I have never doubted you. Men of sanity and capacity — men such as you — will prevail and endure."

From the rough beginning of WBTV, Jefferson — with Bryan as the chief executive of broadcasting — opened or purchased television stations in Florence, S.C. and Richmond, Va. That led later into television cable ventures and newspaper ownership. Bryan was the catalyst for it all.

But there were problems other than profitability in the early days of Jefferson ownership of both the radio and television operations. Severe labor union disputes hit the company within months of the TV station going on the air after Crutchfield and Bryan fired 10 station engineers for "misconduct and disloyalty." Problems continued for years and in late 1950, an attempt was made to bomb the television station transmission tower. Sterling Hicks, a member of the Charlotte parks and recreation commission and a church deacon, was charged with conspiracy to bomb the tower. A house painter was also charged after police, operating on a tip, caught the man literally hurling dynamite sticks with lighted fuses toward the tower. All the burning fuses fizzled before exploding.

After the arrests, the station's labor unrest faded.

By 1955 when WBTV's new studios were dedicated — with the

address at One Julian Price Place — just off Wilkerson Blvd., profits were a regular staple and the station was respected as a top CBS affiliate in the state and region.

The building dedication was a major event for Charlotte at the time with CBS network stars on hand and accolades galore spread all around. Warren Hull, the then popular TV quiz show host was the master of ceremonies. One congratulatory telegram came from entertainer Jack Benny, a well-known tightwad, who asked that the audience be advised he did not sent his message collect.

The station's address was the only visible sign of Julian Price's impact on either the radio or television stations and, in fact, the only visible recognition of his influence on any Jefferson properties until a park in Greensboro was named for Price and his wife in 1999.

Price may not have had his name on properties, but Crutchfield loved the anecdotal tale of the impact he had on Jefferson employees. Price was their drill sergeant and they marched to his drumbeat. At one Jefferson Club dinner shortly after the purchase of WBT radio, Price was slow to begin his meal as he made the rounds of handshaking with corporate executives present. Guests were fidgeting over their fried chicken dinner with knife and fork until Price sat down, grabbed his chicken breast with both hands and dug into the white meat. "You could hear the clatter of men throughout that room dropping their utensils and following the leader by going after chicken with their hands," Crutchfield said. "I learned from that a whole new way of following the leader."

Bryan also developed a strong following among WBT and WBTV personnel in the formative years of the stations. Among the accolades was his willingness to stick with the talented Crutchfield despite their differences and fits of temper to help mold a quality enterprise. Two Bryan's loyalists were WBTV personalities Doug Mayes and Loonis McGlohon. Mayes was a long-time trusted news anchor and McGlohon established himself nationally for his musical talents. Both lament the fact that Bryan's reputation for creating a high quality station with Crutchfield is either not known or forgotten by more recent generations. Bryan's portrait was years ago removed from the station's lobby because then current employees didn't know — or care — who he was.

Without what Mayes called "an ounce" of broadcast experience in his background, Bryan recognized broadcast talent and surrounded himself with such people. Some people at times feared him, but everybody always respected him, Mayes said of Bryan. "He was tough, but fair. He was a class act. Charles Crutchfield ran the station, but he leaned on Bryan for ideas and assistance. People today don't realize the influence Joe Bryan had on this station and its quality or on the growth of television in this region of the country."

McGlohon's relationship was somewhat different, but no less reverential. "He was an icon in the television industry," the nationally known musician said in a TV station interview in 1999. McGlohon learned early on that while Bryan may have been wealthy, he didn't throw money around.

That happened when Bryan asked McGlohon to find a musical band to play for a Bryan granddaughter Laura Edwards 16th birthday in July 1978. Bryan mentioned a few bands that his granddaughter said she'd like to have, but he never mentioned a price ceiling. McGlohon figured money was no problem. He figured wrong.

McGlohon spent part of two weeks dealing with band booking agents. He suggested Bryan should consider from among the Rolling Stones, Creedence Clearwater Revival and some less well-known groups. But he failed to mention that the fees ranged from $25,000 to $60,000.

"He just said to me that his granddaughter said she would like to have a live band and asked me to find one among the names she had mentioned," McGlohon explained. "It was not easy finding one that was interested. Those bands didn't play for private parties

134

but I told them about Joe and that money wasn't a problem. I finally got one band to agree to play at the birthday party and told Joe I thought I had him a good deal on the price."

McGlohon told Bryan the price would be $60,000. "What?" Bryan asked incredulously. "Huh, you must be joking," Bryan responded with an indignant huff at what he obviously felt were outrageous prices. Bryan said he had expected to pay no more than $5,000. Needless to say, McGlohon had to cancel the band.

McGlohon was never again asked to book a party band. He later said he never had the nerve to ask Bryan what kind of music, if any, was arranged for that birthday party. To be sure, there was no live band.

Bryan not only pushed for television industry expansion at Jefferson — once it started making money and directors' fears were quieted — but he was also an early advocate of color broadcasting. In 1954, calling himself "bullish" on color, Bryan advised Crutchfield to explore the purchase of color equipment. "To supply only black and white is like offering a Model T Ford when a colorful Cadillac is in order," he wrote in one office memo.

Bryan, however, was not high on what he considered quirky marketing gimmicks to advertise Jefferson's television stations. In the early 1950s, Crutchfield failed in his attempt to convince Bryan to buy dozens of shelters, which would provide cover for students waiting for school buses, at $110 each with WBTV logos painted on the side. Bryan rejected the offer, saying he figured it would cost $35 a year to maintain each shelter, too much for his taste. Instead, he offered to loan Crutchfield the money to buy the shelters personally, but nothing ever came of the loan idea.

One idea that did catch on with Bryan was the creation of a public television channel even though many people in the commercial television viewed it as direct competition. Not so with Bryan who saw university-sponsored television as a complement rather than competition.

When he was asked to help, he took a giant step forward, giving money, corporate talent and equipment. That action, some would concede, may have been one of his most important legacies even though through the years his early generosity in this specific area has remained pretty much a secret. University television supporters in North Carolina know of his help in financing the new studio and production facilities in the Research Triangle Park that bears names of Joe and Kathleen Bryan. His real support, however, was much earlier and much less well known. But it may well have been more significant.

9

PUBLIC VS. PRIVATE TELEVISION

When the Japanese bombed United States military installations and personnel at Pearl Harbor on Dec. 7, 1941, the attack set off an outpouring of patriotic response across cities and farms in North Carolina. Tar Heel soldiers by the thousands were anxious to join the war effort. Many of the state's young men were victims of the slaughter on that fateful Sunday morning and their deaths or others to come at the hands of the enemy were not to be in vain.

A common sight in homes across the state during World War II was the window stickers symbolizing that brave and proud young men — and some women, too — who once lived there were off fighting, and in many cases dying, for their country. Their sacrifices were for a dedicated cause to help preserve freedoms for current and future generations.

Despite an enviable record of fighting strength and faithfulness to the flag, however, North Carolina's men in the military had a major blemish to overcome. They were, in a word, unhealthy.

The willingness of many of the state's soldiers to fight often surpassed their physical ability to do so. Many veterans nationwide, of course, had shown health problems when they were called to active military service and submitted to physical examinations, but those from North Carolina were regrettably — embarrassingly — among the worst. Health records among soldiers from the then 48 states showed that North Carolina was sixth from the bottom.

From that starting point emerged something called the Good Health Campaign. And from that effort, remarkably, came the birth of public television. The direct connection between those two seemingly unrelated enterprises was the small group of visionary and determined individuals who caused those joint efforts to succeed.

It was North Carolina's two energetic UNC graduates and Tar Heel natives Billy Carmichael and Kaye Kyser who spearheaded the success of both. Their determination to improve the health of North Carolina residents helped create the medical training programs at the University of North Carolina in Chapel Hill. Their same dedication to the cause of improving education led them to Joe Bryan in Greensboro who took the lead in forming university television.

Kyser was a child of rural North Carolina, born in the flatlands near the tobacco fields of Rocky Mount, who would become a nationally known big band leader of the World War II era and beyond. Kyser was a popular student at UNC, serving as a cheerleader and general fun-loving man about campus and town. His indifference to academic pursuits was shown in his response, late in life, when he was asked what his major was at UNC. He said he wasn't sure. It was either English or business, he said, but he couldn't remember which. For him, it didn't matter.

Carmichael was born in Durham, son of a tobacco company executive who wound up as an investment broker on Wall Street in the middle 1920s before returning to the state as an official with the UNC crown jewel campus in Chapel Hill. He was a member of the UNC basketball team, as was his younger brother Richard, the first North Carolina native named to the All America team.

Kyser was a bundle of boundless energy who had all the right

138

entertainment industry connections. Carmichael was so smooth as a university pitchman that he could have marketed milk to a dairy farmer. The two made a dynamic duo.

Carmichael and Kyser were determined to help improve the health of North Carolina soldiers, and everyone else, after learning of and discussing the dismal physical condition of Tar Heel veterans, and those physically unable to join the military, during and after WW II. The state in those days was mostly rural with pockets of poverty that were appalling because of a shortage of doctors and few medical facilities. The university campus in Chapel Hill offered some premed courses, but there was no medical school and virtually nothing to ensure that citizen health would get much better anytime soon. It was Kyser and Carmichael who coined the Good Health Campaign slogan and set out to convince the public and public officials it was essential to create a medical school at UNC. Carmichael put his marketing skills to work inside the state and Kyser called in some green stamps within the entertainment industry to put their plan in place.

Carmichael received most of the recognition for the health campaign just as he later did in creation of public television with the assistance of his friend Bryan. While his efforts were pivotal, it was Kyser's musical connections that may have been as critical as anything else in bringing the effort to fruition was. A song and some dance steps that Kyser arranged with the right people is what helped turn the tide.

Kyser asked his friends Sammy Cahn and Jula Styne to put together the lyrics and music to a song about the state's poor health records and called on his friends Frank Sinatra and Dinah Shore to sing the jingle. It worked. Radio stations across the state made a regular hit of the song about the need to improve health care with a punch line of "It's all up to you." The goal, the upbeat lyrics from the voices of Sinatra and Shore stressed, was to bring the state from 42nd to 1st in health care.

139

But as popular as the Kyser-produced musical set was, there was the political problem of convincing state legislators that funding of a medical school was the right and essential thing to do. Carmichael put his silky-smooth lobbying approach to work, figuring the quickest way to the hearts of lawmakers was the appearance of a pretty woman. Once more, Kyser was right by his side.

At a legislative dance in the ballroom of the venerable downtown Sir Walter Raleigh Hotel in Raleigh in the fall of 1947, a vivacious and photogenic Hollywood starlet was the hit of the evening. She waltzed across the floor with dozens of legislative leaders — without knowing who any of them were. But you could bet that Carmichael knew as she unintentionally worked his plan.

The belle of the ball on the dance floor that evening was 27-year-old Georgia Kyser, the talented and pretty wife of the bandleader Kaye Kyser. She had been featured on the covers of national magazines for her stunning beauty. She was having a grand time on the dance floor and said she didn't realize until later she was part of some political sales pitch by her husband and Carmichael to promote legislative passage of a bill to create a UNC medical school.

When the dance was over, Mrs. Kyser learned she had been part of a calculated plan to charm lawmakers.

"You did a fine job," Carmichael told her. "You did it just right."

"I did what just right?" she inquired.

"The dancing," Carmichael replied, with a nod of agreement from her husband. "We think you put it (the medical school bill) over."

"That's ridiculous," she replied. "It's scary if dancing with the legislators is all it takes to pass legislation."

Maybe that is all it took. Shortly after that dance, members of the N. C. General Assembly agreed to enact a law creating the UNC Medical School and provide initial funding for it.

"All this (the dance) was just a little side thing that amused me then and now," Mrs. Kyser said from her Chapel Hill home in the spring of 1999. She and her husband moved to the edge of the UNC campus after they ended their professional careers in New York and California.

"I was just enjoying dancing that night. I didn't know who the men were. But for whatever their reasons, they voted for the Good Health Campaign and the medical school was part of all that. And that campaign changed the university and Chapel Hill. The hospital started bringing in doctors and all kinds of medical people and buildings started going up all around."

Not long after the success with the health care issue in the state, Kyser hit upon the idea of selling education in his home state by way of television. The idea had never been tried here, and not many other places either, but Kyser was intrigued with the prospects. He was at the time doing a regular television show on NBC with Ford Motor Company as the primary sponsor. If people will listen to someone pitch the merits of new cars in a video spot, Kyser asked, why can't they learn math and English and history the same way? Not surprisingly, among the first people Kyser discussed his educational television idea with was his friend Carmichael who was a willing listener and immediate advocate. Once more, it would take the support of state lawmakers. But that was only the beginning.

There had been some discussions and limited efforts within the university on the possibilities of forming a public television station prior to Kyser and Carmichael joining arms, but mostly it had been all talk and no action. The dynamic duo changed that. And Joe Bryan enthusiastically stepped up to the plate with a big bat.

Carmichael had known Bryan since the middle 1920s and their days as bachelors together in the commodities markets in New York City where Carmichael formed his own brokerage company and Bryan was the youngest member of the Cotton Exchange. They and their wives remained close friends throughout their lives. Carmichael and Kathleen Bryan also shared an abiding faith in the

Catholic Church. Tragically, both Kathleen Bryan and Carmichael's wife May would later suffer the same fatal disease and be inextricably linked in death to a far greater degree even than in life. Bryan also had met Kyser through mutual friends in the middle 1940s. Both Carmichael and Kyser, of course, knew that Bryan was head of the largest commercial television station in the state at the time, WBTV in Charlotte that was owned by Jefferson Standard Life Insurance Company in Greensboro.

The timing was fortuitous. The Federal Communications Commission was interested in opening up new television outlets nationwide and had lifted a four-year ban (1948-1952) on such expansion. Of the 2,053 additional TV outlets approved by the FCC, public universities were invited to apply for 242 new channels.

Bryan's corporate ties and expertise were naturals for Carmichael and Kyser to tap. He was one of a limited number of people in the state at the time that seemed to understand the potential of television. And he and his associates at Jefferson Broadcasting had proved their capabilities by turning a once financially struggling commercial station they had started from ground zero into one that was both profitable and respected for high quality.

But the Carmichael and Kyser plan still faced significant hurdles. Not many legislators were enthusiastic about spending tax money to start a television station. A lot of university faculty members — despite their theoretical belief in enhanced educational standards and freedom of expression — strongly opposed the idea because they saw university television as competing against and siphoning off money from other academic programs. Faculty members argued there was no guarantee the public was ready for such a risky venture even if the money could be found to start it.

Against such odds, however, Jefferson Standard and Bryan had already begun to show their support of the prospects for educational television, unlike some other broadcast owners who viewed it as direct competition, by helping with initial planning. The Jefferson

Foundation was the first corporate entity to contribute money to the university for research of educational television. Jefferson had also created a scholarship program at UNC for in-state students interested in pursuing broadcast careers.

One of the early applicants for the Jefferson scholarship was a Charlotte teenager named Charles Kuralt. He, of course, later became a popular, down-home kind of broadcast journalist for CBS, but his national fame never led his heart far from his beloved UNC alma mater. Kuralt, who died in 1997, is buried among UNC faculty and alumni in a cemetery on the edge of the Chapel Hill campus.

Even as UNC was pushing ahead with plans for starting a television station, Bryan and associates at Jefferson were busily expanding their commercial enterprise. With WBTV becoming profitable, Jefferson purchased a second station in Florence, SC, and began pursuit of a third in the Chapel Hill area. That's when Carmichael and Kyser learned they were facing another roadblock, perhaps the biggest one of all.

In applying for a license for a specific public channel frequency, Carmichael was shocked to learn he was seeking the exact same channel Jefferson has chosen for its new commercial station near the university. Jefferson had put its application far ahead of UNC although the FCC had not decided which applicant would be approved. Anxiety among university officials reigned. With Jefferson already seeking the same channel after investing huge amounts of money and proving its success in its commercial venture, what would that mean either for the UNC cause or Jefferson's past support of the university's efforts?

It turned out to be a baseless fear. Bryan once more rode to the rescue, this time in a magnanimous move that would then and for years come at great expense to Jefferson Standard.

Carmichael and Kyser first went to see Charles Crutchfield, the top official of WBTV in Charlotte, in search of advice on how to

Joseph M. Bryan Sr. and Charles Crutchfield. The two founded North Carolina's first commercial television station in Charlotte and were instrumental in the creation of public television as part of the University of North Carolina in Chapel Hill.

resolve the dilemma of dual applications for the same TV channel.

Crutchfield went straight to the phone to call his boss Bryan at Jefferson headquarters in Greensboro.

Bryan's one-word response was "ugh".

"What does that mean? What do you want me to do? "Crutchfield asked.

"There's only one thing to do," Bryan responded without hesitation. "We'll just give up our application and give it to them. And we'll also give them our legal group in Washington working on it. Just do everything you can to help them."

Crutchfield later marveled at the quick decision Bryan made to help the university's effort. "The biggest decision and most important decision Joe ever made was being responsible alone for the beginning of the UNC network," Crutchfield said in a June 1998 interview. "He just did it without hesitation. It was a great and wise decision. Joe didn't make bad decisions on things like that and he made it just like that (snap of finger.) In my judgment that was one of the greatest things he ever did for the people of this state."

Others involved in the early workings of the formation of the UNC TV network don't give Bryan quite the full credit as Crutchfield did. But all involved with the station's formation agree that public television would have come later and with far more difficulty even if the FCC had approved the public channel if Bryan had not shown his support and benevolence. Bryan may not have been the key to UNC's initial television success, but he was an important key.

With the FCC in support of public television channels, the university might well have won in a battle for that channel even if Bryan had insisted on fighting to keep it for Jefferson, but it would have been costly and undoubtedly prolonged battle.

But Bryan made it easy. Jefferson had at that time already invested three-fourths of a million dollars in its Channel 4 application through legal fees and negotiations of land purchases for placement of a commercial TV tower. Bryan said that expenditure was not a problem. In addition to withdrawing his company's application, Bryan provided the university with legal help for several months in transferring the license request and offered Crutchfield's efforts to work with the university to speed the process.

Based on Jefferson's investment in starting WBTV, the company could have started its commercial television station near Durham for several million dollars. At Bryan's death some four decades later, the value could have grown to as high as $300 million.

"That's what Joe gave up for educational enhancement and for university television," Crutchfield said. "It's just one of the most meaningful things he ever did in his life as a broadcast executive. It was his decision alone and he didn't hesitate at all."

There were, of course, others who played roles in the success of UNC getting the license and in securing public funding for the public television network that started as a three-tiered piecemeal operation with limited access and fuzzy signals. One of those players was William Friday, at the time an assistant to Carmichael on the Chapel Hill campus who later became a 30-year president of the UNC system and a force throughout the state on behalf of literacy and philanthropy. Friday worked his magic with certain legislators whose votes were essential for public funding, a trait he carried out with grace and success for decades as head of the university system.

The key vote in the General Assembly came from state Sen. Thomas White of Kinston. A savvy, no-nonsense lawyer, White was not a fan of public television, but he was willing to give it a chance to prove its worth. Friday and Carmichael persuaded White that public television within the university was a collateral undertaking similar to other forms of extension services offered to citizens under university sponsorship. Initial funding was squeezed through a legislative appropriations committee by a single vote, which came from White. "His support was pivotal. Legislatively speaking, Tom White saved public television," Friday said.

Crutchfield also got into the political lobbying effort with the strong Mecklenburg legislative delegation. "Once Joe Bryan made the decision, Charlie really went to work for us," Friday said. "He was very supportive and deserves a lot of credit although a lot of people have no idea what he did. But without Joe Bryan and Jefferson, public television would not have begun when it did, as easily as it did or be where it is today. It would not be an exaggeration to say his decision to support UNC TV made it happen. It was a typical kind of new project that brought on all the dissenters, but there was no war because of Joe Bryan."

Friday, as is his habit, discounted the significance of his own role in the formation of public television, but his unending persistence was critical with lawmakers. "Bill Friday saved it in the legislature because he wouldn't give up and kept it going," said John Young, one of the first public television's employees. "Billy Carmichael and Joe Bryan got it started, but Bill Friday kept it going."

Friday first met Bryan when Carmichael asked Friday to accompany him to visit Bryan in Greensboro to discuss Jefferson's support for public television. It was the beginning of a 40-year friendship that ended only at Bryan's death. Friday became Bryan's link to university television after Carmichael's death.

"I walked into that office for the first time and there sat this great big bear of a man with a heavy mustache, and those shaggy eyebrows. He could scare the daylights out of you," Friday said. When Bryan learned that was Friday's initial reaction, he apologized.

"I don't mean to frighten anybody, but that's just the way I am," Bryan said.

Underneath that gruff exterior was a different personality. "He had a very soft heart and a very generous heart," Friday said. "Sometimes it was hard to know just how he felt about things, but few people have had his impact for good. Joe Bryan has been as much a part of the fabric of this state as anyone. He had a quiet generosity and his good works will live on. His spirit of giving is what his foundation is trying to carry on. He cast a long shadow over this state and his most enduring legacy is in the good that he did. He raised the level of life in North Carolina and we all should be grateful."

Bryan later said what he did for public television was primarily a business decision. "It was long our philosophy that growth and expansion of educational broadcasting would have a far-reaching effect on the progress of the state," he told university supporters shortly after the station went on the air. "We are conscious of the fact that the continuing progress of our organization depends largely on the continuing progress of the state. The advancement of educational television will give stimulus to the growth of Jefferson Standard and its ability to serve more people."

Once UNC's hold on Channel 4 was secure, other battles began. Carmichael and Friday dreamed of miracles in the legislative halls, but both realized they would never be able to secure adequate financial support from Raleigh alone. Carmichael began a series of visits to corporate offices across the state. The first office he visited was Bryan's at Jefferson, the day he took the young William Friday to meet the man with the booming voice and shaggy eyebrows. Bryan and his wife Kathleen made the first private donation to a fund Carmichael was establishing to supplement legislative financing.

Carmichael went in search of $1 million from the state's corporate boardrooms, a move that earned him the nickname of "Tin Cup" Billy, and raised anxiety in the mind of then UNC president Gordon Gray. Carmichael and Gray worked as the two top UNC administrators, but they were about as different as night and day. Gray, also owner of radio station WSJS in Winston-Salem and later WSJS-TV, had none of Carmichael's verve. Crutchfield would in later years, with Bryan's blessing, advise Gray on how to secure his own television station license.

Gray was quiet, conservative and careful in everything he did. Carmichael was a risk taker who routinely swung for the fences, conceding that at times he'd strike out but also believing he'd have some big innings and hit some home runs.

He scored big on his corporate UNC television drive, bringing in $1.315 million. That success was essential because the General Assembly provided only $108,000 a year, 50 percent of what Carmichael said was needed to get the station on the air. The Carnegie Foundation, headed by John Gardner, and the Ford Foundation both rejected requests for financial help. William McPeak at Ford predicted that public television would never survive.

Greensboro companies and families followed Bryan's lead in helping with the $1 million fund. Greensboro names on the original list of donors were the Britt Armfields, Wilbert James Carters, the Benjamin Cones, the H. Smith Richardsons and the Spencer Loves.

Other individual family names included the Hills of Durham, Kenans of Chapel Hill, Cannons of Kannapolis and the Moreheads of Chapel Hill.

Greensboro area corporate donors to the original campaign were Burlington Industries, Jefferson Standard, Security Bank (which Jefferson then controlled) and Wachovia Bank.

UNC television went on the air on January 8, 1955. The first live broadcast was from the state Capitol where then Gov. Luther Hodges made his State of the State speech. The FCC had granted UNC eight channel outlets across the state, but there was money enough to operate on only three campuses — Chapel Hill, Raleigh and Greensboro — and then for only 40 hours a week. Equipment was primitive, some bought through deals that Carmichael found through friends at RCA, and some donated by Jefferson Standard through Bryan. The first mobile unit was a converted Trailways bus.

Among the early popular programming were Bernard Boyd's Bible study, a Sunday School lesson from UNC Chancellor Robert House, and a regular farm hour. The early programmers had help that most viewers and even some university people didn't know about, thanks again to Kyser's entertainment world connections. Kyser arranged, without pay or much public exposure, to bring in scriptwriters for initial programs and to assist faculty members in better ways to teach by videotape.

At the 25th anniversary show of UNC television in 1980, Kyser watched the accolades being poured on the early supporters of the network. His name was not mentioned.

"You know, that makes me angry," his wife Georgia told him. "You got no credit for all that you did."

"Don't worry about it," Kyser responded. "I know who did it and God knows who did it. That's all that really matters." Kyser died in 1985.

The first video of a sporting event in the spring of 1955 was achieved, literally, through a hole in the wall. Carmichael was excited about showing basketball games even though many said such broadcasts would be boring and not generate any viewers. Furthermore, commercial broadcasters complained that the university was usurping their privileges. As a compromise, Friday and Carmichael arranged for a hole to be knocked in a retaining wall of Wollen Gym on the UNC campus, then the campus basketball arena, just large enough for a single camera lens. That camera showed the game, but commercial stations carried the sound.

"We (the university television staff) didn't say a word during the game," Friday explained. "We just stuck a camera in the hole in the wall, invented the term broadvision, and let the commercial stations do the talking."

That first game was between UNC and Wake Forest and included what could be considered an embarrassment because educational TV was the source. Someone painted a sign with the two team's names as part of the video, but the name of Wake Forest was misspelled as Wake Forrest. Whether that was the hand of a poor speller or the calculated work of a UNC partisan will never be known.

Among the loudest critics of public television were faculty members within the university. They predicted fearfully that money for television would come from their own budgets. One unidentified faculty member lamented: "The university must take care to avoid robbing a faithful and deserving Peter in order to pay an intriguing but yet new and untried Paul."

But Joe Bryan never doubted the merits or potential of what was being done. Carmichael saw to that. "My father was constantly in contact with Joe and Kathleen Bryan about university matters, especially in the early days of the television station," said Carmichael's daughter Mrs. Margaret Lester of Chapel Hill. "He'd get in bed at night and work the phones. I can hear him now. He would always call Kathleen first. He would say 'Kathleen, Billy here' and then go into one of his appeals."

Bryan later acknowledged his initial gifts to public university came with encouragement of his wife. "I can't help but think of Kathleen when I think of public television," Bryan said when the new television studios bearing the names of Bryan and his wife were dedicated in Research Triangle Park. He contributed $1 million for those studios.

Bryan never attempted to micromanage the university television network even though his generous contributions would have given him ample opportunities to do that. He did, however, keep a close watch on what was happening there just as he did in everything he helped build or support.

Bryan didn't like some of what he called fluff programming. He didn't hesitate to let Friday know of his disdain for Lawrence Welk shows and felt the so-called experts commenting on fishing skills didn't have many of their own.

"I'm tired of Lawrence Welk," Bryan said in one conversation with Friday. "I've been looking at that same program for 20 years. And the fishing shows are amateurish. I know more about fishing than some of those folks do." And he probably did, too. But Bryan never asked that any program be eliminated or added. "He never attempted to coerce anybody into something because he had given money. He was not that way. His heart was as big as his head," Friday said.

Bryan remained faithful to public television until his death. "There is much more to be done," Bryan said of his $1 million donation to the new television studios. "This is really just the beginning."

He kept his word. Bryan stipulated in his will that at his death that another $1 million of his assets be donated to the university television network. His support was critical from the beginning and will stretch well into this century. Without him, the network wouldn't have started when it did or run as smoothly as it has. Bryan's generosity and spirit live on in the state's public television arena just as in other fields of philanthropic endeavors.

151

10

LEADERSHIP SHAKEOUT

J oe Bryan's ongoing support for creation and development of public television in North Carolina came amid a period of turmoil within Jefferson Standard Life Insurance Company. For policyholders and investors, the corporate structure seemed solid; business was growing and profits were increasing.

But underneath the surface were pockets of boardroom minefields that threatened to weaken if not devour executives. In fact, the bitterness did chew up and spit out some at the top and raised doubts among those who remained.

There was the trauma of overcoming the death of company patriarch Julian Price and the selection of his son Ralph Price as company president. While few within the company hierarchy felt Ralph's tenure was wise or should be long lasting, but there were uncertainties on just how to proceed. Ralph and his sister Kathleen Price Bryan owned significant chunks of company stock, not enough to control boardroom actions but enough to make others squirm if they dared to challenge too much too soon.

Bryan, meanwhile, took it all in stride. The problems lay primarily within the insurance side of the business, not the broadcast side where Bryan was in charge and where things were running smoothly. It is certainly true that Bryan and his wife Kathleen —she more than he did — once had hopes that he would be named president to succeed patriarch Price, but both realized that wasn't in the corporate cards with Ralph in the picture. Bryan would just await another opportunity.

Furthermore, Bryan's resources — thanks to the Jefferson stock price rise and his wife's generosity at helping support his outside investments — were enough to allow him to pursue his varied interests in associating with the rich and famous on golf courses and game preserves around the world. Bryan had become a regular patron at the Master's Golf Tournament in Augusta, Ga., and had joined several prestigious fishing and hunting clubs in this country as well as in England, Spain and Scotland.

Life, in short, for Bryan was quite good. He didn't need the Jefferson presidency to prove his success. He had shown that in many other ways. Furthermore, he expected his situation to get even better, and had ample reasons to believe it would.

His benevolence toward university television was just the beginning of what would follow under his direction. His philanthropy would expand greatly over the next decades with a focus on education and recreation for thousands of people. That would remain the case throughout his long life, and beyond, through the creation of his private foundation whose purpose is to carry on what he started and to maintain his philosophy on giving.

In the Jefferson corporate offices, however, life was not that way. Divergent factions among executives and directors were choosing sides and the friction was becoming known outside as part of the regular street gossip. As it became clear after four years of boardroom infighting and disgruntlement that Ralph Price's presidency was doomed, Bryan had begun lining up directors' votes to assume control of the entire corporation. For awhile, he felt he had enough support for the presidency with his wife's block of stock and a growing acceptance of him as a viable part of the corporate structure because of his success with broadcasting.

Bryan, however, had not counted on the quiet — some would say conniving — and calculating impact of Jefferson director J. Van "Jack" Lindley. Known as the "gray fox" or quite often less flattering names, Lindley suddenly became a force within the company far beyond what might have been expected because he was neither an employee nor a major stockholder. Lindley's stealth role was both dominant and long lasting both within Jefferson and later in the formation of a series of bank mergers that resulted in what by the end of the 20th Century was the financial giant Bank of America. But he worked in mysterious and secretive ways his wonders to perform.

Lindley has never garnered much attention in the corporate world of either Jefferson or the bank boardrooms — which is precisely the way he wanted it. But if he had not been clandestinely on the cutting edge of insurance and bank deals in Greensboro and Charlotte in 1950s and 1960s, Jefferson Insurance might well have become a different company and Bank of America might never have been formed. That's how powerful he was.

Lindley, whose family ties with Jefferson date to its beginning, put together deals involving millions of dollars affecting thousands of people, but he never enjoyed much of the fruits of his labor. He died deeply in debt and family members and lawyers were still sorting out his convoluted maze of financial entanglements a decade after his funeral in 1990.

Jefferson directors had concluded by the late 1940s after several years of lethargy from Ralph Price that he had to go. But they wanted to ease him aside to avoid adverse public response. He had been ineffective as president and had irritated directors by asking for a year's leave of absence with pay to work on his hobby to promote a world peace movement. Directors refused to grant his request for time off, but offered him an alternative as their way out of the dilemma of keeping him as president.

154

If Price would agree to move up to the exalted title of chairman of the board — the title his father had at his death — the directors would provide him an annual salary of $50,000 and few responsibilities so he could carry on his interests outside the company as he desired. Either that, directors said, or he would be dumped altogether.

Price refused the new title because he would have retained none of the power his father had with that title. Uncharacteristically, the normally docile Price decided to fight his dismissal. That set off another round of public turmoil within the company. But the die was cast. Price was on his way out.

Bryan, while not directly a party to booting Price aside, agreed with the plan. He was ready to take Price's place, even though he never publicly said he wanted the job and later expressed doubts about his ability to handle it. But he had begun what he felt was an appropriate step toward the presidency if the opportunity came. Bryan was made chairman of the company finance committee, replacing Price, and word in corporate offices at the time was that if Bryan performed well as head of that money committee he would be later be considered as president.

"Joe and Kathleen very much wanted him to be president. They thought he could and should be," said Jefferson's longtime attorney Bob Koonts. "He and Ralph were pretty much opposites. If Ralph said go left, Joe would say go right. Joe eventually lost out for the presidency and later concluded he had been sold out by Jack Lindley." Bryan went into the director's meeting the day of the selection thinking that he had the job. But he underestimated the Lindley influence.

Directors picked a new president, but it wasn't Bryan. They made, at least for Bryan, a surprise choice when they elected Howard "Chick" Holderness. Bryan privately confided to his colleague Roger Soles, who would himself 17 years later become president, that he (Bryan) had no inkling that Holderness would be cho-

155

sen or was even a candidate until the vote was taken. Lindley had put the Holderness plan together without any advance word or warning except within his coalition on the Jefferson board.

Soles said Bryan never received serious consideration for the presidency because, as finance committee chairman, he was regarded as uncooperative with his colleagues. "Joe was given a chance, but he began to take up some old grudges against people who had been against him in the early days," Soles said. "So directors turned against him, took him off the finance committee and brought in Chick Holderness with Lindley's backing."

That was in July 1950.

Lindley owned little Jefferson stock personally, but he had control of large amounts through various family members. He discreetly secured support for Holderness through Lindley family interests on the Jefferson board and other major shareholders in his own family. Lindley's grandfather was an original investor in Jefferson and a long-time director. His father was a director and his father's sisters and their spouses controlled large amounts of company stock. Lindley pooled those collective stock holdings and had all that voting power in his pocket on the day of the vote for a new president.

Bryan, despite his surprise at the choice of Holderness as president, once again accepted his fate without bitterness or reprisal. He and Holderness worked together for 12 years before Bryan retired. Their wives remained close personal friends until Mrs. Bryan's death. But the two men spent little time together outside the corporate offices and there was always a lingering coolness in their relationship. The same was true for Holderness and Ralph Price after the corporate coup.

Kathleen Bryan never forgave Lindley for slamming the president's door on her husband. "Don't ever turn your back on Jack Lindley," she told friends. "He'll stab you."

The Holderness years at Jefferson were steady and solid, but he was never able to establish himself in a leadership role the way

156

Julian Price had done. Holderness was capable, but was not a risk taker. He was far more timid and less direct than the senior Price. Better to be safe than sorry, might have been his motto. While Holderness held the title of president for 17 years, he was under the influence of Jack Lindley —without whom he would never have obtained his job — for much of that time and gradually gave increasing responsibilities to his savvy investment replacement Roger Soles before officially turning over the title.

There are those who say Lindley, in effect, ran the company because of his influence with Holderness. Lindley served as chairman of the Jefferson executive committee and finance committee and maintained an office in corporate headquarters even though he never received a salary from the company.

Holderness had worked for Jefferson years earlier, but left to join his brother in an investment business before Lindley put together the plan to bring him back as president. Holderness' father had been one of the original founders of Jefferson when it was created in Raleigh.

The beginning of the Holderness tenure at Jefferson was anything but peaceful even though his later service maintained a period of tranquility. For awhile, both he and Ralph Price claimed to be president. Each had an office with the title of president on the door, just down the hall from each other on the 14th floor. At directors' meetings both men sat at the table, Price at the head and Holderness to the side. Price initially refused to give up his title because he claimed Holderness was illegally elected in violation of company bylaws that required an officer to be a member of the board of directors. Directors who booted Price out resolved that conflict by calling another director's meeting, voted to elect Holderness as a director and on the spot reelected him president. That made it legal.

Price still didn't give up without a fight, however, and in his effort to hang onto his office showed more spunk that he ever did when he was the president. He mailed a series of letters to stockholders in the fall of 1950 alleging poor management by directors and explaining how his own decisions to make the company stronger had been routinely rejected. Price also later went to court against Jefferson and what was then Security Bank, which Jefferson controlled, claiming the bank had mishandled his father's estate. Kathleen Bryan sided with the bank against her brother.

Price also dumped his entire block of Jefferson stock on the market, some say in an apparent effort to reduce the price and put Jefferson in a bad light. His plan didn't work. It cost him money, but had little impact on the company. He also hired a Raleigh lawyer in the losing effort defend his presidency.

The lawyer charged him $25,000 in the losing cause, a figure some of his friends chided him for spending. "If it cost you that much to lose, it's a damn good thing you didn't win," Pierce Rucker told Price. "If you had won, you couldn't have afforded the fee." Rucker was a close friend of Price's father and for years served on the Jefferson board. An early advocate of Julian Price as president, Rucker was a familiar figure standing on the street corner near the Jefferson building and urging friends to buy Jefferson stock.

"Unfortunately, he never followed his own advice," Rucker's son Walker said about his father. "He never owned much of the stock. He was close to Julian Price and offered Ralph Price good advice on how to function as president, but Ralph wouldn't listen. Ralph was a little like King Edward VIII, just having to abdicate his throne because he would not listen."

Among the ironies of the Ralph Price/Holderness feud was that they had been close friends in their earlier lives. They were roommates while students at the University of North Carolina in Chapel Hill and again in graduate school at Harvard University. The fathers of the two had jointly decided both their sons should attend Harvard for business training and should room together. Price had been the rowdy one in their undergraduate days and earned a reputation as a party man on campus. After one drinking party, he was transported by friends like a shot deer, tied on the hood of a car, from Duke University to the UNC campus.

As a young man, Price battled an alcohol problem, a fact his mother blamed on the liberal influences of UNC and Harvard. He used self-discipline to wean himself off alcohol in later years and became a teetotaler except for champagne at special celebrations. His adult aversion to strong drink extended to company social functions, a point that wasn't well received by other executives.

Price was obviously embarrassed over his ouster by Jefferson directors, but there are those who say it also brought him a sense of relief and gave him freedom from a burden he didn't want to carry. "My father was a creative intellectual who became president of Jefferson because it was expected of him," Price's son Julian Price said. "He never really wanted that job but it was inappropriate for him to say he didn't want it. He was never temperamentally suited to be a chief executive. He was hurt by what happened to him, but he was much happier after the change because he was not suited for that job. He wanted to do other kinds of things."

Ralph Price, according to his son, idolized patriarch Julian even if the feelings were not mutual and was constantly as a young man under terrific pressure to live up to his father, a role he could never fulfill. "I have great warmth and feelings for my father," Price's son Julian said. "He was always reasonable, never mean or irrational. But he was just pushed into the wrong business. He just wasn't interested in running the company. He had other interests."

After the turmoil of Price's departure from Jefferson was settled, he moved into other areas, all far more pensive and befitting his personality than running a large insurance company. He brought a farm on Fleming Road near Guilford College, named it Hillside, and raised Angus cattle and Hampshire hogs. That farm was later developed into the upscale Cardinal residential subdivision. He bought Greensboro radio stations that didn't take much time to manage and devoted much of his time to his first love of promoting world peace after the United Nations was created. He wanted to turn continents into commonwealths.

Price was passionate on his peace plan and personally presented it to Pope Pius XII at the Vatican. "Well, it's a good plan and could be adopted," Price quoted the Pope as telling him. "But you'll have to have help from above," the pope added as he pointed skyward toward heaven. Price never received Divine intervention and the plan withered away. Price later gave huge sums to establish world peace and world law center at Duke University and create world peace lecture series at UNC.

Price and his wife Martha had two sons, Julian, who was named for his grandfather and Clay, and one daughter, Louise. Louise, like her father before her, once took Jefferson to court over stock prices after she became irritated with then company president Roger Soles. But unlike her father, who lost his battle, Louise Parsons won a handsome settlement when the company, after Soles retired, allowed her to exercise a quantity of stock options for handsome profits.

Price endured his share of personal tragedies in addition to his business problems at Jefferson. His wife, like his father, was killed in an auto accident in 1963 enroute home from taking their daughter to college. His son Clay died three years later of an aneurysm at age 27. Price remarried at age 62 in 1966 to Janie Poag, an acquaintance from Florida 20 years his junior whose husband had committed suicide a decade earlier after battling mental illness. Her father had once worked for Ralph Price's father at Jefferson offices in Texas.

Price died in September 1989 following a year of incapacity following a stroke. He also, according to Bryan, had symptoms of Alzheimer's, the horrific disease that claimed the life of his sister Kathleen Bryan.

Problems surrounding Ralph Price's removal as president in

1950 represented the second time people within the company had acted to remove the company president. Seventeen years earlier a dissident group of directors led by the company's lawyer had attempted to shove patriarch Julian Price from power. That was a foolish mistake. That attempted coup failed abruptly once the dominant Price got wind of the move. He promptly deposed the instigators.

In February 1933, Jefferson corporate lawyer and director A. L. Brooks, who publicly labeled himself a friend of Julian Price, quietly began plotting to gain control of the board from Price. Brooks' law partner Julius C. Smith, who was not part of the plan, inadvertently spotted some documents dealing with the planned clandestine takeover on Brooks' desk. Smith concluded the takeover attempt was wrong and immediately advised Price. Within a month Price had crushed the move, fired Brooks as company attorney and removed Brooks from the board of directors.

Price was so appreciative of Smith for telling him of the plan that he hired Smith as corporate attorney although Smith retained his private law practice, but as might have been expected no longer as a partner with Brooks. Brooks, a proud man accustomed to getting his way, never forgave his former law partner for blocking the takeover move. "Julius, thy name is Judas," Brooks said disdainfully to Smith after the episode.

While Price and Brooks never spoke to each other after that failed takeover attempt, family and friends say, they wound up close in death. The two men are buried within a few feet of each other in Greensboro's Green Hill Cemetery.

There would also be one additional failed try 18 years later to wrest control from executives during the early tenure of President Roger Soles. That, too, failed because Joe Bryan changed his mind about being a part of the plan.

The later attempt to take control of Jefferson occurred in the early 1969 and involved a coalition of well-connected individuals that included former Gov. Terry Sanford, Joe Bryan, Bryan's daughter and son-in-law and UNC benefactor and political insider Walter Davis whose primary business was oil investments in Texas. Davis initially was the out-front leader of that effort, but Sanford, Bryan's daughter Nancy and her husband Lauch Faircloth were silent participants. So was Joe Bryan, at least for awhile. But Bryan retreated in the middle of the negotiations and without his and his wife's support, the plan was doomed.

It was on a cold and snowy February in 1969 when Bryan called Roger Soles from Bryan's rented vacation house in Palm Beach. Bryan asked Soles to come to Florida to discuss a plan by Davis, Sanford and others to gain control of Jefferson. Soles was asked by Bryan not to alert Holderness, then board chairman, of the meeting.

Bryan had arranged for Davis' private jet to pick Soles up at the Greensboro airport. Soles, reluctant to discuss any takeover and even more reticent about being spotted boarding the Davis plane in Greensboro, agreed to the trip on one condition because he was intrigued with who was behind the attempt. Soles said he would drive to the Raleigh-Durham Airport to meet the plane, lessening chances of being seen by people who knew him. Bryan and Davis agreed to that.

Soles didn't know who else was involved in the possible deal until he walked into Bryan's Florida condo.

"What the hell are you doing here," Soles said as he walked into the house and saw former Gov. Sanford sitting there with a smile on his face.

"Well, I wasn't sure about the weather at home so I took a train down last night," Sanford replied. "I wanted to make sure I could get here."

The plan was for Davis, then an official at Occidental Petroleum Company, and Armand Hammer, who at the time owned the majority of Occidental, to gain control of Jefferson through stock purchases and majority director support. Sanford and Bryan family members were to play roles in running the company, according to the preliminary discussions. Bryan was interested because he initially felt this was his only way of becoming a more prominent player in company matters even though he had retired eight years earlier.

Initially, Davis had said he and Hammer were not interested in running the company, but just wanted control for economic gain. Soles was told he would be allowed to remain president. At one point in the Palm Beach meeting, Davis casually referred to what might happen when he became president. Bryan abruptly stopped Davis in midsentence and reminded him that he had earlier said he didn't want that title or authority.

"Well, whoever," Davis said. "It really doesn't matter."

But it did matter — a lot — to some in the room. Bryan at that point expressed second thoughts about the plan, as did his wife Kathleen. They were clearly bothered by the thought that Davis or Hammer might be in charge. Soles made it clear he wanted no part of the deal. But Sanford persisted and was not willing to give up. Faircloth and his wife Nancy also were interested in pursuing the plan, but realized that without Bryan it would never fly because he and Kathleen controlled too much stock.

Bryan eventually backed away, saying he just couldn't do it. He later told friends that he liked the idea, but didn't want to go through the hassle back home where Kathleen was friends and played bridge with the wives of Jefferson officials who might be adversely affected by a change in power.

"When Joe Bryan backed out, I pulled out," Davis said. "There was no use in continuing. I was told things about some stockholders (Bryan and his wife) that turned out not to be true. I was told that Bryan and his wife were for the thing, but they backed out. We thought we had votes among stockholders (Bryan and his wife) that we didn't have. That was the end of it for me."

Kathleen Bryan, in fact, may have been the key to killing the plan even without consideration for her bridge partners back home.

163

After Davis commented about his possible presidency, Mrs. Bryan lost enthusiasm in a hurry. "I remember the time that someone (A.L Brooks) once tried to take control away from my father," she commented. She was not interested in someone other than her family maintaining control.

Soles made it known he was opposed to the plan from the start. Within hours of his return to Greensboro, Holderness was at Soles home discussing the role Bryan had played in the plan. Neither Holderness nor Soles was pleased that Bryan had helped hatch the plan, even though he would later back away. But they never discussed it further with him.

Sanford was determined to push on against the odds even after Bryan retreated. He wanted a share in company management. So did his then friend Faircloth, although Faircloth would later discount any particular interest in the plan. Sanford sent his law partner Hugh Cannon to Jefferson offices to secure stockholder names and other pertinent data. That effort turned into something of a comical fiasco, although it was a private one within the corporate structure. It frustrated Sanford, but pleased Soles who thought the whole idea was nothing but a nuisance.

Soles was determined to do the Sanford group no favors. While corporate laws involving public companies required that Sanford's aide Cannon had a right to see certain documents, the law didn't require Jefferson to turn over any documents. Soles refused to make copies of records that Sanford wanted. Cannon was forced to rent a copy machine to obtain his documents. Then Soles refused to allow him to hook the copier into Jefferson's electrical outlets, saying he wasn't required by law to do so. Cannon was then forced to purchase copy paper and electrical cable and run the wires down the street from another building to the Jefferson offices in order to turn on the copy machine.

Soles chuckled as he recounted the Cannon and Sanford maneuverings and his response.

Cannon laughed, too, about the incident in the fall of 1999 when asked about it, but he didn't find it funny at the time. "I had this big moving van parked on the street," Cannon explained. "The law required them to show us the documents, but they didn't have to give us copies or allow us to use their copying machine. They refused to even provide us the electricity for the copier. I had to do all that myself, running electrical cords down the street and printing and hauling off thousands of records. It wasn't easy, but we did it because we felt it was an attractive business deal. We just thought we had some blocks of stock that we didn't have and the plan didn't work out. Walter Davis said the numbers (of shareholders) did not work, so we ought to just drop it. But Terry (Sanford) didn't want to do that."

Davis and most of the others involved in the plan sold their stock holdings when the takeover fell through. Sanford held on to his, and lost roughly $100,000 after the stock price dropped in ensuing months. He is one of the very few Jefferson shareholders who ever lost money on the stock. Soles just smiled years later when he learned that Sanford had lost money on the deal. "Served him right," Soles said in his cryptic style.

After leaving the practice of law, Cannon moved to Charleston, S.C. to open a new car dealership. Reflecting on the attempted Jefferson takeover, he said he fully understood Soles' adamant defensive actions. "He surely didn't help us, but I can't blame him. The company was totally justified in their lack of cooperation and assistance. If I'd been in their shoes, I'd have done the same thing, or maybe even worse to us."

That failed takeover episode closed the door on such efforts and Soles settled in for a relatively quiet tenure as president for almost two decades. Soles ran a conservative company, but his rock-solid investment strategy kept Jefferson in top financial shape while some other insurance companies were falling on hard times with risky investments and rising interest rates in the 1970s and 1980s. Bryan

165

was by that time, of course, in full retirement and in pursuit of his own personal investments and hobbies with friends. Oil drilling, sports shooting and fishing and golf were high on his list of interests.

But Lindley was not finished with his plans effecting Jefferson. He would once again weigh in with his quiet but effective influence in company matters when it came to a bank merger involving Jefferson. Bryan also was an active participant in the bank transactions but, once again, he lost out to Lindley's behind the scene actions.

"Jack was sometimes known as the 'evil genius' because he had lots of power and he used it to his advantage," said Dr. Shahane Taylor, a friend of both Lindley and Bryan. "Joe, on the other hand, was a very thoughtful person who was dedicated to what was best for Greensboro."

If Bryan had gotten his wishes with the bank merger, his ideas would have served Greensboro much better for much longer. But it was not to be. Nevertheless, Bryan would remain an important and increasingly influential link to Greensboro's future throughout the reminder of his life and beyond. In fact, it was in retirement that he really made his mark on the local community. Philanthropy became his true legacy.

11

BUILDING A BANK

Joe Bryan never intended to get into the banking business when he joined his father-in-law Julian Price at Jefferson Standard Life Insurance Company in the early 1930s. But neither he nor Price had much choice.

When the collapse of banks across America hit on March 6, 1933 in what became known as the national Bank Holiday as part of the Great Depression, Greensboro and Jefferson Standard were affected like communities and businesses everywhere. It was much worse in Greensboro, however, because not only did the existing banks close that day, they never reopened.

Two banks in the city failed, one of them twice. United Bank folded, reopened once and failed again. North Carolina Bank and Trust Company closed never to even try to reopen. Greensboro, for a lot longer than most cities, literally was devoid of all banks. Cash was scarce; some people had no money and little hope of getting access to any. Scrip became the means of payment in some places. The nearest bank was some 15 miles away in High Point where available money was rationed to customers as a means of ensuring that it wouldn't run out.

Jefferson Standard was especially hard hit, as were textile mills in the city. Everybody from corporate executives to mill workers and insurance secretaries had trouble securing cash. Jefferson and the city's major textile mills had to go to New York to obtain operating funds. The money shortage in Greensboro was so bad that national attention was focused on the city when Lowell Thomas reported on his CBS radio newscast that Greensboro was the largest city in America without an operating bank. Such negative attention was so discomforting to Julian Price as head of Jefferson Standard that he decreed that the city had to have a bank and if it meant that Jefferson had to create one, so be it. So that's exactly what happened.

Security Bank, with the backing of Jefferson Standard and $300,000 in aid from the federal government's Reconstruction Finance Corporation (RFC), was set to open its doors on Friday, August 25, 1933 in downtown Greensboro, ending a five-month drought when there was not a single bank operating in the city. Security was a replacement for the failed N.C. Bank and Trust. But in keeping with the government's habit of tardiness, official approval didn't reach Greensboro until the next day, a Saturday. Federal banking regulations required that in order for a bank to begin business, at least some business had to be carried out on the day of official authorization. So new Security president N.S. Calhoun opened the bank's doors just long enough to make the first token deposit on Saturday, the only transaction of the day.

Future Security president C.M. Vanstory later said that Calhoun's cash for that deposit on the weekend was always a mystery. "Nobody knew where he got the money," Vanstory said. "All of us were broke."

Jefferson Standard for a while controlled all initial Security operations, initially owning 100 percent of the stock, before repaying the RFC loan from bank profits and making small amounts of stock available to others.

Six months after Security National Bank opened for business, in

168

early 1934, the RFC stepped to the forefront once more to help start a second bank in Greensboro. Guilford National Bank, controlled by Pilot Life Insurance Company, opened in the spring of 1934. Guilford Bank was a replacement for the failed United Bank. The two banks run by the two insurance companies clearly eased the pain of money shortages for the city and its workers as they competed for business, but the competition was determined to be a long-range detriment with so much of the community's economic base tied to only two companies. Jefferson and Pilot had merged into a single insurance conglomerate in the early 1930s, meaning that Jefferson directors controlled both banks.

Pilot would later split off from Jefferson, but rejoin for good in 1945.

Security Bank slowly but surely became the dominant financial institution in the region over the next two decades stretching into the middle 1950s with offices in five cities across North Carolina, including the Capitol City of Raleigh where Jefferson was founded in 1907. One Security branch was more than 125 miles to the east in Tarboro, the hometown of Jefferson president Howard Holderness whose father had been one of the original investors in Jefferson almost 50 years earlier. Security, with headquarters on the first floor of the downtown Jefferson Building, emerged as the leader, despite some stringent rules on lending in the early days of operation. In the Security High Point office, for example, loans were limited to no more than $1,000 to any individual borrower because of credit risks as well as shortage of actual dollars at the bank.

Despite the solid foundation of Security with control by Jefferson — or perhaps because of it — corporate customers as well as investors in Greensboro were becoming increasingly anxious about the bank's future. With so much control in the hands of so few and with the dominance of Wachovia Bank based in Winston-Salem, directors agreed that changes were necessary by the middle 1950s. More diversity of ownership was critical.

169

Among the early directors at Security was Joe Bryan, by then holding dual titles as president of Jefferson Broadcasting and board chairman of Pilot Life. Also on the board was Jack Lindley, a long-time thorn in Bryan's side when it came to business dealings. Lindley, then as later, held no official paid position at Jefferson, but his influence was no less significant as a director and executive committee member than when he later engineered the selection of Holderness as Jefferson president. When Security Bank was formed, Lindley stepped into the center of its operation as an aggressive director. The late 1950s was a time when both Bryan and Lindley were interested in strengthening Security's position, but they differed over ways to achieve their goals. Both were looking at a merger with other banks. Bryan was interested in what was best for Greensboro. Lindley simply wanted a merger to give the bank more clout and the impact on Greensboro, at least for him, was secondary. His stance was one that would prove critical in later years.

Lindley began working his clandestine magic in search of a bank merger. He worked independently of other bank directors, particularly Bryan. He was interested in any almost any merger except with Wachovia, an institution for which he held contempt for reasons he never fully explained. Lindley, whose habit was to use his inside coat pocket for a filing cabinet and to work his business deals out of phone booths to ensure more privacy, spent years off and on in meetings with bank officials around the state, including those at First Union and First Citizens. He claimed he was just a naive country boy who knew virtually nothing about banks except that customers could write checks and borrow money. But he was cunning like a fox.

A Phi Beta Kappa graduate of UNC Chapel Hill, Lindley was a member of the state banking commission during his search for a merger for Security, and maintained an insider knowledge of the workings of the state's financial situation through his close friendship with then State Treasurer Edwin Gill. Lindley had earlier served on the State Highway Commission and his political ties reached directly into the office of then Gov. Luther Hodges who named him to both commissions.

Lindley's penchant for secrecy became legendary. Not only would he refuse to conduct much business from his office in the Jefferson Building — where he was the only non-employee director with his own private space — but he would often borrow his secretary's car to drive to phone booths to make calls to avoid being seen in his own vehicle.

Greensboro businessman and Jefferson stockholder William Jones, with a serious tone that hid his devilish intent, once admonished former Jefferson President Roger Soles that Soles ought to do something about Lindley who had doubled the cost of the company's expenses.

"What do you mean?" Soles inquired.

"Well, the cost of using a pay phone has doubled from a nickel to a dime and that's twice the cost of doing business because Lindley does everything from a pay phone," Jones responded with a laugh. Even the normally serious Soles thought that was humorous. Lindley had doubled his cost of doing business, but he was using his own nickels.

As Lindley scouted out possible bank mergers, both through his phone booth calls and private small hotel room meetings often under the cover of darkness, former Greensboro mayor Huger King gave Lindley the leverage he needed. King, a lawyer who was elected head of Greensboro-based Richardson-Merrill Corporation in the summer of 1958, made it known to Lindley that the Richardson family was interested in owning a chunk of Security stock. That was quickly arranged — with a special caveat from Lindley — primarily because of the close family and friendship ties among those who ran the two companies. The affluent Richardson family in Greensboro founded what would later become Richardson-Merrill in 1905, seven years before Jefferson moved to the city, under the name of Vick Chemical Company. Jefferson and Richardson officials had numerous connections in local civic and corporate affairs as well as personal friendships.

Lindley promised King he'd work out plans for Richardson-Merrill to purchase some Security stock provided that King would agree buy shares only on condition that Security pursue a merger.

"Why, of course," King said. "That's the only reason I would buy it."

That was music to Lindley's ears. With Lindley handling arrangements, the purchase of Security stock was promptly made and King was immediately named to the Security board. That amounted to one more chit in Lindley's merger arsenal, but it was a slow process because he had been stirring the bank merger pot for some five years without much success.

The first official step in the merger was to put the two competing Greensboro banks together, a relatively easy task because Jefferson controlled both. Security and Guilford banks became one in April 1960. But while directors of the two banks were comfortable with the merger, the move caused some turmoil at the top as the officers jockeyed for leadership.

Patrick Calhoun who was the top officer at Guilford Bank had been privately negotiating a merger of his own, but not with Security. He had been dealing privately with Addison Reese who headed American Trust Bank in Charlotte. Regrettably for his own job security, Calhoun had not bothered to tell his own directors of his deal-making and once they learned of his actions and the Security-Guilford merger was in place, Calhoun found himself without a job. C. M. "Neil" Vanstory was chosen head of the merged Greensboro banks that operated under the name of Security National Bank.

Lindley, meanwhile, was still cooking up other deals. He, too, had been talking with Addison Reese in Charlotte at the same time Reese was working on a plan to merge American Trust with Commercial National Bank, next door neighbor banks in downtown

Charlotte. The Charlotte merger was accomplished under the name of American Commercial Bank in the spring of 1960 at roughly the same time as the Security-Guilford merger was sealed.

Lindley saw that as yet another opportunity. If he could wed the newly merged Charlotte banks with the recently merged Greensboro banks, it would give him and Jefferson the kind of financial advantage he felt was needed to offset Wachovia. Wachovia at the time seemed to have locks on state investments and major lending, a point that bothered Lindley and his pal State Treasurer Gill.

Bryan was sensitive to concerns of merger, but he was interested in what it would mean to Greensboro. Charlotte was a Federal Reserve City and the two merged Charlotte banks had more total assets than the two merged Greensboro institutions. Whatever happened, Bryan urged, Greensboro's interests ought to be uppermost.

As Bryan wondered what might happen with the merger negotiations as he pursued his personal travels and outside investments in oil wells in the Deep South, Lindley was moving yet again in the shadows with a singular focus of finding the right bank marriage. To avoid public attention, Lindley called a series of meetings with bank officials from Greensboro and Charlotte at the Holiday Inn on Interstate 85 in Salisbury, halfway between the two cities and a place where none of the bank directors would likely be recognized.

"Merging a bank was almost like talking about somebody's wife," Lindley said of his stealth meetings in Salisbury years after the fact. "You don't speak it out loud and you're pretty circumspect in what you do." He also said his only interest was in getting the merger move off the status quo and he didn't realize the risks. "Since I was just a farmer and didn't really know what I was doing, I just didn't think about it beyond getting something going. I guess I could have played hell several times."

But when asked if he was also having fun playing the power broker role despite his claims of naivete, Lindley didn't dispute the suggestion.

The closing deal on merging the Charlotte and Greensboro banks was, quite literally, sealed in a smoke-filled room at the Salisbury Holiday Inn, this time with Huger King being the point man because Lindley was out of the country on a trade mission to Europe with his friend Gov. Hodges.

King and Harold Lineberger, a director at the merged Charlotte bank were at that meeting, both smoking cigars. "I had tried to break the cigarette habit and had taken up cigars," King said of that eventful meeting. "Harold was also smoking cigars. We got poor Addison (Reese) in there and stayed all morning. The smoke was so thick you couldn't see across the room when we finished."

That meeting brought forth agreement from all participants that the banks would be merged, but there were some sensitive details to be resolved. Both banks had some powerful businessmen on their boards, all with clout and none that wanted to give up their power. Furthermore, both Greensboro and Charlotte wanted to be the headquarters city. Both sets of directors also had to agree on a new bank name.

Lindley, as usual, had a plan. Federal banking laws allowed up to 25 directors, but did not require that number. Lindley proposed a full slate, 13 from Charlotte and 12 from Greensboro. Some Greensboro interests wanted an equal number from each city or fewer than 25, but Lindley insisted that Charlotte should get one more than half because those merged banks had been larger than the two in Greensboro. It was also apparent that the Charlotte group wanted that weighted vote on the board; Lindley agreed to allow Charlotte one extra director as insurance against any collapse of merger plans. And he had the majority backing — but not unanimous support — of the Greensboro group. As a concession for having fewer directors, Greensboro would get the new board chairman in Security's Vanstory while Charlotte's Reese would be president.

Reese had to carefully negotiate through a committee process to find directors to represent a majority stock interest. Lindley didn't have such difficulties at his end. He had enough power among Jefferson and Security interests that he could just call the shots as he chose. "If I had had to come back and get a decision every time, we never would have gotten it," Lindley said later. "I didn't owe any obligation to anyone but me."

Lindley proposed dual headquarters, one in each city. Directors meetings would be split between the two cities. That way, Lindley said, no city would have an edge. Vanstory wasn't convinced of that, but he felt it might help negate Charlotte's total control if Greensboro had at least a part of the corporate headquarters. But that wasn't to be—not for long, at least.

Bryan, who had not been directly involved in the merger negotiations because of his many travels, and Vanstory soon saw the handwriting on the wall. Both personally opposed the planned merger if Charlotte had control of the board in numbers even though Vanstory would be board chairman. Greensboro, they feared, would eventually be relegated to second tier, despite what Lindley kept saying about equality. Their fears soon became reality as more and more power shifted southward.

Bryan also didn't like the proposed merger because Lindley was so much a part of it. Bryan had never trusted Lindley since the Jefferson presidency issue years earlier when Lindley had privately engineered the selection of Holderness over Bryan.

There was pride of ownership, so to speak, in Greensboro from Bryan's point of view. "I didn't want Charlotte to get control of the bank," Bryan said. "I had pride in the bank and wanted it here (in Greensboro). It was a valuable asset. I wanted the control to stay in Greensboro."

Vanstory felt the same, even though he agreed to serve as chairman under the dual headquarters arrangement. It was something of a hollow victory for him. Vanstory had a title, but not much to go with it, and that was not something that set well with the strong-

175

First meeting, Board of Directors, North Carolina National Bank, Charlotte City Club, June 30, 1960 - Seated, front row, l. to r.: Frank Dowd, Julian Robertson, William H. Barnhardt, C. M. Vanstory, Jr., Addison H. Reese, C. T. Council, Fielding L. Fry, Orton A. Boren; standing, l. to r.: H. F. Kincey, John C. Erwin, J. Van Lindley, Jas. G. Cannon, David R. Johnston, James J. Harris, Thomas M. Belk, J. M. Bryan, W. C. Boren, III, T. A. Upchurch; seated, center row, l. to r.: Wilbur L. Carter, Jr., John B. Hatfield, James M. Peden, James L. Coker, J. H. Lineberger. Lower right inset: W. G. Clark, Jr. and Huger S. King.

Directors of what was then North Carolina National Bank, at their first meeting on June 30, 1960, at the Charlotte City Club. Joseph M. Bryan and Jefferson Standard Life Insurance Company were involved in the creation of that bank, which later became Nations-Bank and then Bank of America.

willed man who had been in charge at Security as well as in charge of the city while earlier serving as mayor.

As mayor of Greensboro in the 1940s, Vanstory was a strong leader who didn't suffer fools gladly. He was part of the Julian Price slate of candidates and well connected with the city's elite of the corporate community and a dynamic spokesman for Greensboro's financial interests. One legendary story from Vanstory's term as mayor involved a woman who once called him at 3:30 a.m. to complain that a street light in front of her home was not working. The mayor assured her he would get it repaired the next day, and he did. Then he waited until 3:30 a.m. the following morning to call the woman to ask if her street light was fixed. She never bothered him again.

Vanstory felt betrayed with the merger results, and by his former friend Lindley. "They just shoved my father aside," C. M. Vanstory III said of the way his father was treated. "They gave him a title and a desk that didn't even have drawers and he had virtually nothing to do. That Charlotte gang and Jack Lindley just outvoted him. That's why he never had any respect for them after that. Lindley had lots of power and he used it the way he wanted to use it."

The senior Vanstory once said to a friend about Lindley: "The S.O.B just sold the bank out from under me." Lindley never made excuses or offered apologies for what he did. He was satisfied that he had pulled it off.

By April 1960, agreement was reached on the number of directors, location of headquarters and officers. The final hurdle was choosing a name. That took awhile. Directors wanted the word national in the name and they preferred to retain parts of the names of the original banks. The first suggestion was American Security National Bank, but it was considered cumbersome and omitted the state angle. Lindley suggested National Bank of North Carolina, striking either of the original bank names, but retaining the state and national connection. There was opposition to that name because some directors from Greensboro felt it was too closely tied to the former North Carolina Bank & Trust that failed in 1933. But no director at the time could come up with a better name, so Lindley's recommendation was approved – temporarily.

Federal officials in Washington rejected that name. When the board met again, Joe Bryan recommended a new name.

"Why not," he said, "keep the words we chose but flip the sequence?" Directors agreed. National Bank of North Carolina became North Carolina National Bank.

Both the directors and federal bank officials approved Bryan's recommendation for the name of North Carolina National Bank. Thus, NCNB was born out of the mind of Bryan who could claim

177

at least one victory from the lengthy negotiations.

NCNB began operations on July 1, 1960. Two of the directors were Bryan and Lindley.

Reese promptly hired former Federal Reserve employee Tom Storrs to run the Greensboro end of the new bank as part of the dual headquarters arrangement. Storrs remained in Greensboro for 10 years, but when he returned to Charlotte to direct the bank from there and Vanstory retired, Greensboro's hold on the bank management evaporated, never to return.

NCNB later became NationsBank and by the late 1990s had become Bank of America under the leadership of hard-charging ex-Marine Hugh McColl following Storrs' retirement.

But it all began with the phone booth calls and after sunset meetings in the Salisbury hotel, spearheaded by Jack Lindley. Without his persistence, those initial mergers might never have happened. Almost certainly, the mergers would not have occurred in the same fashion without Lindley's activism. In one sense, then, it was Lindley who deserves considerable credit for creating what is now Bank of America just as it was Lindley who is largely responsible for the bank's location in Charlotte instead of Greensboro.

It is only conjecture what Greensboro would be like today if the bank had remained in that city instead of slowly creeping southward to Charlotte. But there is no doubt if NCNB headquarters had remained in Greensboro, the city would be different from what it was on the eve of the 21st Century. Greensboro leaders have frequently lamented the fact that the city has never been headquarters for any major financial institution. Charlotte has gradually become the state's banking center, thanks in large part to Lindley.

"Lindley was more responsible for those initial bank mergers (that ultimately resulted in NationsBank and Bank of America) than any other one person," Storrs said in an interview. "He was the consummate power broker. It was almost as though he had influence simply because he had influence. When it came time to get things

Joseph M. and Kathleen Price Bryan, in one of the last photographs taken of the couple prior to her affliction with Alzheimer's disease a decade before her death in 1984.

Joseph M. Bryan, right, with Ike Granger, left, and Blake Clark of Greensboro at The Masters golf tournament in Augusta, Ga., in 1992, three years before Bryan's death. Bryan and Granger were the two oldest members of the club at their deaths. Clark was a friend of both.

Ann Rambeaut, Bryan's longtime administrative assistant, and Roy Hay, Bryan's personal chauffeur from London, at a mid-1980s Greensboro celebration in honor of Hay.

Greta Medlin, Bryan's closest confidante in his later years, and Bryan at his 90th birthday celebration.

Bryan and his attorney, Carole Bruce. Bruce handled Bryan's personal and business finances for decades and is a member of his foundation board of trustees.

Joseph M. Bryan with his trusted English Spaniel, Jason, at a shooting site in Guilford County in 1986. Bryan was 89, and his eyesight was failing, but he would watch Jason, who would spot birds first, then alert his master to the oncoming flock.

Joseph M. Bryan (with his guide) at the end of a day of successful fishing along the Watchichou River in Canada when Bryan was 91. The Atlantic salmon weighed 14 pounds and was the largest caught on the river at that point in the season. Bryan hooked the fish, then had his guide motor near the shore where he stepped into the water and continued fighting with his catch before reeling the fish in.

done, he had the (Security and Jefferson directors) votes in his pocket. He was a very pragmatic man and he knew right much about the banking business (despite his protestations to the contrary). And my impressions are that as a director he also got into some management issues as well as oversight."

Lindley kept his finger in the new bank's personnel office, too, influencing some of the hires, including Storrs. Contrary to rumor, however, Lindley did not play any role in hiring McColl, the man who later took the bank to the top of the nation's financial hierarchy. McColl was hired by American Commercial Bank in 1959, a year ahead of the merger with the Greensboro banks. Legend has it that American Commercial executives initially rejected McColl when he applied for a job. When that happened, McColl's father who was a major customer of the bank called Reese to ask why his son had not been hired. No one knows the exact content of that conversation, but shortly after the phone call Reese reversed the rejection and the younger McColl was hired. The rest, as they say, is history.

While Bryan opposed the merger if it meant that Charlotte would gain the upper hand, he was not present the day directors voted to approve it. He was at the time on a shooting trip out of the country. "They did it in my absence," he later explained to a friend. "Had I been present, I would have fought hard to prevent it." Maybe so, but it might not have mattered. As Storrs said about Lindley, he had the votes in his pocket before they were ever counted.

Storrs agreed, however, that Bryan was opposed to the merger, even though not opposed enough to remain in town for the vote or fight the merger instead of leaving the country for a recreational excursion. "I can't say that I ever directly asked him," Storrs said. "But from his demeanor and attitude that were reflected in what he said, he was not in favor of merging. I think Joe would have been against anything that, in his eyes, diminished the role of the City of Greensboro."

Lindley has received little public recognition for the role he played in the bank merger. That's as he said he liked it. Others have attempted to give him credit, so far without success. Ironically, with all he did with Jefferson and the bank mergers, when Lindley died in 1990 he was virtually bankrupt with debts in the range of $8 million. At his death, he held title to assets valued at far more than his debts, but his properties were all heavily mortgaged. He owed NCNB, the bank he helped create, $967,000. He held a $2 million certificate of deposit at another bank, but owed that same bank $1.968 million. When the CD was cashed in, his debt was paid off and the remainder went toward another debt at yet another bank.

Lindley was continuously buying land, always with borrowed money, and never selling any of it. Bryan never liked the fact that Lindley was always in debt to Jefferson because as far back as the early 1940s, Julian Price loaned Lindley money to purchase property. Lindley paid interest on his debts, but seldom paid off principal. "He was not a seller," said his grandson Cope Livingstone III who was still settling his grandfather's complex financial estate at the end of 1999.

Among Lindley's debts at his death was an unpaid pledge of $460,000 to Guilford College. The money was to be used to construct a new entrance to the West Side of the campus. Lindley originally pledged the money for a campus building, but when it wasn't needed for that, he agreed to finance the new entrance. That pledge was the latest in a long line of Lindley family ties to Guilford. Lindley's grandfather, a devout Quaker who refused to fight as a soldier during the Civil War but agreed to serve as a hunter of buffalo meat for soldiers, was a Guilford trustee for 33 years and Lindley's father also served as a trustee.

Lindley's friends Seth Macon, former Jefferson executive, and Stanley Frank, a Greensboro businessman and strong supporter of Guilford College, have appealed to Bank of America officials to pay that pledge in a show of appreciation for Lindley's role in creating the bank. The bank steadfastly has declined to fulfill that request.

While Lindley didn't or couldn't pay his pledge to Guilford College, Joe Bryan did pay his pledges to the college where a dormitory is named for Bryan and his wife. His son Joe Bryan Jr. has followed his father's lead in showing generosity to that Quaker institution where he received a degree and serves as a trustee.

Bryan Sr. was once a strong supporter of Guilford before turning his attention in later life to Duke University and the University of North Carolina at Greensboro. He contributed $250,000 for the new dorm at Guilford that bears his name. The building cost $237,000, but Bryan donated $250,000 and asked that his gift be invested at a higher rate of interest than the debt Guilford had incurred at Pilot Life — before Bryan made his pledge — to pay off the new building. That way, the school paid off its debt at a low interest and earned money at a higher rate, thanks to Bryan.

Former Guilford President William Rogers learned early the importance of knowing Bryan. "My first day on the job in January 1980, some members of my board advised me I ought to meet Mr. Bryan," Rogers said. "They said he had been very helpful to the college and I would enjoy getting to know him. They were right on both issues. He always weighed his options carefully, but always had a lot of thoughtful ideas and always wanted to learn more. I always enjoyed his companionship in our many meetings over the years. He was very helpful with scholarships in addition to the dorm contribution."

Bryan also had one other, unannounced, connection to Guilford College. When he was hoping to become president of Jefferson Standard in 1950, Bryan discreetly hired then Guilford President Clyde Milner to teach him ways to improve his public speaking abilities. Bryan wanted to learn how to better present himself in front of an audience, whether at Jefferson or elsewhere, if he became company president. He later told Milner that although his hopes of becoming Jefferson president never became reality, he felt his speech lessons were beneficial and he never regretted asking for help.

Bryan would often lament in later years the fact that Greensboro lost its hometown bank that he and others at Jefferson had founded. He laid most of the blame for that on Lindley. While the bank headquarters shifted south to Charlotte, Jefferson's presence and Bryan's heart remained integral parts of Greensboro and its future. Jefferson continued to grow as a thriving insurance and broadcast company and a major stockholder in the profitable bank that got away. At the end of the 20th Century, Jefferson was still a large stockholder in Bank of America. The bank, once the largest Jefferson stockholder, sold its Jefferson stock in the middle 1990s and used those resources to pay costs of starting banking operations in Texas.

Bryan officially retired from Jefferson on July 1, 1961, one year to the day after NCNB opened its doors with dual headquarters that he didn't like and with the gradual shift southward that he feared.

In retirement, Bryan's network of good works was really just beginning. His name would soon become synonymous in Greensboro and across the state with good deeds. He would obtain after age 65 through his benevolence a degree of pleasure and satisfaction that he was seldom ever able to reach as a corporate executive or as a father.

12

GREEN SPACE AND OIL RIGS

Joe Bryan's presence in a room was like a flash bulb on a camera: hard not to notice. He was an imposing figure, tall and muscular with a booming voice that never lost its distinctive, up-town sophisticated sound of his New York years. He didn't sound British, but he sure looked the part. A few of his friends teased him that if the British had not already been there, he would have invented them. He considered that a term of endearment and never attempted to disabuse anyone of the thought.

He sometimes wished, he once said, that he had been born early enough to live in the Edward VII days when he would have appreciated — and he added with a smile deserved — the splendor of it all. The two men, a generation and a country apart, shared a common love of sport and travel.

Bryan's snow-white, bushy eyebrows didn't dance as rapidly or as often as North Carolina's nationally known and respected U.S. Senator Sam Ervin's did, but they were just as pronounced. His matching gray hair and mustache and immaculate wardrobe of tailor-made suits gave him just the touch of class that he enjoyed.

At one Jefferson Standard social gathering, a company executive apologized to Bryan for not putting him at the head table. "Don't worry about it," Bryan said with a touch of good humor. "You don't need to designate a head table. Where ever I sit IS the head table."

Throughout adulthood, Bryan thrived on the lifestyle he led, perhaps in part because it was much more comfortable and pleasurable than his earlier years as a child in a family constantly on the move and then later divided. He was a regular attendee and early member of Augusta National Golf Course. He fished for salmon in Canada, shot grouse in England and Spain, maintained annual visits to a resort in the Bahamas and to a plush and elegant private sports club in Pennsylvania, dined with the Queen Mother in London, once visited with the Pope and hobnobbed with the rich and famous at every opportunity. His regular sporting friends were the heads of giant corporations or top governmental and political figures.

"He was very impressed with his friends," one Bryan acquaintance "I never met a person who wanted to be associated more with important people." Other Bryan friends dispute that assessment, saying that while he had friends in high places he more readily enjoyed associating with average people. There's some truth in both views. Bryan always seemed able and willing to adjust his actions and mannerisms to fit the circumstances.

Surrounding all his opulence and elegance, however, Bryan maintained a soft spot in his heart for the little people who most needed a guiding hand. In that respect, he was more like Edward VIII who was a champion of the downtrodden. While Bryan's sophistry was at times clearly pronounced, he never let that interfere with his benevolence for those less fortunate. He was always willing to lend a hand, but never content just to give a handout. He wanted to help, he said, but only to help those willing to also help themselves. He also wanted results.

A little child, in fact, may well have been the one who led him. It was in 1969, well into Bryan's retirement years and his 73rd birthday, that then freshman Greensboro city councilman E.S. "Jim" Melvin drove Bryan and his wife Kathleen to a struggling public school in the poor section of the city to witness some of Bryan's earliest generosity. It was just a year earlier that Melvin, who later became mayor as well as the city's biggest promoter and would eventually go on to lead the Bryan Foundation, had first met Bryan and, somewhat frightened, asked for his first charitable donation.

That first meeting of Bryan and Melvin was a fortuitous one that resulted in large and long lasting benefits that neither expected nor intended at the time. But there is a lesson to be learned from it.

Bryan, by then a wealthy man from his Jefferson years although his assets would later grow much larger through astute oil well investments, had a history of giving relatively small donations to charities. But Melvin felt Bryan could and should do more and asked the assistance of then Congressman Richardson Preyer.

"The first time I ever actually met Mr. Bryan was when I asked Rich Preyer to go with me to request Mr. Bryan's help with an idea we had come up with to start an enrichment fund through the United Way," Melvin said. That fund was to allow the United Way to provide unrestricted grants to non-United Way agency community groups wanting to try new and innovative projects to improve the lives of people in their neighborhoods. Bryan had been giving $5,000 annually to the United Way, but Melvin and Preyer aimed higher, asking for $25,000 a year for the enrichment grants.

"I didn't know what to expect. I took the congressman with me because Mr. Bryan didn't know me from Adam's house cat," Melvin said.

Bryan listened intently to their request and, without much enthusiasm, agreed to the donation as he added a somewhat caustic comment about lack of appreciation.

"Well, I assume you will be like everybody else who comes in here asking for our money," Bryan said with a serious tone. "You'll get our resources and we'll never hear from you again."

That comment struck Melvin as both unexpected and, if literally true unfortunate. And it stuck with him. "That comment surprised me. I paid attention to that and remembered it, " Melvin said. "I told the United Way people we ought to pick good projects and keep up with what was happening. I was committed to taking the Bryans to see the results of what their contribution had achieved. I was determined not to allow him to believe we didn't care or appreciate his help as apparently some others had done."

From that day forth until Bryan's death age 99, Melvin never let a Bryan gift go unrecognized, at least privately but most often publicly. The show of appreciation paid manifold dividends. Melvin has always wondered how much more Bryan might have given much earlier for more worthwhile causes if recipients had just said a simple thank you.

Part of that initial Bryan grant went to Caldwell School in East Greensboro where it allowed children, then all black, to have resources for enhancements that the school could not provide. Melvin fulfilled his pledge to show Bryan and his wife firsthand what their gift had accomplished. He drove the Bryans to the school so they could personally watch the children show off their achievements. Bryan seemed bemused at what he saw, but Melvin was unsure of his true feelings as they prepared to leave. That changed as they left the classroom when a 10-year-old boy ran up to the regal Bryan, clasped his huge hand and said he wanted to sing a song.

"OK, let's hear it," Melvin remembered Bryan saying as they wondered what would occur next.

The child sang "Jesus Loves Me." "You could have heard a pin drop," Melvin recalled. "It was wonderful and gave all of us a warm feeling. There were tears all around that room, including from Mr. Bryan. That little boy was saying thanks the only way he knew how." As Melvin drove away from the school, Bryan turned toward him and said, "Jim, I believe that was $25,000 well spent."

That well-spent $25,000 donation was the tip of the iceberg. Bryan was obviously pleased with what he saw his gift accomplish and he later increased the annual enrichment gift to $100,000.

Since his death, the Bryan Foundation directors have tripled the amount to $300,000 a year in his memory.

That school gift was the start of Bryan's major philanthropy in his adopted community. The gifts live on in large part because Melvin listened when Bryan said he would appreciate seeing some positive results and hearing a word of thanks. It was a little thing at the time, but it became huge and significant over time. From that little child and the cultivation of the practice of showing apprecia-tion sprang many millions in contributions to hundreds of worthy causes. From that, in fact, a Foundation was conceived and Melvin began a close personal and warm relationship with Bryan that last-ed until Bryan's death. The feeling of respect and genuine concern for Bryan's philosophy and philanthropy continues through the Joseph M. Bryan Foundation where Melvin serves as president.

A year after the enrichment grant success, Melvin came up with another idea that really put Bryan's name in the forefront of Greensboro's public recreational endeavors. The Greensboro City Council had earlier sought and received voter approval for a $1 mil-lion public park and golf course on 480 acres of city-owned land along the shores of Lake Townsend, a municipal water supply, on the northeast edge of the city.

"Somebody asked what name we (the city) ought to put on the park," Melvin recalled. "And so I said well, golly Pete, there is no question is there? There's nothing in town with the Bryan name on it so why don't we name the park after Mr. and Mrs. Bryan? They hadn't put a nickel into the park at the time, but I just felt it was the appropriate thing to do."

Melvin agreed to ask the Bryans for permission to name the facil-ity in their honor. He still didn't know Bryan well and for security on his second trip to the Bryan home he was accompanied by then-Mayor Jack Elam.

"We went in there, to that nice quaint little den at his home. The city election had just been held and I had beaten Elam by 12 votes or something like that and Mrs. Bryan took great delight in bringing that up," Melvin said. "I let Jack do the talking and ask their permission to put their names on the park. Mr. Bryan just sat there and listened without saying a word. Then he just looked at us for a minute."

"Well, how much is it going to cost me?" Bryan asked with a touch of sarcasm in his booming voice. Little did he know how important that question would become.

"It's not going to cost you anything," Melvin replied. "The park is already committed and is already being built with city money. We just want to name it in your honor. I think that meant something to both of them, especially to Mr. Bryan. From that point on, he and I had a sort of ongoing relationship."

That's how Bryan Park was named for the couple before they had donated a dime. The park opened with the golf course among the amenities and Bryan's interest began to grow. Bryan was hooked because golf was among his passions. One day near the end of 1969 when Melvin was visiting in Bryan's office, Bryan asked if the city ever planned to construct a building for recreational use or business meetings on the property.

"Yes, someday we're going to do that when money is available," Melvin replied.

"Well, how much do you think something like that would cost?" Bryan inquired.

The city had shortly before that time built two other recreation centers at municipal parks for approximately $300,000 apiece. Melvin had hoped for something nicer at Bryan Park so he suggested to Bryan that it would likely cost $600,000 to build a really fine recreation center at the park.

"Well, let's do it," Bryan said.

"Mr. Bryan, you didn't hear me," Melvin responded. "We don't have a lot of flexibility in a city budget to just find $600,000. Someday we'll have another bond vote and hopefully get the money."

188

"No, Jim you didn't hear me," Bryan said. "I said let's do it. I'll pay for it."

Melvin, saying he was delightfully taken aback with Bryan's proposal without even being asked, politely thanked Bryan and left the office. "I literally ran to the city manager's office to tell Tom (City Manager Tom Osborne) of Mr. Bryan's offer," Melvin said. "We went straight to the architect's office and then went back to Mr. Bryan's office that same day and just sat and talked and dreamed about a building and what ought to be included."

Greensboro Architect Hyatt Hammond was asked to draw plans for what would ultimately be the Enrichment Center at Bryan Park. But Melvin's cost estimate was not even close. Hammond made it clear that what was requested would cost $800,000. Melvin broke the news to Bryan.

"Well, I didn't think you could do it for what you said, so just go ahead and build it for the $800,000. I'll pay the extra cost."

Bids came in a few weeks later, but not at the anticipated price. "The dadgum low bid came in at $1.3 million," Melvin said. "I turned pale. I asked how that could happen and the architect said, well we had a very elaborate building."

Thirty minutes later a chagrined Melvin walked into Bryan's office. "He just looked up and said the bids came in didn't they and I said yes sir they did. And he said they came in high didn't they and I said yes sir they did. I told him we could cut some things out."

"How high were they?" Bryan asked.

"At $1.3 million," Melvin replied sheepishly.

"What the hell happened to that $600,000 building you had said you would build?" Bryan asked.

"I again told him we could scale back and cut some things out and try to get the price down," Melvin said.

"Then he looked at me and said don't cut out a thing, just build it," Melvin recalled. "We did exactly that and he paid $1.3 million and never complained."

As Melvin left Bryan's office that day, Bryan couldn't resist a deserved dig. "By the way," Bryan said, "you need to take a course on cost estimating."

"Yes sir," Melvin replied without any hint of disagreement.

The Enrichment Center construction was started and Bryan make regular, sometimes daily, trips to the park to watch progress. His impatience became a trademark; once he was committed to something he wanted it finished in a hurry. "He was in his 70s at the time and he didn't know how much longer he was going to live. He wanted to see it finished."

On one trip to the site with Bryan, Melvin repeatedly commented on how nice various sections of the building were going to be. "After about the third of those comments, Mr. Bryan grabbed my arm and asked me never to say that again," Melvin said. "I asked him why and he very pointedly said for what that building cost it ought to be nice. So I never said that again."

The Enrichment Center contribution was actually the second major Bryan contribution at the park once his name was attached. The first was for additional land in an acquisition that Melvin says seems predestined.

It was on a beautiful fall afternoon with the sun glistening off the coloring leaves that Melvin, then City Manager Tom Osborne and Bryan visited the park for the final inspection of the new golf course, along with contractors, architects and city parks department officials. They were discussing the beauty of some 120 acres of adjacent land owned by private businessman Russell Hall when Hall walked up and joined the conversation. Melvin said he still doesn't know why Hall showed up at that particular time.

"You know, Russell, one day we ought to buy that land from you and add to the park," Melvin commented.

"Well, it's for sale," Hall replied, "for $2,500 an acre." Melvin, a banker at the time, thought that was a reasonable offer, maybe even a little low.

190

"That's a good price," Melvin replied, "so I'd like for you to hold it for us. Some day I hope the city can buy it."

Melvin at that moment felt a tug on his arm. It was Bryan who was pulling his sleeve.

"Buy it," Bryan said.

"But we (the city) don't have the money," Melvin replied.

"I know you don't, but I do," Bryan said. "So just buy it. Send somebody to my office later today and I'll give you a check." That was done and the deal was closed in less than two days with $300,000 of Bryan money.

Less than a month later, Hall suffered a stroke and died shortly afterward. "Think about something," Melvin said in recalling that incident. "Who invited Russell Hall out there that day with Joe Bryan standing there, so shortly before Hall died. I don't know. The odds of that happening are rare indeed. I consider that to be one of the great stories about Greensboro. It just happened, like maybe it was predestined."

Bryan was a constant thorn in Melvin's side about the need to purchase additional land surrounding the park property and to get facilities at the park in place rapidly. Bryan said he wanted the surrounding to be secure so that wealthy people couldn't buy it for residences and turn the public park into their private country club. That, Bryan insisted, would discourage people who don't have access to a private club from using the public park. "This is just typical of his thinking and his desire to keep the park open and available for as many people as possible," Melvin said.

Bryan Park was officially opened and dedicated in ceremonies on May 20, 1971. Bryan later contributed another $300,000 for a soccer complex at the park. Since Bryan's death, directors of the foundation he created have purchased still more land and donated it for park use in keeping with Bryan's desire to keep the land pristine and undeveloped. Bryan Park is considered one of the finest facilities in the state.

With all Bryan's personal interest in and generous contributions to the park that bears his name, he insisted that his money not cover all the expenses. The city, he insisted, ought to do its part, too. Bryan took the same approach with his other donations. He would help with projects, but not do it all.

"He did all these things by himself, from his own mind and without any staff," Melvin said. "I did some leg work for him and got him information on some things he was especially interested in, but he made the decisions himself. He would just sit and listen to people make requests, but if he didn't think they were committed, and just wanted his money, they didn't get far with him. If he invested in you, he wanted to make sure you were doing your part and to show him you were doing the best you could. He wanted to see tangible results. He also sometimes supported projects that he really wasn't too fond of, but he felt they were the right thing to do."

One of those was Bryan's support for the Hayes Taylor YMCA in East Greensboro that serves primarily racial minorities. In the early 1990s, ongoing expansion and upgrading of that facility was fraught with cost overruns, construction delays and bickering among board members. Bryan repeatedly bailed the project from the ashes of incompleteness and confusion.

"He went back to the table three times on that one," Melvin said. "He didn't like the way it was being handled, but he felt it was critical to finish the project and that it was an important symbol to the community that someone cared enough to complete it. How many people would do that? I think that says something really important about him. That's just the kind of person he was."

Of all the projects Bryan helped produce, Bryan Park was always at or near the top of his list. He was adamant in his desire to see it grow and expand with his resources supplementing that of the city. In his latter years, Bryan asked friends to drive him to the park virtually every day to watch as the development continued or, often, just to watch children at play. There are numerous stories of both children and adults at the park who went out of their way to stop Bryan and thank him for his generosity. Those times, he said, were among his finest moments.

Bryan also wanted constant additions to the facilities at the park, frequently asking if there wasn't something else needed. "And when we agreed to start something, he was always pushing to get it started," Melvin said. "He'd tell me I had better get on with it. He'd go out there every day and if he didn't see something happening and didn't see progress he was always asking what was holding things up. We were working on engineering plans and the like, but he wanted to see action.

"One time when he was getting so inpatient about lack of progress on the soccer fields, I asked the staff at the park to get a bulldozer and push some dirt around while the engineering was being finished. All we did was just move some dirt every few days. We were not really trying to deceive him or anything, but we wanted to show him something was happening. We did that for about 60 days while drawings were finished. He was reasonably happy because were doing something he could see."

On one occasion, however, Bryan's visit to the park literally came within a car length of perhaps costing his life. For all Bryan's attributes, care and attention behind the wheel of his Lincoln convertible was seldom paramount. While driving from the park on a spring day in the late 1970s in the company of his then son-in-law D. M. "Lauch" Faircloth, Bryan was bragging on the facilities and inattentive to the surroundings as he whizzed across a railroad track near the park's entrance. He either didn't hear or ignored the sound of the train whistle.

"He barreled across that track without ever looking or hearing the train and the engine missed us by maybe a car length," Faircloth said. "Scared the devil out of me." There were two pieces of good news in that incidence. One is that the train missed the vehicle. The other is that Faircloth was at the time Secretary of Transportation for North Carolina and shortly after the near crash, highway officials quietly installed an electronic crossing gate with flashing signals at that location.

At one of Bryan's last public functions, he sat in a wheelchair under an overcoat draped over his shoulders on a chilly and cloudy day at the park as he listened to friends extol his virtues at the unveiling of a life-size statue of him in front of the Enrichment Center.

Bryan took as much interest in that statue as he did in other aspects of the park. He was a stickler for statue precision, insisting that the artist redo parts to his liking. He sent the sculptor a pair of his shoes so she could get them just right. He insisted on chiseling off some hair on his neck and demanded that a three-button jacket be changed because he never wore coats with three buttons.

Because of Bryan's love and devotion to the park in life, it seems fitting that part of him remains there even in death. Half of his ashes are buried at the foot of his statue in the park. Buried beside Bryan's ashes there are the ashes of his prized English Springer Spaniel, Jason. Jason, ill with a fatal disease at age 14, had been put to sleep by Veterinarian Ken Eiler three years before Bryan's death, but Bryan couldn't bear to part with the dog's ashes; he just wanted them saved. After Bryan's death, Eiler and Melvin agreed it would be appropriate to place Jason's ashes with his master in the park. The remainder of Bryan's ashes is buried at his gravesite in Greensboro's historic Green Hill Cemetery.

Bryan Park came into existence almost a decade after Bryan officially retired from his duties at Jefferson Broadcasting and he had started what became a lucrative second career as an oil investor. Unlike his role at Jefferson where he was frequently in the limelight and on public display, his oil field dealings were low-key and private, but highly profitable.

He made, based on estimates of one of his key oil-drilling partners, in excess of $30 million in oil investments, all after his 70th birthday. He could have possibly doubled that except for bad timing when he pulled out of one drilling operation just before it hit a major gusher.

It was some of Bryan's profits from oil fields that helped support Bryan Park and also added to his own and his wife's wealth.

Bryan didn't wait until retirement, of course, to begin his other investments outside Jefferson — once saying as far back as 1933 when he bought his first Jefferson stock that he always kept himself broke buying stocks — but few of his investment ventures paid off like those in oil drilling.

Bryan put his own and his wife's money into oil and gas drilling in Mississippi, Louisiana, Alabama and Texas. Mrs. Bryan was never keen on the idea, thinking the ventures were overly risky, but Bryan continued cautiously and made a lot of money for her portfolio as well as his own. On one well he turned an $8.1 million profit in a six-year period and on another $7.4 million profit over eight years.

His interests in oil came through some of his sports friends who encouraged Bryan on shooting and fishing trips to invest. "Joe was a major investor," said Dudley Hughes an oil drilling executive in Jackson, Miss. Bryan became an investor with Hughes in Jackson and Hughes brother Dan in Texas in the 1970s after learning of their oil drilling operations while on shooting trips to England.

"He called and asked to invest with us and we became great friends," Dudley Hughes said from his office in Jackson. "He was all business, and we never had any problems. He paid his bills the instant he got them and if he had any complaints he'd talk with you. I remember one wild cat drilling we had and he became dissatisfied, saying he didn't feel like we would ever hit oil. He withdrew and we promptly hit the biggest strike we'd ever hit. If he had stayed in, he could have doubled everything. But he didn't complain about it. It was his decision to get out of that one."

Bryan's oil dealings were for both fun and profit. "I really think that once he made a lot of money in oil that he sort of stayed as much for fun as for money," Hughes said. "I'd say he made some-

195

where between $25 million and $50 million in profits beyond the money he actually put in. I would estimate he put in about a third of that amount. He dealt strictly in trust. He never really looked at anything once he made the investment. He trusted us and just left it up to us. The only difficulty I ever had with Joe was in communication because he couldn't hear worth a durn. He had been on all those shooting trips for years and never considered ear protection. He had ruined his ability to hear."

Bryan took his oil investments seriously even though he was also having fun and became something of an expert on the minute intricacies of drilling operations. His friend Kemp Reece Sr., a stockbroker in Greensboro, learned just how much Bryan was involved in oil investment to his (Reece's) own surprise.

"I called Mr. Bryan one day to say I had a really good investment potential for him in oil," Reece said. "He didn't seem too enthused although I was excited, having just returned from an investment course about one oil drilling company. I went to his office and gave him my assessment. He just listened for awhile. Then he turned around behind his desk and said he wanted to show me something. He pulled out a portfolio of oil investments far beyond the total value of the company I was pushing. He knew a lot more about oil investing than I did. He didn't need me to help him. But he was willing to listen and was polite about my efforts although he was far ahead of me in his own knowledge about oil stocks."

Bryan began backing away from oil investing by the late 1980s after having made handsome profits to help support his benevolent causes and adding to his wife's stock portfolio after laws were changed making it harder to gain tax advantages on drilling projects.

By that time, he had accomplished his mission of turning a profit and enjoying the friendships made and preserved. Bryan Park, summer youth programs, university campuses and public schools are all better off from his oil field risks. Charities and children over a wide area are reaping the dividends from his oil field investments.

13

GOOD TIMES AND THE GOOD LIFE

Joe Bryan, in many respects, could only be called an enigma.

He never owned but one house, always saying that second homes were overly expensive. But he regularly forked over huge sums for plush rental units in some of the most expensive conclaves in this and other countries. He harrumphed when people left unneeded lights on in his office, but he never gave a second thought to spending up to $50,000 on a week's worth of entertainment with a dozen affluent friends.

He would spend lavishly on imported custom-made suits, but would wear them for up to 40 years or more, sometimes even after moths had feasted on the fancy fabric.

His personal tailors from Hong Kong came to Greensboro to fit Bryan, as well as his staff, with custom suits because his purchases were well worth the trip. Bryan was more inclined to buy new clothes for his hired help than for himself, however, and his friends frequently would buy him new ties because he insisted on wearing worn, faded ones even as he bought new clothes for them.

He would spend hundreds on a bottle of fine wine, but would ask his secretary to erase names on greeting cards he received so he could send them on to someone else. He recycled the cards not just to save money, although that was an incentive, but to get double use out of cards he especially liked. He said he did that more for fun than frugality.

He also was habitually sending people memos and messages on hotel notepads and scraps of paper rather than company stationery, saying that saved money. And it was not uncommon for Bryan to circle words on mail he received, then return the same letter to the sender with his comments — positive or negative — on word choice as his way of having fun with language use.

When he received a check, he wanted it deposited immediately to avoid losing even one day's interest of a few dollars, but he would the same day write out checks for thousands to some benevolent cause that appealed to him.

While Bryan would sometimes spend lavishly on some social gatherings with his friends, he lived frugally at home where he routinely ignored the need to improve or upgrade his own living quarters.

He didn't seem at all bothered by worn out household equipment, tattered drapes or even a leaky roof. But he enthusiastically contracted for a hand-dug, elaborate thermostatically controlled wine cellar in the basement where he kept huge quantities of the finest imported wines. The labels on the shelves were still there years after his death, as a kind of memorial to his desire for fine wines.

He spent thousands a week on recreational trips at exotic hotels and private resorts in this country and abroad, but was also content sharing a single bathroom with couples in a small rustic fishing cabin on the Santee Cooper River in South Carolina.

He could project an image of a rough and gruff corporate boss or demanding father or grandfather one hour, yet turn into a purring kitten with a heart as soft as fur later the same day. He was considered absolutely immovable by many of his business associates, but could spread charm like warm butter among social friends.

He often complained that the household help in his employ was so aged that they needed their own nursing care, but he kept them on salary years after they were of limited productive value and showered them with gifts on holidays.

He enjoyed lavish living in some of the world's most elegant hotels and finest upscale shops, but equally enjoyed visiting Kmart and other discount shops in his later years. He spent time with some of the country's most influential corporate giants and socialized with elected presidents in the White House, but also seemed content to listen to blue collar workers and the downtrodden talk about their families and lives.

"He had a certain grace and understanding that drew people to him like a magnet," said his adoring friend Greta Medlin. "I never saw him look down on anyone or speak condescendingly. He had a way of making everyone feel like a king or queen. What made him unique was not the money he gave away, but the kind of person he was. He was the most charismatic person I have ever known."

Bryan frequently carried only a $100 bill in his wallet when he was in town, meaning that friends had to pay for snacks and sodas. He liked to joke about not having any smaller bills, but to him it was only a game. More often than not it was Bryan that picked up the tab for expenses, large or small, when he was with friends.

A sign of his quiet and private benevolence toward friends was an occasion when he discreetly covered the sizable investment loss of a casual acquaintance to prevent public bankruptcy disclosure. Bryan's only assurance of repayment was a verbal promise, which was later kept. On another occasion, he paid for the wedding reception for a single mother who had no money for the celebration of her daughter's wedding. He also arranged for another wedding reception on short notice for a frantic young bride whose new husband was shipping off to war.

"He did things like that all the time for people, never wanting any recognition," said his devoted long-time administrative assistant Ann Rambeaut.

People who knew him described him in terms ranging from sugar lumps to shark's teeth. It was all part of the Bryan persona, one that he never tried to amend. Rather, he seemed to enjoy it in a kind of Napoleonic quality of never wanting the opposition to know exactly where he was at any given moment.

"He could deliver a sword with a velvet glove the best of anyone I've ever known," Rambeaut said with reference to the often tough and unpopular — but what he called important and essential — decisions he made in the business world.

Bryan never forgot his humble beginnings even though he kept that part of his life a carefully guarded secret except for a select, small number of intimate friends near the end of his life. But once he overcame those early difficulties through a combination of shrewd investments and marriage, he never made excuses or offered apologies for a lifestyle that only the elite could ever expect to achieve or afford.

Golf was a special passion, even though his desire to play well more often than not exceeded reality. Bryan was among those, in fact, who said that Mrs. Bryan was the better golfer in that marriage. But that didn't keep Bryan from the links as a player in early adulthood or from becoming a respected connoisseur of the game well into his late 90s even as he needed a wheelchair and help to maneuver the spectator routes.

Bryan was an early visitor and among the earliest members of the status-conscious Augusta National Golf Club. At his death at age 99 in the spring of 1995, Bryan was the second oldest member of that club. For years at Augusta, Bryan wore the "Number 1 Official Observer" badge at the annual Masters Tournament, the only member ever to have that designation. That allowed him virtual free rein of the grounds during each tournament. Not even President Dwight Eisenhower could claim such privileges when he held membership there.

Bryan was a long-time member of the prestigious Rolling Rock

200

Club near Pittsburgh, an elegant English-styled lodge and game preserve initially built by the Mellon family and used under strict rules by a limited number of select wealthy members. He made annual visits to Lyford Cay, an exclusive resort in the Bahamas. He regularly rented a standing condo in Palm Beach, Fla. for relaxation several times each year. He was a member of a private hunt club in Camella, Ga. He made annual trips to a little-known fishing resort in Canada where the purportedly best salmon fishing in the world was confined to a limited number of fishermen with the wherewithal of Bryan and a handful of corporate giants across the country. Bryan was the only salmon fishermen at that exclusive Canadian resort who was invited without ever being asked to pay, an indication of how strongly the paying members felt toward him. He maintained that exclusive lifestyle for more than half a century. Only failing health stopped him.

When Bryan made regular trips to London and Spain solely to shoot grouse and hobnob with the wealthy of the world, he employed his own private driver for his own Rolls Royce. And not just any Rolls Royce either. He used a vintage model.

But after growing weary of seeing haughty British officials in and around 10 Downing Street driving around with British flags attached to their limos, Bryan showed his sense of humor with a bit of fun and frivolity of his own to make a point. Prior to one trip to England, Bryan obtained miniature flags from the City of Greensboro from the mayor's office. Once in London, he attached the city flags to the front of his Rolls and had his chauffeur drive him around Downing Street with the Greensboro flags flapping in the breeze. While the Brits gawked at the sight, Bryan just leaned back and enjoyed the inside joke, often his favorite kind of fun.

"Joe was in many ways always bigger than life," said Jim Becher, a well-connected Greensboro businessman and one of four North Carolinians who were members of the Rolling Rock Club at the beginning of the 21st Century. "People at Rolling Rock idolized Joe for his mannerisms and style. They were asking about him until his death. They still talk about him."

It's debatable whether there are more membership rules at Augusta National or Rolling Rock. It didn't matter to Bryan. He was generally loyal to and a stickler for rules, but on rare occasions couldn't resist ignoring those who found overly silly or unnecessary. And on a few occasions, he helped secure changes in rules he disdained.

Bryan made his first trip to Augusta National in 1937, just three years after the inaugural Masters. He joined the club in 1941 and was a faithful and recognized member until his death, never missing a tournament even in the face of physically impairment shortly before his death. In his latter years, he chartered two planes from Greensboro to the Masters, one for himself and friends and a second for luggage, personal household help and his wheelchair.

Until their deaths in 1995 and 1999 respectively, Bryan and North Carolinian Ike Grainger were the two oldest members of Augusta National. Bryan was older by a few months in membership, but Grainger, a former New York financier and president of the U.S. Golf Association, was 13 months older in age. Grainger died in the fall of 1999 at age 104.

For years, Bryan rented a private home in Augusta for the tournament where he lavishly entertained friends. Only officials of the tournament and their wives were allowed to reside in homes on club property. That didn't suit Bryan who felt he deserved the perk of staying on the grounds because of his long-standing support. Masters cofounder Clifford Roberts, never having been accused of passing a charm course, refused to listen to Bryan's request for more favorable housing or treatment.

"Dammit, Joe is not an official of the tournament. We have rules and that's it. No exceptions," Roberts groused when asked to bend the rules for Bryan. Roberts didn't bend rules for anyone. He once demanded that one of his closest friends change from shorts to long pants because he didn't allow anyone to play Augusta wearing shorts. He was perplexing to his friends, but no one ever doubted his love and loyalty to the Augusta course. If you didn't love Augusta and his rules, you could just leave. That view caused some tense moments between Roberts and Bryan through the years and it was a well-known fact among friends that the two were never considered close friends. While they each held a degree of respect for each other, their personalities were starkly different. Bryan was engaging and enjoyed people and crowds. Roberts was much more reserved although he could be quick to anger at the slightest hint of criticism of the Augusta golf course or tournament. Roberts was once described by an acquaintance as having personality of a delegate to an undertaker's convention. Such a style was hardly Bryan's forte.

Roberts, in failing health in 1978, tragically took his own life with a handgun. It was after that that Bryan's friend Blake Clark from Greensboro and other tournament officials created a "No. 1 official observer" status for Bryan as the oldest member still attending tournaments regularly. That got him residency and total rein on the grounds.

"Blake, you have made an old man very happy," Bryan said to Clark when the honorary badge was presented. Bryan wore that badge with pride and held onto it until his death a month after his last Masters in the spring of 1995.

Bryan's conflict with Roberts was not the first for Augusta members and the irascible Roberts. When President Eisenhower was a member and frequent player at the famed course, the president routinely commented on how he despised a huge pine tree at the edge of the 17th fairway, some 125 yards from the tee. Most members didn't seem bothered by the tree, but the president was habitually slicing his tee shots into the tree. He wanted it removed. Roberts steadfastly refused the president's repeated requests to cut the tree.

At the conclusion of an Augusta governors meeting in 1956, Roberts asked if there were any further business to discuss. President Eisenhower stood and raised his hand. "About that damned pine tree at 17," Eisenhower said as Roberts abruptly interrupted the president's words.

"This meeting is adjourned," Roberts ruled emphatically, leaving the president of the United States standing speechless.

The tree still stands and, as of 1998, became even more of a hazard for Masters players when the tee at the 17th hole was moved back 25 yards.

Despite their disagreements over that tree, however, Eisenhower employed Roberts, a former Wall Street broker who took a financial bath in the Crash of 1929, to create a blind trust for Ike's holdings while he was president and to handle the Eisenhower estate. Roberts' friendship with Eisenhower afforded him overnight accommodations in the White House long before William Clinton made them available to Democratic fundraisers. Roberts once sent Eisenhower a note that said "You're the best player in the club, bridge (not golf) that is."

CBS sportscaster Jack Whitaker once drew Roberts' wrath when he referred on a radio broadcast to the "mobs rushing" the 18th green during a tournament. "Get that bastard off the air," Roberts roared. "We don't have mobs at Augusta. And even if we did, they wouldn't rush." Roberts banned Whitaker from broadcasting the Masters for the next five years. On another occasion, Roberts heaped verbal abuse on another CBS commentator who referred on the air to the Augusta County Club. "Golf club dammit, not a country club," Roberts shouted.

Bryan ignored one of Roberts' strict rules that assigned members responsibility for monitoring security at certain holes on the golf course during the tournament. Growing bored at his assigned 18th green during one slow tournament round, Bryan discreetly made his way to a nearby bar and ordered a scotch. Before his drink was finished, another member in a panic rushed in to inform Bryan that a problem was erupting in the crowd at the green Bryan was assigned to protect.

"Joe, they're storming the 18th green," the agitated member shouted. "We need your help out there." But Bryan wasn't bothered. He saw it as no problem.

"I just turned back to the bar and ordered another scotch," Bryan later told friends.

"Mr. Bryan was revered by members and players at the Masters," said University of South Carolina law school professor Alan Medlin who frequently was a Bryan guest at the tournament. "He had a commanding presence."

Bryan was certainly one of the more popular members of Augusta, much admired and recognized by golfers. Before one tournament, golfer Ray Floyd from Fayetteville, N.C. ran down a hallway to stop Bryan and speak to him.

"I just wanted to shake your hand for good luck," Floyd said to the smiling Bryan. Tar Heel golfer Billy Joe Patton called Bryan a regular presence during the tournaments. "He was just always around. Everybody knew him. He stood out among the members," Patton said.

John Derr, former Professional Golf Association official, CBS broadcaster and journalist, called Bryan one of Augusta's most admired members. "Joe Bryan was highly regarded at Augusta, more so than Roberts. Both were big wheels there, but Bryan was a wheel without portfolio," Derr said. "He was liked for who he was because he was so kind to everyone. He was a good friend of the golfers and was a fixture around the clubhouse at every tournament. He was as well known and well liked as any member."

Derr also said Roberts held a fondness and respect for Bryan, although Roberts never acknowledged that fact. "Joe never knew that because Roberts never let him know, but it was there," Derr explained. "I always felt that Joe represented the kind of lifestyle that Cliff wanted. Joe was so regal looking. He looked British, cutting a striking pose everywhere he went."

Derr also said Bryan's subtle sense of humor came out in his association with golfers and members he met and became friends with while at Augusta. Golfers and spectators at Augusta often bragged about the great golf courses of Scotland, but not Bryan. He traveled often around the world and viewed and played golf on some of the famous courses. Those in Scotland, he said, were nothing special. "The best thing about Scotland," Bryan said often, "is the strawberries. They're the sweetest in the world."

"That's just the kind of person he was," Derr said. "He was just a great fellow, kind and friendly. I loved the wonderful cards and letters he would send. He went to England in July and bought Christmas cards to send to friends. They were classic. I still have some of them. He was a wonderful man, a great friend to everyone."

The Masters is the premier golf tournament played each spring on the renowned course created by Roberts and golfing great Robert Tyre "Bobby" Jones on what was once a fruit farm for Confederate soldiers during the Civil War. The property became a Southern winter resort for wealthy Northerners in the 1920s. Once the golf course was developed with Jones in charge of the layout and Roberts keeping a thumb on finances, the first tournaments were known as the Augusta Invitational. Jones wanted what he called the masters of the game to play there, but he detested the suggested name of the Masters Tournament because he said the title sounded haughty. He yielded to the wishes of others once many of the game's "masters" began to play there.

The name not only stuck; it has become revered. Winning the Masters is a ticket to stardom and a ticket to the tournament is a status symbol that evokes jealously in corporate offices and golf courses across the land. Masters membership put one in an elite circle and Bryan was always in the center.

Jones and Roberts, despite their vastly different backgrounds and personalities, formed a good match to develop the Augusta golf course that has become legend. Jones, one of the nation's all time great golfers because of his grace and talent on the course, was a Georgia Tech engineering major who also held a Harvard English degree and a law degree from Emory University. He died in 1971 at age 68 of a rare spinal ailment. Roberts, the same age as Bryan and with a similar background of frequent moves as a child, died in 1978 at age 83, of the self-inflicted gunshot wound. Fittingly, he took his life at the place he loved most: Augusta National.

As religiously as Bryan made his annual spring trek to Augusta and the Masters, he made his fall excursion to Rolling Rock Club, a private 100,000 acre sportsman club in Ligonier, Pa., a two hour drive from Pittsburgh. Membership is limited to an elite few of some of the country's richest men (no women members) where sports activities include bird shooting, golf, fishing, horseback riding and consuming fine wine and food. Wives are allowed to travel to Ligonier with spouses, but they aren't allowed in the club's bar and must spend their nights in other lodging places while husbands spend nights at the lodge.

Rules are strict, particularly involving women. One guest once brought his mistress, not his wife. The man was allowed to stay that week, but he was never invited back.

Members reserve certain weeks each fall of bird hunting season. Game shot is pheasant and duck, sometimes hundreds of pheasants and ducks a day. Bryan always chose the peak week of fall color for his shooting trips, usually the middle week of October. Bryan was careful to label his trips to Rolling Rock or places in Europe as shooting activities, not hunting. He, with good humor, chastised those who mistakenly referred to his recreation as hunting. "Hunting is what you do on horses when you shoot foxes," he said. "I do not hunt. I shoot."

The Andrew Mellon family whose resources came from Mellon Bank, Gulf Oil and Alcoa Aluminum built Rolling Rock and endowed the upkeep beyond what membership dues covered. Membership is carefully monitored. Members are not allowed to sponsor their own sons, out of concern that some sons of wealthy members wouldn't be of sterling enough character.

Dave Phillips of High Point, whose father was a close Bryan friend, was voted in as a Rolling Rock member on the recommendation of Bryan. "I was lucky enough to be sponsored by Mr. Bryan, a man who was greatly respected and well liked at Rolling Rock," Phillips said. "He took time to teach me to shoot. Some say he could appear pompous, but I never saw a negative side. Rolling Rock is an elegant place and Joe fit right in."

When Bryan picked his October week at Rolling Rock, he also picked his friends and picked up the tab. He personally arranged who would shoot with whom, what the schedule would be, what wine would be served and often led spontaneous humor and jokes on his fellow shooting pals. He insisted on the finest of everything.

His guns for bird shooting were not just ordinary guns. He owned Churchills, the Cadillac of weapons. In fact, Bryan owned matching Churchills. "He sometimes let me shoot with his Churchills," Phillips said, remembering the experience with fondness.

A week at Rolling Rock at Bryan's expense could run as high as $30,000 as far back as the 1950s and 60s. Bryan insisted on paying for everything. "He even got a shooting license for everybody he invited and wouldn't even let you pay for a phone call," said his oil investment partner Dudley Hughes of Jackson, Miss., a frequent Bryan guest. "After Joe had to stop going because of his health, I tried to have his type of Rolling Rock party, but I couldn't get the class of people he had. He had the finest."

Bryan also had an ulterior motive in his financial arrangements at Rolling Rock, according to his at-home shooting friend Jack Rochelle of High Point. "He wanted to show up the really rich folks, to let them know he was as good as they were," Rochelle said. "And by paying for everything, he could control everything. When the wine steward would ask why a certain vintage was being served, Joe would say that it was, by God, because he was paying for it and that's what he wanted. He was knowledgeable about what he was doing. He tested your intellect. He drank deeply from the well of life, although not as fully as he might have. While he was entitled to it, he never showed his hubris as he might have. He never flaunted his money to most people, but he spent it the way he chose."

Ranking with the elegance of Rolling Rock were Bryan's annual trips to London, Scotland and Spain for more shooting, entertaining friends and consuming fine wines. In Europe each shooter paid his own way, but Bryan was most often the one who provided the wine.

Shooting in Europe was mostly for a particular species of grouse indigenous to that part of the world. Shooters, called guns, were expected to wear coats and ties while shooting which was arranged by hiring young men, called beaters, to line up for as much as a mile wide in huge fields and flush out birds for shooters to kill. A grouse shooting day could cost hundreds of dollars because shooters had to pay for each bird they killed, but they were not allowed to keep the game that was then sold in markets as a delicacy.

"Joe always went first class, the finest in everything," Hughes said. "He had connections and enjoyed the finest and best. But he was also kind of humble even when he invited some of the most important people in the country to shoot with him. He taught me a lot about wines and class. He was a fine gentleman."

Hughes also recounted an example of what he meant about Bryan going first class. "I learned on our very first trip to Europe what he meant about first class," Hughes said at Bryan's 90th birthday party in Greensboro.

"We met at the Claridge Hotel in London and Joe asked me to arrange to get us to Edinburgh the next day where we were to shoot," Hughes said. "I made train reservations and told Joe and he said he was not riding in any train. So I arranged seats on a shuttle flight and Joe said he wasn't taking any shuttle where he had to handle his own luggage. I asked him how he expected to get us there and he said charter a plane. So, I did."

When Hughes and Bryan reached Edinburgh by chartered jet that day, Bryan's chauffeur Roy Hay with Bryan's Rolls Royce was already there to meet them. "How did he get here so fast," Hughes asked.

"I sent him up last night by train with the car so he would be waiting for us." Bryan explained. For the chartered flight, Bryan had arranged for serving of Dom Perignon champagne, Buluga caviar and a five-course meal with vintage wine.

"That's when I began to learn what he meant by first class," Hughes said of that experience.

Bryan's fondness for chartered flights once was on the verge of taking him to Greece from London instead of to Edinburgh. That occurred when Bryan and Hughes were told to go to a different gate from their usual one, but neither questioned the decision.

"We went to the terminal as instructed and unloaded our gear," Hughes said. "They said, 'Oh, you have guns' and I said, 'of course, that's why we're here.' They whispered for awhile among themselves before letting us on the plane. The pilot said the flight would take more than two hours. I told him it couldn't possibly take that long because the distance to Edinburgh was only one hour."

"We're not going to Edinburgh, we're going to Greece," the pilot said.

"We're supposed to go to Edinburgh," Bryan responded.

"Aren't you General Pompous Lottas from Greece," the pilot asked. "No, I'm Joe Bryan from Greensboro," Bryan replied with more than a touch of agitation as well as a sense of price.

"Oh my God, we've got the wrong passengers," the pilot responded. The pilot stopped the plane, ordered Bryan and Hughes off, piled their luggage and guns on the runway and taxied away.

"There we stood in the middle of a Heathrow Airport runway, a mile from any building with nothing in sight but 747s taking off," Hughes recalled. "Joe and I just looked at each other, mainly distressed because they had taken the champagne with them." After a 30-minute or so wait, a car picked up the stranded pair and delivered them to the right plane for their trip to Edinburgh.

In London, Bryan regularly employed Hay as his personal chauffeur with his own Rolls Royce. The car was special, like so much of what Bryan enjoyed. It was a 1958 silver wraith touring car which is one of the most elaborate Rolls ever built with walnut paneling inside and a fold out bar.

When Bryan became physically unable to travel to London by the late 1980s, he directed Hay to sell his Rolls Royce. Some Japanese businessmen purchased it, a fact that disturbed Hay greatly because he felt it wouldn't get the care he and Bryan had given it. Hay and Bryan kept in contact until Bryan's death when Hay moved to Paris.

"My husband was always so fond of Joe," Hay's widow said of Bryan in the summer of 1999. Hay died suddenly of heart attack while visiting his native London in April 1999 at the age of 73.

Despite his taste for the finest and his tendency to spend lavishly when necessary, on trips with friends Bryan could be frugal to the point of pinching pennies. One caviar story that brings chuckles from his friend Jere Ayers of Greensboro, son of Bryan's shooting buddy Nathan Ayers, illustrates the point.

Bryan prided himself on knowing quality caviar and was especially fond of Buluga, which is what he ordered for the chartered trip from London to Edinburgh. He once complimented Ayers on his Buluga.

"This is really great Buluga," Bryan congratulated Ayers at a cocktail party. "I can't even afford to buy it very often."

"It isn't Buluga," Ayers responded. "It's off the shelf at Marlow's Store at Pawley's Island, S.C. Bryan was unconvinced and added what Ayers called some choice words about his knowledge of exquisite cuisine. "I know Buluga when I taste it," Bryan insisted.

Once shown the original package and convinced the caviar was

Joe Bryan Sr. (left) and his salmon fishing buddy F. Stuart Molson in Canada. The headgear netting Bryan is wearing is designed to fend off stinging bites from mosquitoes. Molson, a descendent of the founder of Molson beer, holds a can of liquid refreshment as he discusses the day's catch.

not what he thought and learning that it was also not expensive, Bryan began ordering it by the case from Marlow's. He served it to his friends for years. He loved to listen to them brag about the quality caviar before telling them it wasn't what they thought and boasting that it was as good as any but a much better bargain. The taste of Buluga by any other name to him was just as sweet, tasty, and far less costly.

"Some people have money and don't know how to spend it," Ayers said of Bryan. "Joe had it and knew how to enjoy it. He appreciated the finest, but he spent his money on things he preferred." Store shelf caviar was good enough if it tasted good enough.

Bryan also made regular trips to Riverview Club, a private game preserve in Georgia where a week of shooting could cost $15,000 as far back as 1950. Riverview, since closed, was limited to 28 members who used a 4,000-acre shooting area at a 31,000-acre plantation.

There were also decades of annual fishing trips to Canada, again to a private domain where only select persons were allowed to fish for salmon each June and July. The Grand Romaine Club, limited to 8 members, is on the northern shore of Quebec opposite Anacosta Island on the Olemoane River at Etamaniou, Canada. Bryan was never a member of Grand Romaine, but fished there as a guest of his member friends. He also salmon fished at the Watchichou Club, limited to 6 members.

At age 91 while fly-fishing from a canoe, Bryan caught the largest salmon recorded that summer on the Watchichou River.

Bryan was introduced to Canada fishing by Tristan Colket Jr., nephew of Bryan's friend Jack Dorrance who was president of Campbell Soup Company.

"Joe was a wonderful friend to my uncle and a wonderful man to me," Colket said. "He was respected for his ideas and his warm friendship." When Dorrance died in April 1989, his family sent a private plane to Greensboro so that Bryan could attend the funeral in Philadelphia and sit with Dorrance's widow.

Bryan's endearing friendships with his shooting and fishing buddies extended to their widows, too.

"He had a real love affair with his friends, you could just feel it," said Mrs. Margie McBain, widow of former Brystol-Myers chairman Gavin McBain who was a regular shooting partner of Bryan's in Scotland. "Gavin and I both treasured his friendship. He was an absolute gentleman, a real Southern gentleman. He was just fun to be with. He loved to have parties and have fun." After McBain's death, Bryan treated his widow to dinner in New York at least once a year until his own health failed.

"I always considered him sort of like a father," said Mrs. Lucy Sharp, whose husband John and father F. Stuart Molson, a descendent of the Molson brewery family, were shooting and fishing partners with Bryan. "Joe served the best wines and caviar. I miss him dearly and think often of him. He was such fun and I always felt sad that he didn't seem to have a very happy life with his own family. It is sad about his family, but he was a most lovable gentleman."

Bryan and Molson shared common characteristics beyond their love of sport. Molson, like Bryan, never considered himself an insider in the family beer industry or within his own family. Molson, labeled a rebel by family members, was a director of the family-owned brewery, but he was never an officer or held top responsibilities within the company. "My father never liked people telling him what to do," Mrs. Sharp said. "He and Joe were a lot alike in that regard. I think that's why they got along so well together."

While most of the men who fished in Canada were wealthy corporate executives from across the country, Bryan took his friend and next door neighbor, Dr. David Patterson, on several salmon trips. "They were wonderful," Patterson said of the trips.

"Joe was as good a friend as a person could ever expect to have," said his shooting friend Tim Ireland, a former Wall Street banker. "He was generous to a fault. He would do anything for you. He was always thinking of others. He was a great companion when we shot

214

grouse in London and Spain. He was always the best company, making people happy with his good humor. There was never a dull moment with him."

Bryan's annual winter, sometimes more often, trips to Lyford Cay resort on the Island of Providence in the Bahamas were not for fishing or shooting, but for golf and relaxation. Bryan and his wife Kathleen spent time there for many years, and he continued to go after her death in 1984. The trips were not inexpensive. The place Bryan rented cost a basic $14,000 a month with any extra service adding to the cost. Receipts Bryan saved from those trips showed he spent $16,500 on his 1985 trip there and $20,000 in 1987.

Those winter trips were in addition to regular visits he made to a rented condo in Palm Beach when Kathleen was alive and well. Those trips ended when she became too ill for travel. Bryan's one-home ownership philosophy didn't keep him from enjoying the luxuries of plush residences owned by others. He paid handsomely for those homes, but he never tired of the enjoyment of it all.

Bryan was also a member of the Metropolitan Club in Washington, D.C., the Bath and Tennis Club and the Everglades Club in Palm Beach.

It was that lavish kind of spending that generated at least some of the resentment within his own family, but it was just one of many things that caused friction in his household. Family difficulties plagued Bryan throughout most of his adult life, difficulties considerably different from those of his childhood years, but none the less disheartening. His family's inability to function in a way that all could enjoy the fruits of his labors was, by all accounts, regrettable and a constant source of disappointment to him even as he conceded that he contributed to some of the discomforts. The problems at home, all of his friends continue to say, were unfortunate and caused him hurt and public humiliation for years. That hurt ended only at his death.

14

HEARTACHES AT HOME

"I was not a good father," Joe Bryan said in a candid conversation with a newspaper reporter in the summer of 1982, decades after his two daughters and one son had grown into adulthood. "I wasn't paying as much attention as I should have. I am aware of it now as I look back. I could have (better) used the time to better advantage, to learn more about my children."

That was not an easy self-assessment for a man of Bryan's pride and stature in the Greensboro community. He obviously was proud of his many business and community achievements. He was both conscious and concerned of his image. Discussing his personal disappointments within his own family was not something he had ever done before in public. But, friends say, it was a comment straight from the heart of a man who wished for what might have been even though he knew all too well that it would never be. He was 86 when he made that confession about his failures at home. It was too late to turn back.

Bryan also offered another, unsolicited, burst of candor in that same interview as he discussed his philanthropy. "I've often wondered," he said. "I just wonder, and you didn't ask this question, I did. But wonder if I'd done all this on an anonymous basis, would I have gotten the same satisfaction. Somehow or other, I don't know. Maybe I like my name connected with all this. I guess I do. Well, then I'll say it. Yes. Yes, I do."

Bryan's unhappy, some might even say unhealthy, family situation and his perceived desire for positive public recognition — the latter prompting some of the former — hover as blemishes over his incredible and enduring benevolence and generosity.

As Bryan readily conceded, he enjoyed public recognition for much of his giving. But he said that, at least in part, was a way of encouraging others to contribute to their communities, too. He also gave away a lot of resources without public notice, mostly to friends and for needs that didn't draw a lot of attention or notoriety.

There are stark differences of opinion about Bryan as a businessman and community leader among his friends, family and former associates. He was, at times, a revolving contradiction, being magnanimous and engaging one moment and unbending and intractable the next. But there is unanimous agreement that his inability to coexist in harmony with his children, and to a lesser degree some of his grandchildren, is a sad and regrettable chapter in an otherwise fruitful and rewarding life that has meant so much to so many in so many places.

"There were two sides to him," eldest daughter Kay Bryan Taylor Edwards of Greensboro said of her father. "My mother always said he was an angel on the streets. We frankly never saw the street angel at home. He was a very strict father, what you might expect of a German parent (Bryan's ancestors were Irish-Catholic), who expected immediate responses and never accepted misbehaving. Dad had a terrible temper and we were subject to a barrage of temper tantrums. It was difficult, but it was what was expected. We did not have a TV, 'Leave It To Beaver' kind of upbringing."

Bryan's friends say he once was close to daughter Kay, doting on her as a teenager and young adult. She attended prestigious schools and was popular as an intelligent and beautiful young woman. After two failed marriages, both to men her father disapproved of, and eight children, the father-daughter relationship grew steadily more estranged. Family friends and family members say that Bryan and his daughter Kay were at odds partly because they were so much alike: at times headstrong and unbending. Like some other family members, Kay Edwards has always felt her father was receiving too much credit for doing too many philanthropic things with her mother's family money.

The obvious bitterness still lingers. After Bryan's death, Edwards supported, some say even encouraged, two of her own children who filed a lawsuit against trustees of her father's private trust. The court suit sought public disclosure of more details on how and why Bryan created the trust partly for the benefit of his grandchildren and great grandchildren after greatly reducing the originally scheduled inheritance to each.

The suit eventually was withdrawn, but not without rancor by plaintiffs and not until after a lot of dirty family laundry was aired in public through newspapers and street talk.

Edwards said nice things about her father, however, in a 1986 interview with a Raleigh newspaper reporter. "We (the children) always thought he was superb," she said of her father at that time. "He always treated me as an adult and didn't look down on me."

Edwards also readily acknowledged that she was something of a spoiled child at times during her teenage years. At her debutante dance in Raleigh, for example, her parents reserved rooms in the Carolina Hotel that they owned through inheritance from Mrs. Bryan's father. "I refused to stay there," Edwards said. "It was not as nice as the Sir Walter Hotel where the other girls were staying. I demanded my father rent our rooms at the Sir Walter. And of course he did to make me happy. I was spoiled. I got what I wanted." The Bryans later donated the Carolina Hotel to the City of Raleigh for municipal use.

Edwards also said her father objected to both her husbands because he thought the men were marrying her for her money. "And as it turned out, he was probably right," she conceded. Bryan had experienced first hand, of course, the feelings of a father not being happy with the man his daughter married. That's exactly what had happened to him with his father-in-law.

Kay Edwards first married Ray H. Taylor Jr. of Greensboro, a handsome man with a deserved reputation as a happy-go-lucky playboy. Actually, she married Taylor twice. The couple first secretly married in July 1948 in York, SC, a marriage they didn't disclose to either set of parents. Three months later, in October, they were publicly married in a Catholic ceremony at St. Benedict's Catholic in downtown Greensboro with parents and friends present. The new Mrs. Taylor was pregnant when the church wedding was conducted. The couple divorced on October 26, 1960 after six children and 12 years of a stormy marriage.

Taylor, who died in October 1982, is said to have stayed away from his wife and family more than he was home during those 12 years.

Ray Taylor, never with a regular job or income during his marriage, was usually found on a golf course or a bar. "His work was whatever he could fall into," Mrs. Edwards said of her first husband. "Mostly he was a golfer. He was called a playboy, but he didn't have enough money for that. He never made as much money as he spent. He spent my money and was a philanderer, slept around."

While anxious to extricate herself from the Taylor marriage after a dozen years, Edwards didn't wait to wed her second husband. She married Roy Edwards on October 27, 1960, one day after her divorce from Taylor, in Holy Trinity Episcopal Church because her earlier divorce prevented marriage in a Catholic ceremony. That marriage lasted six years and produced two children. Shortly after her second marriage, Edwards financed her husband's entry into a retail men's clothing store in Charlotte, but the business failed. The

Edwards' divorced in June 1966. Roy Edwards, a native of Mount Airy, died in November 1989.

Son Joseph McKinley Bryan Jr., whose primary residence is in Greensboro although he owns homes in Florida and New Mexico, was less blunt than his sister Kay in discussing his father, but his assessment was generally the same. "Outside the house he was a charming, pleasant, commanding sort of person," Bryan Jr. said of his dad. "Inside the home he was different. There wasn't much communication. Not much to talk about. He was very structured with a strict set of rules. There was not much affection shown in our family.

"My relationship with him was strained. It was formal, not casual. I remember one time he allowed me go with him to Augusta (to the Masters Golf Tournament). That was fun. But we didn't go to football games and things together. He was a man of hard knocks. He expected his son to be of the same school, and I wasn't like that. I just wasn't what he wanted in a son. Jim Melvin is the son he wanted. I have given away a lot of money just as he did, but I don't care about having my name on what I've done. He wanted his name plastered all over the philanthropic world."

Bryan Sr., friends say, was never especially close to his son although his mother adored him both as a child and adult. Mrs. Bryan, her friends said, often pleaded with her son to make more frequent visits to their home after he became an adult, a request he often declined because of ill feelings between father and son.

Daughter Nancy Faircloth of Raleigh declined repeated requests to discuss her parents, saying through her own daughter that she just didn't want to talk about her parents. Nancy was the darling of her father's eye in the 1960s when she was a writer at *Fortune* magazine, and her husband D. M. "Lauch" Faircloth was a close friend and associate to Bryan until Bryan's death, long after the Faircloths were divorced. Faircloth, a wealthy businessman and farmer from eastern North Carolina, served one term in the U.S. Senate with strong financial backing from his former father-in-law.

Associates of Nancy Faircloth said that Bryan and his daughter became estranged primarily over her displeasure of his wanting his name on all his major philanthropic endeavors. "She is a very private person and simply detested the fact that her father always wanted his name on everything," one Bryan friend commented. "That's what split them apart."

The two Bryan grandchildren, Mary Price (Pricey) Taylor Harrison and Joseph McKinley Bryan Taylor, who were lead plaintiffs in the court suit against the Bryan trustees over disclosure of inheritance trust documents, each said their grandfather was hard to understand. Both insisted that while they would have preferred not to take court action, they felt the lawsuit was necessary to help clear up distrust within the family over the trust agreement. Each also said Bryan was not the warm, cuddly grandfather of storybooks, although he had positive attributes.

"I have fond memories of family events as a child," Harrison of Beaufort, N.C., said. "But I felt closer to my grandmother than to my grandfather. She was a warmer personality. My grandfather was not very affectionate toward the grandchildren. I don't think it was from lack of real feelings, but that just wasn't his personality. He was always so regal. When we visited we always had to be on our best behavior, careful not to do the wrong thing. It was almost like having an audience with him. I don't mean this negatively, but that's just the way he was. He was not the warm, cuddly, charming persona I thought that maybe he conveyed to the public in general. But he filled a surrogate father role for me because my father was banished (by family members) from Greensboro when I was just a child. My grandfather filled in for sage advice from an older male that I needed. I consulted him for a lot advice and he was always helpful. I genuinely appreciated his help and he filled an important void for me, maybe for a lot of us (other grandchildren).

"I think he was suspicious as he aged that all we wanted from him was his money or other material things and that we were just waiting for him to die so we could inherit his money," Harrison continued. "Nothing could be further from the truth. He was certainly in many ways a very generous man. I don't know what created this feeling that he had about his family. The way he set up the foundation and the deliberate exclusion of our participation is an odd thing to me. I think when I moved down here (to Beaufort) that he felt I was just hanging out at the beach or something."

Pricey Taylor Harrison worked as a lawyer in Washington, D.C. for awhile after obtaining her law degree at UNC Chapel Hill, before moving to the North Carolina coastal town of Beaufort with her long-time partner DeSales Harrison, a twice divorced older man. They lived together for 10 years before marrying in September 1998 after he was diagnosed with lung cancer. He died eight days after their marriage. Taylor Harrison is an active environmentalist and serves on dozens of non-paying boards and commissions, all designed to promote and preserve the environment through planned and limited growth and development.

Bryan Taylor of Charlotte, named for his grandfather and with a son of his own with the same name, said both his grandparents in many ways were considered larger than life when he was a child. "My grandfather was a bit more stern, playing everything closer to his vest," Taylor said. "He was fairly formal. I think he was of the opinion that children should be seen and not heard. We didn't go to his house much unless we were dressed up. He was fairly regimented, like a good military officer. I think that given his own background, maybe he didn't quite know how to react with a family. I get the impression that he never had much involvement in his children's lives as he didn't in our lives. Looking back, I just think he didn't know any better. That's just the way he was."

Harrison and Taylor each said they went forward with their lawsuit not out of lack of respect for their grandfather, but because of what they felt were unreasonable actions from Bryan Foundation trustees. Trustees objected to grandchildren seeing full details of the documents that created their grandfather's trust and provided for their inheritance because Bryan had asked that the document details be kept private.

"I was reluctant to go forward with the lawsuit in the sense that I knew it would turn into a free-for-all (in public) that would be unpleasant," Harrison said. "That was uncomfortable and not pleasant. I was OK on the narrow legal issues that the lawsuit was going to address on the rights of beneficiaries to see the trust. The courts allowed us to do that, but there was nothing glaring in there, no smoking gun. I think my grandfather just decided he wanted his money and money he inherited from my grandmother to go toward causes and concerns that he felt like needed help instead of to the family. Maybe he was just unhappy with some of the grants (the original family fund) had been making. I know that bothered him some. But I do feel there is a chunk of my grandmother Price's money in his foundation, which is unfortunate, because I think my grandmother would be upset with that."

"The newspapers kept writing about greedy grandchildren," said Taylor, acting director of the Bryan Family Fund between the firing of the previous director and the breakup of the fund in late 1999. "That was unfair. We didn't sue grandfather's estate or his foundation. We sued the trustees, just asking to see the documents. But we were challenging an icon in my grandfather. It was difficult. It was emotionally draining. It wasn't something I relished. But I certainly have a strong feeling that in his foundation there is Price money. That's not grandfather's money. It's family money."

Two other Bryan grandchildren, Ray Howard Taylor of Great Falls, Va. and John Taylor of Madison, Wis., offered similar views of their grandfather, but neither was a party to the court action. They said they respected their grandfather and admired his successes, but each said they didn't know him well and never felt close to him as a family except for brief encounters that never lasted. Each offered

223

examples of both general aloofness as well as occasional acts of kindness from their grandfather.

"He was not your Norman Rockwell grandfather," said Howard Taylor, a stockbroker and one of the few Bryan grandchildren who has held onto a steady paying job for any extended period of time. "We had formal dinners at his house, more like employees than grandchildren. I don't have many loving memories. It wasn't always easy being a Bryan grandchild. But his Christmas Eve parties were great affairs. I enjoyed them even as an adult."

Bryan's Christmas Eve gatherings have become legend among his neighbors and friends outside the family. It became a tradition over decades for Bryan to invite in dozens of neighbors as well as his own grandchildren each Christmas Eve when he would sit on the floor and read "The Night Before Christmas" and distribute gifts to all the children.

Taylor chuckled in recalling one encounter with his grandfather concerning a gift as an example of his feelings. Bryan had promised Taylor a new car when he graduated from high school in Charlotte. A month following the graduation while Taylor was visiting his grandparents in Greensboro, Bryan admonished his grandson for never even writing a thank you note for the car.

"But you haven't given me the car yet," Taylor told his grandfather.

Mrs. Bryan laughed at that reply and said, "Joe, he's right you know."

Bryan, although promising the car, had apparently forgotten to arrange for the vehicle to be purchased and delivered. Within days after that conversation, Taylor had a new Mercury Cougar. He then sent the note of thanks.

After graduating from Charlotte's Country Day High School, Taylor applied for admission to Duke University and the University of Virginia and was accepted at both. Following the letter of acceptance from Duke, his grandmother asked him to write a personal note of thanks to the Duke admissions office.

"Why?" Taylor asked.

"Because your grandfather and I used all kinds of pull to get you in there," Mrs. Bryan replied without any hint of apology.

"I was shocked at that. That sealed my decision for me," Taylor recalled years later. "I was offended they had done that. There was no way in hell I was going to Duke after that. Sometimes it was a blessing and sometimes a hindrance to be a Bryan grandchild. When I graduated from college (UVA), my mother said I should just go down to the bank (in which Jefferson Standard owned a huge portion of stock) and get a job. I said no. I wanted to succeed on my own. That's why I left North Carolina." Taylor is now a successful stockbroker in Alexandria, Va..

On another occasion, Taylor asked a favor of his grandfather in what began as an unpleasant encounter, but turned out to be what Taylor called one of his most memorable and satisfying moments with his granddad. "I had asked him for some basketball tickets and told him I'd be by his office to pick them up," Taylor recalled. "He phoned me three times that afternoon asking where I was, sounding more impatient with each call and asking why I had not shown up yet. When I walked into his office, he coldly handed me the tickets and said 'here's what you came for'. But then we just started talking. We talked about a lot of interesting things. We were really clicking, finally, for one of the first times. We talked for more than two hours. It was a rare occurrence, but wonderful and pleasant."

"I think our grandfather just tolerated us," John Taylor said. "We were always on stage kind of like a theatre troupe, held up in public as rich kids. He mostly seemed not to have time in his life for us. He didn't pay us a lot of attention. It wasn't always easy."

Taylor acknowledged, however, that he and his siblings didn't always make it easy for their grandfather. There were eight of them of stair step ages from 1949 through 1962. Furthermore, John Taylor admitted he was something of a discipline problem growing up.

Shortly after Bryan had donated $10,000 to Oak Ridge Military Academy where Taylor was a student, Taylor was kicked out of school on suspicion of selling illegal drugs. "And that caused a lot of attention," Taylor said in an understatement. "I was not selling drugs, but I was smoking pot and was high on cough syrup. Although the charge against me was the wrong one, they were right to throw me out of school. I later thanked my commandant."

Taylor was also arrested for illegal drug possession while attending Guilford College before his mother sent him to the Institute of Living in Hartford, Conn., hoping to restore discipline and focus to in his life. "I was kind of a neurotic kid," Taylor said of his younger years. "I had a kind of crazy and peculiar life as a child." While in Hartford, in the early 1970s, he received a surprise phone call from his grandmother Kathleen Bryan that, he said, helped him rethink aspects of his own life.

"She called me after her initial medical treatment at Duke," Taylor said. "She was crying, saying she was so depressed at what was happening to her. She couldn't understand the treatment. She poured out her feelings to me. I thought at the time it was strange that she would call me, of all people. I thought I was the one with problems. I had never heard anyone talk about feelings like that. It made an impression on me. I am a different person now."

One reason Taylor was sent to school in New England was the result of a summer when he was, in effect, a homeless rich kid in Greensboro. He was banned from his mother's home that summer because of his wildness. It was ironic, however, that during that same summer he enjoyed an endearing tender moment with his grandfather following an auto accident.

This was after Taylor had taken his older brother's car without permission and crashed it, sending him to the hospital for medical treatment. That happened while he was living in a friend's Country Club neighborhood garage in exchange for yard work, eating a diet of canned food that he clandestinely charged to his mother's grocery store account and taking showers at the Greensboro Country Club. Bryan visited the injured Taylor in the hospital the night of the car crash. "I think he really cared about me and was concerned for my safety," Taylor said of his grandfather on that occasion. "He put his arm around me and just held me for awhile. At that moment, I sincerely felt he was genuinely interested in me as a person."

On another occasion, Taylor said his grandfather pleaded with him to stay in Greensboro where he was visiting. "He grabbed my hand and asked me to please stay and take care of him. I think he was very lonely and isolated after my grandmother died. He didn't have large numbers of friends."

Bryan had friends, of course, but he outlived most of those near his age. He developed friends much younger. He also in later life chose not to go out a lot because of physical impairment. Not unlike most people afflicted with infirmities of old age, he hated giving up his independence and mobility. His rebellion at not being able to do things he once did was at times strong. Once confined to a wheelchair, however, he accepted his fate. Even as his body failed him, his mind remained active until shortly before his death.

Taylor outgrew his rambunctious teenage years and later worked in a series of restaurants in North Carolina and several other states before moving to Wisconsin to oversee a sandwich shop that has since closed. He is now a part-time business consultant and a grant writer for non-profit organizations in his current hometown.

Bryan also extended kindness to John Taylor's first wife, the former Kathy Few whom he admired and helped secure work even after she and Taylor divorced. Bryan called that divorce "unfortunate" and gave Few, now Kathy Evatt since her remarriage, Jefferson stock both when she married his grandson and later when she obtained her college degree. "He never mentioned a word to me about the stock," Evatt said. "It just arrived in the mail. That's just the way he was. He sometimes could come across as very stern and proper, but he had a big heart. I think he cared deeply for people, including family members, but he just didn't know how to express love and affection."

"He could come across sometimes as a crusty old man, but he could also be extremely sweet at times," granddaughter Laura Edwards, an independent film producer in Chapel Hill, said of her grandfather. "We all had mutual respect and I think he really wanted to be kind and gentle. He just didn't know how. I remember the first time I went to him to ask for money for Special Olympics, I had to schedule an appointment in his office. He treated me like any other appointment. In business, he could be rough and he made sure you knew how to do your job. I think he gave me money for the Olympics only because I was his granddaughter.

"But I also remember fondly that in that same formal meeting he said if I could do something about Alzheimer's Disease he'd give me all I ever needed for that effort. It was painful for him to discuss mental illness and what happened to my grandmother. I remember when my grandmother died, I went to see him and he was just sitting there alone in her bedroom. He told me I was beautiful and asked me to please sit and talk with him. It was a special moment."

Despite the estrangement from his grandchildren, Bryan was generous to them over many years. He gave granddaughter Kathleen Clay Taylor $350,000 for a residence when she moved to New York. Each year he gave each of his grandchildren $10,000 on their birthdays and did the same for his great grandchildren. This is in addition to the $100,000 he gave each at his death.

The Faircloths' daughter Ann, who like her mother worked for *Fortune* magazine for several years until the middle of 1999, also declined to discuss in detail her grandparents. "I would rather just let my memories of them remain memories," she said. "I would just like to let my grandfather rest in peace. There has been too much water over the dam." The last statement was in reference to the lawsuit against trustees. Faircloth was not part of the legal action and, in fact, strongly opposed it, as did some other members of the Bryan family. "She was not interested in participating," Bryan Taylor said. Nancy Faircloth and Joe Bryan Jr. also each objected to the court suit against trustees, as did at least one other grandchild.

"I was never asked to be a part of that court suit," John Taylor said, "but I would not have been anyway. My view is that it was filed out of greed by a bunch of kids who have been spoon fed all their lives. There was no emotional aspect to it. I was not in my other grandfather's will or my father's will. We each got $100,000. That's not a bad gift, especially since we got $500,000 from our grandmother's will. A lot of people don't have that opportunity. Our family is not geared toward trust and some members have never learned that. Often we've lived a lie. All my grandfather ever required was truth and honesty from people. My grandfather was a hero to keep my grandmother at home all those years as he did during her illness. My (present) wife is a psychiatrist and she understands the importance of that and what it means."

Three other Bryan grandchildren, all daughters of Kay Bryan Taylor Edwards, also chose not to discuss their grandfather.

Melanie Taylor Farland of Charlottesville, Va., is a divorced mother of three daughters, a community volunteer and substitute teacher. She didn't respond to written questions about her grandfather.

Kathleen Clay Taylor, former employee of Time Life Books, is unemployed following a series of accidents, and resides in Stockbridge, MA. In recent years she suffered three head injuries: one a car accident, one a fall from a bicycle and one from a crash while snowboarding. She said she would discuss her grandfather only if she would help author his biography.

Susan Edwards resides in Greensboro, in late 1999 buying her first home after living with her mother, and is an active equestrian and serves on community boards. She said she was too young to remember much about her grandparents.

Bryan's friends concede that he frequently seemed impatient with his grandchildren, but that that the family members brought on much of his frustration because of their seeming unconcern for him. "He'd sometimes sit for hours and hours and wait for them to come as they promised. They would never show up or call to explain why," one friend said. "Sometimes he would turn down invitations to things because he said one of the grandchildren was coming to visit. And they would never show up. That hurt him deeply."

Bryan was, of course, not known for his patience, with family or business associates. Letters in his family history file show his feelings about his grandchildren and their behavior when they were young. "All the grandchildren were over here Sunday," Bryan wrote in one letter to his sister Anne Stoute in Barbados. "They were all dressed to the nines, but that didn't last long. They are just unmanageable. They get used to their mother's voice for correctness and it has no effect."

In a "Dear Family" letter to his siblings in the fall of 1956, Bryan also expressed his frustration with the grandchildren. "Last Friday Kay and I took her four children to supper at the club," he wrote, "and before the evening was over I swore many times it wouldn't happen again. I sure am getting fussy in my old age."

Bryan also lamented to some friends that he was bothered by the fact that many of his grandchildren had no gainful employment much of the time once they became adults. "It bothered him a lot that he always had to work and earn money and they didn't seem interested in that," said a close Bryan friend. "That also bothered him about Joe Jr. who never really worked at a regular job for long. That's one reason those two had differences."

Bryan's close friend and long-time private attorney Carole Bruce said Bryan had indicated similar views to her about the lack of work ethic of his grandchildren. "He valued hard work and saw himself as a hardworking person," Bruce said. "I think he didn't see his grandchildren working much. That was disappointing to him. I think he also had the same view at times about his children."

Employment was clearly one of the early points of disagreement between father and son. "I went to New York to look for a job in 1960," Bryan Jr. said, "My sister Nancy was working there at the time and we asked our father to make some phone calls to his banker friends in an effort to help me. He said no, let him do it on his own. I didn't want him to get me a job, but he wouldn't even make a phone call to open some doors. That hurt me."

Bryan Jr. worked for Chemical Bank for several years before returning to North Carolina. Bryan Sr. later told friends he did, in fact, make some phone calls on behalf of his son, but just didn't tell anyone because he wanted his son to feel he got the job on his own initiative.

After leaving the banking world in New York, Bryan Jr. moved to Southern Pines where for some 20 years he managed a horse farm where he mingled with a lot of rich and famous people. "I went into something my father knew nothing about," Bryan Jr. said. "That's when he hated me because I got to know and become friends with people he never could. I was moving in a lifestyle that he only dreamed of. My mother was proud of my successes. She thought it was great, but my father didn't."

Others, of course, dispute Bryan Jr.'s assessment of his own social connections compared with those of his father. In fact, both had ties to wealthy and important people, just different ones.

The final collapse in the father-son Bryan relationship came when Bryan Jr. sent his father a Father's Day card that Bryan Sr. apparently found insulting. The card contained a message inside that read "Happy Father's Day. You have made me all I have become."

The senior Bryan took great offense to that message because he interpreted it to mean he was responsible for aspects of his son's lifestyle that he found objectionable. After that card was sent, Bryan

231

Jr. was never invited to his father's annual Christmas parties or other family events.

In recent years, Bryan Jr. has become a philanthropist of note himself, although not as well known as his father because many of his gifts have been anonymous. A long-time trustee at Guilford College, Bryan Jr. has contributed generously to that school as well as to organizations relating to arts and history across the state. The son, in fact, has given more to Guilford College than the father.

Kay Edwards and her children have also been generous in donations through investments and inheritance left by the Price family through the original family foundation that her parents created in 1955. In the summer of 1999, Edwards and her children gave $3.5 million to establish a public park in memory of her grandparents, Julian and Ethel Clay Price. "We were horrified that until now the Price name has just been wiped out," Edwards said of that gift. Edwards personally contributed $2 million for that park and her children gave $1.5 million.

Nancy Bryan Faircloth, after splitting from participation in the original family foundation, in 1985 created her own charitable trust for philanthropic purposes based in Raleigh. She has been generous through the years in supporting the North Carolina Symphony and other causes benefiting people in need. Most of her gifts have also been anonymous.

One of the highlights of Bryan's social season in Greensboro was his annual birthday bash for friends that he arranged in honor of his wife Kathleen at the Jefferson Club. That event drew lavish praise from the invited guests, but it drew ridicule from some family members who felt Bryan was doing it for his own ego rather than his wife's celebration.

"He spared nothing at that party every April 23, Mrs. Bryan's birthday," said Mrs. Frances Carr, who served as Bryan's at-home secretary and assistant for 18 years. "He invited hundreds of friends, the invitation included a stamped reply card and he picked the menu. He was very sweet and kind to Mrs. Bryan even after she became ill. He wanted her to continue her social life. It was an elegant and pleasant party every year."

The birthday galas were both large as well as elegant with both Bryan and his wife dressed in their finest. Bryan was always the official greeter, often not even getting to enjoy any of the variety of food he ordered because he spent the evening moving among guests. Bryan put on the parties for decades, not even stopping when his wife died in 1984. While family members were critical of the parties which they said Bryan held for his own pleasure, friends say they encouraged him to carry on the tradition in his late wife's memory.

Guests who were handpicked by Bryan ranged from a low of 376 in 1979 to a high of 410 in 1984 just four months before Mrs. Bryan's death from Alzheimer's disease. At her death, 147 memorials were made in her name to area charities.

It was the parties after Mrs. Bryan became ill and after her death that bothered the Bryan children. "My mother would never have chosen parties at the Jefferson Club," Bryan Jr. said. "She liked to have parties at home. But he wanted big parties and he arranged the invitation list. He took her there during the years she was sick and she had no idea what was going on. We (he and his sisters) objected to it, particularly late in her life. They were parties for him. He just did it because he wanted to do it for himself."

Bryan said in a letter to a friend that he continued the parties because his wife enjoyed them even after she became ill. But he also conceded it might have all been to no avail beyond the event itself because of her memory problems. "She'll have a great time at the party, but tomorrow she won't remember it ever happened," he said in the letter.

Bryan continued his wife's birthday parties for five years after her death. His friends say it was out of love and devotion for Kathleen. His children say it was his desire for continued attention. No one, however, challenges the fact that Mrs. Bryan was fond of elegant parties before she became ill.

It was Mrs. Bryan who undisputedly started much of the society social scene for Greensboro. She was cofounder of the Greensboro Junior League in 1925 and cofounder and first president of the Greensboro Debutante Club in 1954. She formed those two social clubs after visiting other cities and realizing they had clubs for young women that Greensboro did not have. She participated in parties and social gatherings regularly until she became ill.

There also is no argument among Bryan's Greensboro friends that he craved attention, just as his wife did before her illness. "Many people felt Joe was cold and insensitive," said family friend Mrs. Judy Davis. "But he was very considerate. He also loved parties as Kathleen did. He could be a perfect host and caviar and wine were his hors d'oeuvre of choice. He entertained beautifully. I also think he really cared and was concerned for his family, but he didn't seem to display those feelings very well."

The absence of harmony within the Bryan family, while talked about among friends for years did not become generally known to the public until the lawsuit was filed against trustees of Bryan's trust in 1997. That suit laid bare much of the previously private feuding among family members.

Clearly, Bryan intentionally created his foundation in his own name to ensure that his assets would be used for good causes outside the family. But plaintiffs in the court suit (Taylor, Harrison and two of Taylor's small children) argued they had a right to see documents relating to the trust.

After months of legal wrangling, both a Superior Court judge and a panel on the state Court of Appeals ruled that the plaintiffs, but no one else, could see only documents relating to their inheritance. Plaintiffs were not allowed to see other parts of the trust document and other family members were not allowed to see any part of the trust.

The plaintiff grandchildren argued through their lawyers that they had a right to see all the trust documents because their grandfather had reduced their inheritance and they were entitled to see why and where the other money went. Foundation trustees objected because they said Bryan had carefully planned out his decision and insisted that it be kept private.

The lawsuit actually plowed new legal ground. There had never been a court ruling anywhere in the country on the specific points in this case. Before final settlement, the plaintiffs agreed to drop the suit if defendant trustees would pay plaintiffs' legal fees. The defendants refused that settlement offer.

Once the two lower courts had ruled, and the N.C. Supreme Court refused to review the case, the two sides met to discuss some mutually agreed upon recognition for Mrs. Bryan or other family members separate from patriarch Bryan. They couldn't agree and the case was dropped. Bryan Foundation trustees have since agreed to make a substantial donation to the new downtown Greensboro Central YMCA to be named for Mrs. Bryan although Bryan family members didn't agree with that decision.

There was subsequent debate within the family whether they should also file another legal action claiming Bryan was mentally incompetent when he had documents drawn. Bryan had originally planned to donate $500,000 to each of his nine grandchildren, but reduced the amount to $100,000 (after taxes which he had arranged to pay) after inheritance laws were amended to disallow certain tax benefits.

"There was threatened legal action, but we never knew specifics," Bryan lawyer Bruce said. "There were words like undue influence thrown around, but they were never in any way substantiated. No other lawsuit was ever filed."

Family member plaintiffs hired well-known and respected Raleigh criminal lawyer Wade Smith and his partners to investigate the matter. Those lawyers conducted careful research into the family history and background and into the public perceptions of family members and foundation trustees. That research included focus groups where local citizens were asked their views on the individuals involved. Trustees came out ahead.

One person familiar with some of those focus group interviews put it this way: "When comparing what was perceived as a lawsuit filed by a few very selfish people and the reputation in the community of a respected lawyer like Carole Bruce, Carole came out looking like Mother Teresa."

By the time all this has taken place, even with the lawsuit no longer active, the family friction had become a public spectacle.

The lawsuit also was an expensive undertaking. Legal bills totaled more than the grandchildren's individual inheritance. "Oh, yes, we spent more than our $100,000 inheritance on legal fees," Bryan Taylor acknowledged. "It was a bit of a victory, but there wasn't any altruism involved. It was certainly self-interest." Both sides agree that the money spent on lawyers could have been better spent on community benevolence.

William Massey, director of the Bryan Family Fund for four years until Bryan trustee grandchildren fired him in August 1998, said he was aware of family friction involving Bryan and his children as well as among the third generation, but he never knew specifics. "I never saw any sense of closeness there within the family," Massey said before shortly before starting his new job in New York with the National Charities Information Board that certifies non-profit groups. "I was struck by just a sense of how different their relationships to Mr. Bryan seemed to be. I just sensed a distance in the relationship. Maybe it was just a very different way of showing feelings and emotions. I got the feeling that they (children and grandchildren) were closer to Mrs. Bryan than to Mr. Bryan. I don't know there is any judgment to be gained here, but I had the strong sense that was the case. I think they all enjoyed and actively loved Mrs. Bryan. The emotion that was expressed about her versus him suggested to me they felt Mrs. Bryan was really a very special, warm, wonderful person to them and Mr. Bryan wasn't. But we never discussed it."

"Mr. Bryan always wanted to be liked and remembered in a positive way," said former Bryan archivist Gary Parks. "It is sad the family was never close or got along very well."

"I really believe members of the family genuinely cared for each other," said Mrs. Elise Franklin, a close Greensboro family friend and relative of Bryan's father-in-law Julian Price. "But there was this undercurrent that ran throughout. It was just unpleasant." Bryan in his later years would go to the Franklin home for holidays and other special occasions. He did that, Mrs. Franklin said, because he was lonely and had no family members who would help him celebrate.

There was once a hint of that with lawyer Bruce, too. "One Christmas morning he came by my house," Bruce said. "He probably stayed 15 minutes. I would guess he went to other homes too. Would most people believe that Joe Bryan on Christmas Day would sort of be at loose ends?" For parts of Christmas Day, however, Bryan for several years visited at the home of daughter Kay following Mrs. Bryan's death.

Others close to the Bryans called the family bitterness both sad and regrettable. "Individually they were and are all good people," commented Mrs. Thornton Brooks, a longtime family friend. "But as a family, it is so sad because of all the problems. It is so horrible it sounds like fiction, but unfortunately it is real. It is just sad that this happened because Joe and Kathleen were such fine people who left their marks on this community. The feuding just tarnishes their positive contributions and their good name."

"I know," said Bryan's long-time and devoted administrative assistant Ann Rambeaut, "that Mr. Bryan always wished things had been different within his family. He was a perfectionist. No one can be perfect, but he made the best shot at it of anybody I've ever known. Sometimes his voice was a little gruff, but he was made of much finer stuff." Late in life, Bryan sought to build close relationships with a handful of people who he wanted to transform into an extended family to replace the immediate family that he felt he did not have.

Family disagreements extended even into death. Julian Price purchased a four-vault mausoleum at Greensboro's Green Hill Cemetery when his wife Ethel died unexpectedly in 1943. Price, his wife and daughter Kathleen Price Bryan are interred there. The fourth vault remains vacant. Buried in the ground adjacent to but outside the mausoleum are half of Bryan's ashes. The other half is buried at the foot of his statue in Bryan Park as he requested. Bryan's marble grave headstone at Green Hill is in the specific design he approved. His wife's name is inscribed on the stone although her body is next door with her parents.

Friends of Bryan said he wanted his wife Kathleen buried at his gravesite, but family members made it clear if he did that, at his death her body would be exhumed and placed in the mausoleum with her parents. Daughter Kay Edwards responded with a firm "absolutely not" when asked if the fourth vault space in the Price mausoleum was ever intended for her father.

Edwards says it was her grandmother Price, not her parents, who gave her love and affection as a child. "I was upset that my parents didn't really raise me," Edwards said. "Others did. My grandmother doted on me. The subsequent things that have happened to me that were not pleasant were things that I can only blame on myself. But I feel pretty fortunate, not having to work and being able to try to relieve misery in other people's lives (through philanthropy). But my money didn't come from my parents; it came from my grandparents. Frankly I don't think my parents contributed much to my life one way or the other, good or bad. I don't really want a legacy for myself, but I hope my children will continue the philanthropy that my mother started and that they will continue to put other people first in their lives."

Deserved or not, Edwards receives much of the blame for the internal friction within the Bryan family. She most often was the vocal one with views that it was Price money, her mother's money that her father used for his philanthropy.

Joe Bryan Jr. agrees with his sister on that point. "We always felt (our father) was spending (our mother's) money on his charitable donations," Bryan Jr. said.

The marks Joe and Kathleen Price Bryan left on their community and state are permanent. With time, perhaps the scars within the family will fade. But there is no doubt family heartaches represent a chapter in Bryan's life that he would have much preferred to erase. There's a lesson here for other families to remember.

15

BENEVOLENCE AND BEYOND

J oe Bryan's last day in his office at Jefferson-Pilot Insurance
Company was April 15, 1995. He should have gone straight
from his home to the hospital, as his home health care nurses
begged, but he insisted on one more visit — the one that turned out
to be his last — to the downtown office he had occupied for more
than 60 years.

He knew something was seriously physically wrong that day. But
he was determined to tough it out as long as possible before seeking
medical attention, as was his custom. Meticulous about his health
that he had for years researched just as he did everything else,
Bryan routinely challenged his doctors on their diagnosis, often
arguing that he knew his body better than they did. Usually, he was
right. He regularly and carefully read every prescription label and
side effect label, often phoning his doctor to air his concerns about
medication. He held steadfastly to the belief that when it came to
drugs, the least he could get by with taking was always enough.

Bryan once discreetly questioned his physician after reading on
his pill bottle that the drug he was to take was used in treating herpes. "I'm just ... well ... concerned about this drug and what it is

240

for and what it is supposed to help cure," Bryan said in a telephone conversation with his doctor, seeming a bit embarrassed to be talking about a social disease. "I ... well ... know that (herpes) is not what is wrong with me. I'm an old man. I know that's not my problem." He was satisfied only when he was convinced that the drug would treat his illness as well as the genital disease.

Bryan also had a distrust of doctors he didn't know, and at times wasn't too sure about a few of those he did know. Once when treated in the hospital by a physician whom he had not met at the medical practice he used, Bryan later had someone drive him to the clinic offices to make sure that doctor's name was on the door. It was and he was pacified.

On another occasion after falling in the Jefferson parking lot and injuring his head on the concrete floor, Bryan was more agitated with his doctors for their seeming inattention than he was worried about his bleeding head wound. He waited impatiently on a gurney for several hours at the hospital before a neurosurgeon arrived. Seeing the seriousness of the wound and fearing brain damage, the physician's first question was to ask if Bryan realized where he was. "Of course I know," Bryan replied with agitation. "I'm in the hospital. I've been here for hours waiting for you. Now where the hell have you been?"

On that last morning in the office he had a premonition. He was a realist and seemed to know what was happening, that the end was near.

"Ann," he said with a sound of resignation in his voice to his caring administrative assistant Ann Rambeaut, "come sit with me for a moment. I'm dying." Rambeaut attempted to put a good face on the problem, even though she regrettably felt his assessment would be proved correct.

"We just sat there, hand in hand," Rambeaut said. "I just patted his hand for awhile. I felt so helpless."

Initial treatment in the office by the Jefferson physician confirmed that Bryan needed immediate hospital care. He was, the doctor realized, dying and was rushed to Wesley Long Hospital. It was the last time he would see his office, the last time he would be a part of the Jefferson corporation that he watched evolve — and he had helped build — into a national powerhouse in insurance and broadcasting.

He died ten days later, April 26, 1995, ending one legacy as a corporate executive and creating another as a philanthropist, a word he never learned to like. Those legacies, however, were not exclusive of each other.

The day Bryan was carried from his office for the last time, Rambeaut turned off the light, as he had instructed her to do every day he was there. The morning after his death, when Rambeaut walked into her darkened office outside Bryan's she noticed a strange sight. The light in the chandelier over his desk was burning brightly. "I've often wondered how that light got turned on because my outer office was locked," Rambeaut said. "It was eerie. It still is a mystery. But I just walked to his door and said, Good morning, Mr. Bryan, just as I had done for so many years. But this time I had tears in my eyes."

To say good morning, Rambeaut said, was the natural thing to do because she felt his presence. It was nothing less than he would have expected.

The two people closest to Bryan in his last days were women, both young enough to be his daughters. One was Ann Dixon Rambeaut who had served as his dutiful and devoted administrative assistant for 26 years. The other was Greta Medlin, a former journalist who first wrote a *Greensboro Daily News* feature story on Bryan in 1982 and ultimately became a confidant and beloved friend. The two shared Bryan's most intimate thoughts in his latter years and administered to his daily needs. They were by his side in death just as in life.

To most executives inside the Jefferson corporate offices, Bryan was devoid of any sense of humor, but that wasn't the case around his social friends, even at the end. As he lay near death in his Wesley Long Hospital bed barely able to speak, he slowly turned toward Rambeaut and Medlin who were beside his bed talking incessantly — as they were prone to do whenever together — and murmured with a smile: "Talking, always talking. Can't a man even die in peace and quiet around here?"

"If we stop talking, will you not die?" Medlin asked. "Well ..." he responded, unable to complete the sentence.

In addition to Rambeaut and Medlin, Bryan's two closest associates in his last years were Jim Melvin and Carole Bruce. Melvin is the one who started Bryan on his road toward major benevolence, served for more than 20 years as an advisor and counselor and became president of the Joseph M. Bryan Foundation. Bruce was Bryan's confidential attorney for more than a decade, advising him on finances, taxes, personal matters and creation of his foundation. Melvin and Bruce are two of the six directors of the Bryan Foundation, five of whom were handpicked by Bryan.

The respect and devotion to Bryan by those four confidants was obvious and reciprocal. Nobody spent more time with him in his later years, understood him better and was more helpful or gracious than those four. They served as a substitute family because of estrangement between Bryan and his own children.

Bryan took to Melvin, Bruce and Rambeaut immediately and their relationship and friendship with him grew steadily. That was not the case with Medlin who at the time they met in 1982 was Greta Tilley and was married to Greensboro lawyer N. Carlton "Woody" Tilley, the man Bryan would later work so hard to help secure a lifetime federal judgeship. When Medlin was assigned to interview Bryan for the feature story, she repeatedly demurred, giving her usual arguments about preferring to write about front porches, poor people and underdogs rather than, as she put it "some old rich man."

243

Joseph M. Bryan and his trusted friend and adviser Jim Melvin, who was the impetus behind much of Bryan's philanthropy. Melvin is now president of the Bryan Foundation.

Bryan had the same lack of enthusiasm with the prospect of her doing a story on his life. While he liked newspaper publicity and was friendly with some reporters and editors, he preferred recognition about his recreational trips or business decisions. He had never talked publicly about his personal life and wasn't sure he wanted to start. Bryan didn't know Tilley, but he checked her out with Melvin just to make sure she was trustworthy. Bryan had always been accustomed to positive press coverage about his business dealings in broadcasting and his philanthropy but was wary of some female feature writer less than half his age probing around in aspects of his life that he had always kept private.

He also, of course, was sensitive to the fact that his late father-in-law Julian Price had once owned Greensboro's afternoon newspaper and that Jefferson Standard once owned a share of the morning newspaper. But those family or business ties to the newspapers were long gone when Tilley, at her editor's insistence, requested time from Bryan for an interview. Little did either of them know at the time how that single story would change both their lives.

Tilley was the most talented feature writer on the newspaper staff when she wrote the Bryan feature story in July 1982 when he was 86. She also was charming enough to melt the outer shell of even the crustiest of interview subjects. Bryan was no exception. He told her things that surprised both of them.

Bryan's associates warned Tilley that he would be a difficult interview. She was advised to, as she later described, "butter him up" with praise. She put on her bubbly native South Carolina charm in the phone request for an interview, pouring on comments about his successful business career and generosity to community projects. He saw right through her efforts, and let her know.

"Well, I was told to say those things," she admitted in her usual animated way. She had a habit of talking as much with her hands as with her voice and bouncing up and down with almost every word.

245

"Well, come on over," he replied.

"You mean right now?" she asked. She wasn't ready for the interview, needing to do more research and assuming he'd put her off for days or weeks.

"Well, you called me, didn't you?" he responded. At her request, he agreed to delay the interview for several days.

"I'm very nervous about this," Bryan said on their first meeting.

"Me, too," Tilley responded. But she opened him up as no one ever had. In a series of interviews, she had Bryan confessing things about himself he had never before acknowledged.

"I was amazed at his honesty," Medlin said years after that initial interview. Following her divorce from Tilley, she resumed use of her maiden name.

"She made me feel like I had been to a psychiatrist," Bryan later remarked of those conversations. She kept asking questions and he kept trying to cut her off. He grew increasingly impatient with her probing even as she became more enamored with his responses. At one point, Medlin commented that she agreed with a point he had just made.

"Good," he said, "now that I have your approval can I just get on with my life?"

Bryan got on with his life after the story, in which he confessed he had been a sometimes inattentive father and surprisingly admitted he enjoyed seeing his name attached to charitable giving. But it was a different life, for both the interviewer and interviewee.

Bryan and Medlin obviously hit it off, once the initial interviews were over and the story was published. They slowly but surely became best friends, as Bryan did with Medlin's husband who, at the time, was a private attorney in Greensboro. After Mrs. Bryan died, Bryan drew even closer to the Tilley couple and the three spent increasing hours with each other in ensuing years. Bryan worked diligently through his political connections to help secure Tilley the federal judgeship as Medlin seemed to move ever closer to becoming the daughter Bryan may have wished he had. She played the surrogate daughter role much as Melvin would become Bryan's surrogate son.

In Bryan's latter years, Medlin spent some time with him virtually every day. She would invite him to dinner, drive him to his beloved Bryan Park or around town and attend functions with him at Duke University. Medlin and her husband were among the invited Bryan guests to the Masters Tournament every year. She cared for many of his medical needs, often pleading with him to the point of tears to follow the medical advice of his doctors. Her tears almost never worked, but she kept trying.

Medlin resigned her reporter's job at the newspaper not long after her feature story on Bryan was published, saying she planned to write a novel. Her time until Bryan's death was spent more on his health and well being than on writing. Her book is not written.

Medlin and Rambeaut saw a side of Bryan's gift-giving that most did not. His gifts were numerous to individuals with particular needs, almost always without any public notice in contrast to most of his larger donations.

He once gave a woman a car because she had no transportation. Another time he handed over every cent in his pocket to a woman who needed food, then had to borrow money to get out of the company parking deck.

"He gave a lot of gifts to people he liked," Rambeaut said. "He gave a lot of gifts for which he never received any recognition and for which he received no tax deductions. He liked to give to places and things that really benefited people, gifts that allowed people to help themselves."

"He was always touched when he could see what his gifts meant to people and how they helped people," Medlin said. "He wanted to do meaningful things."

Examples of gifts from Bryan without public recognition were those to the Greensboro Police Department and to Shrine projects.

247

He wanted to give, but not give too much that he would appear out of the ordinary in some cases.

"He once asked me how much I planned to give to an Oasis Shrine Temple campaign," former Greensboro police executive and Guilford County Sheriff Walter Burch said. "It shocked me that here was this man with all his resources asking me what a proper gift would be. He just wanted to be like everybody else and not stand out. He wanted to do the right thing without any special notice."

Burch once encountered Bryan's impatience with giving, but also saw his willingness to help when a need existed. "I once asked him for $2,000 to help the local Crime Stoppers organization, and he didn't seem too pleased for some reason," Burch said. "He was a little gruff and gave us only half what we asked. But then he called me later that same day and apologized for his initial rudeness. He said he was having a bad day and he'd give us whatever we needed. We never asked for any more because we felt he had done enough."

Bryan on several occasions also paid expenses for Greensboro police officers to attend training programs at Northwestern University when he learned the training was needed and the city had no money to pay the costs. He once picked up the entire bill for a police officer and his wife who spent nine months at Northwestern in a special program.

Bryan obviously held Rambeaut in high regard for her dedication and loyalty toward him in retirement and into his latter years. She catered to his every need, day and night, in the office and at home. Her vacations were scarce because Bryan expected her to be available to him at all times. That loyalty paid off. Bryan showed his appreciation for her efforts by ensuring that she would be financially comfortable in her own retirement after his death.

Bryan provided in his will that Rambeaut would inherit his farm off Holden Road, arranging to pay inheritance taxes in advance. In 1998, Rambeaut sold the farm to Koury Corporation for a net profit of $1.2 million. She also inherited Bryan's two cars, a Lincoln convertible and a Mercedes.

Bryan's driving habits, never exemplary according to some family members, worsened with age and finally he was unable to drive at all. That bothered him. He hated the thought of losing his independence.

Medlin, fearing an accident or injury from his driving, promised him in the spring of the early 1990s that if he would promise not to drive for the next eight months, she'd take him driving on January 1 of the following year. He reluctantly agreed. She forgot the promise but he didn't.

When Medlin and her husband returned home from taking a sick dog to the vet on that January 1, Bryan was waiting, impatiently, in the driveway in his Mercedes. He had driven himself to their home and later drove around their neighborhood in Hamilton Lakes in northwest Greensboro, showing he was able to have total control of his driving ability.

That wasn't the case later in the day when he visited a fast food restaurant on heavily traveled Battleground Avenue. He narrowly escaped a crash when he pulled in front of a van because he was too impatient to wait for traffic to clear. Medlin pleaded with him at that point to give up driving. He didn't give it up, but drove less frequently after that and generally avoided busy streets.

Sometime later, after arthritis inhibited his walking and prevented him from driving at all, he was bemoaning the fact that he would never again sit behind the wheel of his favorite black Lincoln convertible with a white top that folded into the trunk. Not true, said his friend Mark Buie who at the time was visiting from New Orleans.

Buie drove Bryan in the Lincoln to the Grimsley High School parking lot where there were no other cars on a non-school day. Buie helped Bryan into the driver's seat. While Bryan steered around the empty lot, Buie knelt on the floor operating the accelerator and brakes because Bryan's legs wouldn't function on the pedals. Bryan sat in his usual dignified and erect position behind the wheel, a huge smile spreading across his face. He called it a thrill.

One of the last times Bryan actually drove a vehicle at night was on Christmas night 1986 when he made a solo trip to the funeral home when Rambeaut's father died. "It was the right thing to do to come here," Bryan said that night after being chided by Rambeaut for driving himself. "And I didn't want to bother anyone to bring me."

Bryan's driving even scared his dogs on occasions. He was once a regular sight driving around town with one of his favorite dogs standing on the back seat of his Lincoln convertible with front legs propped on Bryan's shoulders. Later, the dogs grew frightened of his driving and would cower on the rear floorboard.

Bryan loved his dogs that sometimes, according to friends, seemed more attentive to him than family members. When Jason, a white and liver colored registered English Springer Spaniel officially named Jayembee AKC #640264, became ill, Bryan sent the animal to the vet school at N.C. State University for special treatment. Jason improved for several months before becoming terminally ill. Bryan would not agree to put the dog to sleep, even though he realized the animal was suffering greatly, but instead turned him over to his friend and local veterinarian Ken Eiler for final treatment until death came on Sept.18, 1992.

Jason's ashes, held by Eiler until after Bryan's death because Bryan couldn't decide where to bury them, are buried with those of his master at Bryan Park.

Several years earlier, Bryan's other Spaniel named June was also terminally ill, but Bryan couldn't bring himself to seek humane euthanasia. While on a trip to Europe, his hometown-shooting buddy Claibourne Darden asked the vet to put the dog to sleep.

"That is one of the kindest things anyone has ever done for me," Bryan later said.

Bryan's neighbors, former Congressman Richardson Preyer and

his wife Emily were witnesses to Bryan's attention to his dogs, and the dogs to him. "Jason minded Joe like a Marine," Mrs. Preyer said in a summer 1999 interview, just months before her unexpected death. Emily Preyer was one of the few people in Greensboro as well known as Bryan.

The Preyers also were recipients to Bryan's good humor, something common among social friends although it was missing in the corporate world. "I was sitting with Joe at a dinner one time and I was just talking all the time just like always," Mrs. Preyer said. "I apologized later, telling him I didn't intend to rattle on so much. He told me not to worry because I was talking into his bad ear and he didn't hear much of what I said anyway. I just thought that was wonderful."

Bryan confided to Medlin and Rambeaut of his personal turmoil as a child dealing with his nomadic father who deserted the family and his mentally ill mother who lived for half a century in hospital for the hopelessly insane. He never once spoke of those conditions to anyone else, including his family or Melvin and Bruce.

"He told me that one time he visited his mother in the mental institution," Medlin said. "It upset him so much that he never returned." That was the only time Bryan saw his mother after she was institutionalized when he was age 6 and his father deserted Bryan and his four siblings.

The trauma of his mother's illness played on Bryan throughout his life. When his wife was ill with Alzheimer's in the 1970s and 1980s, he refused to place her in a nursing home as many of his friends and some doctors recommended. He said he would rip out his home library and convert it to a nursing ward if necessary, but he would not permit his wife to enter a convalescent home. "I'll do whatever it takes to keep her here," Bryan said at the time. He never said why. But he indicated to Medlin that one reason was seeing the conditions in which his mother once lived.

Bryan also talked with Medlin and Rambeaut about some rocky

times in his early marriage, a situation that few outside his family ever knew existed. Except for Medlin and Rambeaut, he never discussed that topic with other close associates, business or personal. Bryan and his wife appeared to adore each other throughout their public appearances and seemingly had deep devotion to each other. He provided her with the best care she could receive during her most serious periods of dementia.

But it was not always that way. In the early 1940s, the Bryans temporarily separated and discussed divorce. Mrs. Bryan's father Julian Price drove his daughter and her two youngest children to Florida to live for a year while Bryan remained in Greensboro, continuing to work with Price at Jefferson Standard. Oldest daughter Kay was away in private school near Washington. "I was told in a letter from my mother that they were planning a divorce," Kay Edwards said of her recollections of that disruptive period in her parent's lives. "But I was never given details or reasons for the separation. And the divorce never happened. Mother and dad were useful to each other and were delightful at dinner parties."

After one year's separation, Bryan and his wife agreed to reunite. Bryan would later say he went to Florida and brought his family back. Family members say it was Julian Price who made the trip to Florida and brought his daughter home. Regardless, divorce was never mentioned again, at least outside the home. Whatever the problems, they were resolved. "He loved her very much," a friend said. Whatever the specifics leading up to that trial separation, Mrs. Bryan accepted full blame in a private letter she wrote to her husband as she sought to restore their marriage shortly before her return to Greensboro. The marriage problems, she lamented in great detail, were her fault. She asked forgiveness and pleaded with her husband not to leave.

She put her intimate feelings in a letter to his office, she said, because that was easier for her than talking. Bryan kept that letter more than 50 years and it was found among his papers.

Mrs. Bryan's verbatim letter follows:

I must write to you for I want you to know how I feel and when I talk I don't always express myself as well as I'd like to.

I feel to completely sunk to do anything, for I realize for the first time in seven years that if our marriage has been a failure it has been entirely my fault. I've never been so completely over-whelmed with a fact as I am with that.

You have given me all and have asked for so little in return, and never once have I measured up to your expectations. Oh, I know now more than at any time in my life how utterly selfish and spoiled I am. Forgive me, if I have left a bad taste in your mouth for marriage. I don't blame you. Why you haven't walked out and left me before I don't know, except that as always, you have given in to me, and also maybe you've been able to discern that in my heart, I love you entirely, and despite my being rotten-ly spoiled you are my life.

Don't let me ruin your life. I am not good enough for that, because with the right kind of girl you could go far. I think I real-ize for the first time what a silly fool I've been to let something slip through my fingers, that is the most precious thing in life— the unselfish love, adoration and loyalty of ones husband.

Please dear, don't resign from the Jefferson, and I say that from an entirely unselfish standpoint. You are so respected and well thought of by all officials, directors and employees of the compa-ny and you have a wonderful future with them. It may seem far off now, but it is not. You should and will head it one day, by virtue of merit—and you will carry it on to even greater goals. It will not only be the biggest insurance company in the south, but the most modern, and best managed in the U.S. You have a won-derful capacity for building an organization, and make people work and make them like it, and for that reason you should stay where the future opens up for you to put your grand policies in

253

effect. You stand for a lot in this community. You have the respect and love of many people — they like you and they want you to stay here — please do. You know the reason why, people admire and like you, not alone for your charming and attractive personality, but that they feel your sincerity and loyalty and one knows, one can depend on you. So do I, and how foolish I was not to hang on to it.

I am brokenhearted and feel so alone, but I don't want to appeal to you through your kindness and mercy. I want you to do, for once in your life what you want to do. I couldn't bear the thought of the future without you and if you could give me another chance, if not because you love me, but because your children and house mean so much to you, I'll spend the rest of my life trying to show you how really deeply and devotedly I love you and I will sincerely try never to fail you again. If you don't want me and god only knows why you should, well—oh—I just feel too lost to think of what life would be if you complete that sentence.

This is just a feeble attempt to tell you how dreadfully sorry I am and also to tell you that I love only you, with all my heart.

I love you — always, yours

Kathleen

Once the Bryans reconciled their marriage with Mrs. Bryan's return to Greensboro, the couple began their interest in charitable giving within five years.

Certainly the many dual donations from the Bryans have been of significant benefit to people across the state and elsewhere beyond what either might have done as individuals. Their generosity preceded the creation of their family foundations. While most of their major gifts have been credited to one of the two foundations Bryan and his wife created, that's just part of their benevolence.

Mrs. Bryan's religious faith played a lead in the couple's initial giving. They donated thousands to the Catholic College of Notre

Dame in Baltimore in memory of Mrs. Bryan's mother Ethel Price who obtained a degree from that institution. They contributed thousands to Belmont Abby College in Gaston County where Mrs. Bryan received an honorary degree. That is in addition to the hundreds of thousands given to build Our Lady of Grace Catholic Church in Greensboro following the initial gift by Julian Price for that purpose. They contributed additional thousands in scholarships to Converse College in South Carolina where Mrs. Bryan was a student although she did not graduate.

As the many gifts show, the Bryans, as was Mrs. Bryan's father, were quite generous to Catholic causes in general and to Our Lady of Grace in particular where Mrs. Bryan was a devout member. Bryan, however, never attended church on a regular basis and at his death was not a member of any church.

Mrs. Bryan, at the urging of her friend Billy Carmichael at the University of North Carolina in Chapel Hill, created the women's scholarship program at UNCG in the 1950s, the first of its kind within the university system.

Bryan was the first private contributor of $1 million to launch the campaign to create and open what is now the state's respected School of Math and Science in Durham that is located in the former Watts Hospital building where Kathleen Bryan's mother once studied nursing.

"I wandered around a good deal in my early life," Bryan said of his gift to the Durham school. "But I think the greatest gift you can get is a good education. I appreciate what a good education can mean." Bryan could have added what the absence of a formal education also meant. "I was right proud to make the first contribution to that school. It just shows what can be done if you put your mind to it," he said of that gift.

Bryan credited Gov. Jim Hunt with getting him interested in the innovative Math and Science School. Maybe so, Hunt said, but it was Bryan's vigor that got it going. "It was his zeal and excitement

Kathleen Price Bryan with sisters from College of Notre Dame in Baltimore in 1951 after Mrs. Bryan made a gift to the college library in memory of her mother Ethel Clay Price, who earned a degree from the school.

Kathleen and Joseph M. Bryan Sr. with their three children, Nancy, Kay and Joe Jr., on the day Mrs. Bryan was awarded her honorary degree from the College of Notre Dame in Baltimore in 1953.

for the concept that stands out in my mind," Hunt said of Bryan's gift. "His heart was in this one as much as anyone's and it frankly would never have happened without him. His support was critical. He not only stepped up, but he urged others to give. It succeeded because of him.

"And his response was so typical. He looked at that dilapidated building and said this just won't do. It has to be better. He wanted a first class facility," Hunt said. "He was bold and courageous to get out front and take a chance to do that project. I had always viewed him as a titan in business. It is one thing to help with something that has been there, but it's harder to start something new. Mr. Bryan was willing and ready to take that risk. He just got out there and did it."

When Hunt was on an industry hunting trip to Europe, Bryan loaned the governor his Rolls Royce and driver in London. "I was quite impressed that the driver knew who I was and kept calling me governor. After awhile I realized I didn't mean anything special to him. He called everybody governor. He had no idea who I was."

Bryan was on several occasions generous to Guilford College, likely because so many of his coworkers at Jefferson were supportive of the school. He also owed an allegiance to former Guilford President Clyde Milner who gave Bryan speech lessons when he thought he was in line for the presidency of Jefferson. After some relatively small gifts, Bryan and his wife donated $250,000 to Guilford for a new residence hall.

In later years Bryan retreated from large donations to Guilford in favor of those to Duke, but he included Guilford in his will with a half million-dollar gift.

Since Bryan's death, his son and namesake has contributed generously to Guilford.

When Greensboro College President William Likens and college trustee William Jones first approached Bryan for $1 million for that small private school, they were warmly received, but shocked with a Bryan question.

"Why are you asking for only $1 million?" Bryan asked. Likens was speechless, but the quick-witted Jones wasn't.

"It's because he's cheaper than I am," Jones said as he looked at the startled college president. "If it would have been left up to me I'd have asked for a lot more." Bryan smiled, but only gave what was requested. Greensboro College also received half a million in the Bryan will, just as all other local colleges did.

A November 1983 newspaper opinion column suggesting Bryan might be racially prejudiced because he had not been as generous to N.C. A&T State University as to other local colleges bothered Bryan who was sensitive about negative publicity. He had, in fact, given to that school. He had donated a $45,000 house on Salem

Street in Greensboro to be used by the A&T alumni association and had given $100,000 to various campus causes. A month after that newspaper column was published, Bryan gave A&T $500,000 to the Focus on Excellence campaign. His donations continued the remainder of his life and his foundation trustees have kept those gifts ongoing since Bryan's death.

"He was a man who always came through to give his very best," said retired A&T Chancellor Ed Fort. "He was more than just a philanthropic prince. He genuinely cared about people and was very much aware of needs. Every time we asked, he said yes. He was respected and admired by our student body."

Bryan's total gifts through the middle of 1999 to A&T had reached $5 million.

Charlie Patterson, a former development officer at UNCG who later moved to similar jobs at Wake Forest and Guilford College, met Bryan for the first time in the middle 1970s.

It was not an especially pleasant meeting. Bryan, who had been making regular contributions to UNCG following the lead of his wife 20 years earlier, was grousing about the quality of speakers Patterson had been bringing to the business school. Bryan wanted Walter Cronkite. Patterson was lucky to get Louis Rukeyser.

"We worked to improve the quality and recognition of speakers," Patterson, now at Guilford College said. "We wanted to bring more visibility to the school, but more importantly we wanted to please Mr. Bryan." Patterson's plan worked. In 1979, Bryan gave the school an additional $1 million, plus a lot more later.

There were, however, more stumbling blocks. UNCG started its Prospectus III campaign in 1982 and Bryan stepped up with $1 million. When Ben Cone donated $2 million and was given higher recognition in campus publications than Bryan had ever received, Bryan was displeased.

"Joe was unhappy," Patterson said. But any agitation didn't last and Bryan was soon back on his giving trail. In 1987, UNCG named its new business school building in honor of Bryan who contributed substantially toward its construction.

A bronze plaque honoring Bryan's contributions to the business school, placed in the entrance, reads in part: "Mr. Bryan has had a long business career and held high corporate offices in insurance and broadcasting. His humanitarian and community work is equally striking and original. His gifts have promoted education, cultural enrichment, recreational facilities and medical science facilities. Everyone who believes that business success can and must be integrated with personal concerns for community needs will take heart from the facts of (his) life."

Bryan and his wife in 1983 contributed $1 million to endow student scholarships and professorships at the business school and he made frequent and enjoyable trips to classrooms just to listen and talk with students. He saw his dollars going to help people who had opportunities he never had as a student.

Bryan's latest gift to UNCG came after his death in the form of a $5 million donation specified in his will. His foundation has donated Bryan's Sunset Drive home for use as the chancellor's residence.

Patterson also learned that Bryan could zing you with sarcasm about his many gifts. After Bryan had donated $3 million to Duke in the middle 1980s for a new student center, Patterson congratulated Bryan.

"That was a very nice gesture," Patterson told Bryan.

"Huh," Bryan responded. "I think $3 million is more than a damn gesture."

"That was just so typical of Joe," Patterson said. "He had an outer gruffness, but underneath was a mighty big heart."

Bryan also helped UNCG by sponsoring a pro-am golf tournament each year at Bryan Park to raise money for the school.

Patterson also benefited from Bryan's generosity at Wake Forest University when Patterson worked in development there between jobs at UNCG and Guilford. "He just said we'd be pleased with what he would do," Patterson said of the Wake Forest request for financial help. "I had no clue what he meant at the time." Wake received $500,000.

Bennett College President Gloria Scott had a similar experience to Patterson's the first time she met Bryan. She had been advised by an insurance executive in another state to go see Bryan as soon as she started her job at Bennett.

"I know you're here to ask for money," Bryan said to Scott on their first meeting in the summer of 1991. "Well, I don't have any money. I've given it all away. Everyone else has beaten you here. I'm just an old man who needs money to live on." Like he had done with many before Scott arrived in his office, Bryan pointed to a hole in the carpet and said he couldn't even afford to replace it. That was his standard joke with first time solicitors.

Scott didn't know the hole in the rug joke. She thought the hole ought to be covered and she sent him a small hand woven rug from Iran to put over the worn carpet. Bryan later thanked her and sent Bennett a check. He gave Bennett money every year.

Money was obviously important to many people touched by Bryan's generosity. But one letter in his personal papers at Jackson Library on the UNCG campus may be more revealing of his big heart than any of his financial gifts. In 1966, a Greensboro woman wrote Bryan about a kindness to her 25 years earlier.

"I read with interest the story about you in yesterday's newspaper," Mrs. T. P. Rhyne wrote Bryan on May 23, 1966. "Much more could and should have been said about you as a warm, friendly person, ready and willing to help others. Let me remind you why.

"It was in 1943 and World War II was going on. Our daughter was to be married to a lieutenant in the Air Force. He had only a one-week leave. We wanted to give them a church wedding and reception. With so little time to plan, it was impossible to find a suitable place for the reception. I was desperate. I had never met you, but I knew that you were one of the most influential citizens here. I knew it was a bold thing to do but as I said I was desperate. I came to your office and told you my problem. To make a long story short, you were instrumental in getting the Starmount County Club for us. My daughter and her husband had a few happy weeks together before he was sent overseas. He never came back. Thank you. I am sure there are many others that you and Mrs. Bryan have helped that few people know about."

Ann Rambeaut didn't know about that letter as she stood by Bryan's deathbed that April morning in 1995. But she knew how she felt to see her friend slipping away.

Just as she had done many time before, but this time with more feeling than ever, Rambeaut leaned over the bed, touched his hand and whispered, "I love you Mr. Bryan."

Bryan opened his eyes, looked into hers and gave a soft response with the little remaining strength he could muster as death's shadow widened with each passing hour. "If you didn't feel that way," he whispered, "it would be awfully one sided."

In a little while, Joe Bryan was gone.

16

CHISELED IN STONE

Duke University President Terry Sanford never worked in a rock quarry or as a stone mason, but by the time Sanford had hammered out his first real construction project with Joe Bryan, he may have felt as if he had been pushing boulders around for a long time.

And before the deal was finally done, Sanford had — literally — seen it chiseled in stone.

Former North Carolina governor and United States senator Sanford and Bryan first met in 1954 in the middle of a political campaign. Politics would bind them together for decades, then regrettably force them apart in the final years of their lives.

When they were first met, Sanford was a little-known state senator from Fayetteville who was managing former Gov. Kerr Scott's Democratic campaign for United States Senator from North Carolina and Bryan was still struggling to establish himself among his peers at Jefferson Standard Insurance Company as a legitimate corporate executive.

Sanford was having difficulty in the spring of 1954 finding business owners and corporate executives across the state willing to support Scott, a rough-hewn tobacco-chewing farmer from Haw River in Alamance County. Corporate circles in the state opposed Scott, calling him too crude and too unfriendly to big business. Scott, after all, had won the state's governorship five years earlier as one of the self-described "Branch Head Boys" made up of agrarian interests who favored the rural areas of the state more than more affluent downtown board rooms or country club cocktail parties. Scott thought corporate officials were basically haughty and cared little for farmers and blue-collar workers.

"I recall that Joe Bryan was one of only three people among businessmen in Greensboro who I could find to support Scott," Sanford said. "Most everybody in Greensboro (among corporate officials) was opposed to Scott because of his rough ways. "But Joe liked Scott and in some ways he and Scott were alike in that they were both independent spirits. Joe, you know, really never was quite a part of the Jefferson establishment, never a real corporate insider. He was always looked upon as an interloper it seemed to me. He always gave me the impression that Mr. Price (Jefferson president and Bryan's father-in-law) didn't necessarily approve of him wholeheartedly."

That was undoubtedly a true statement. In fact, Bryan's friends contend it's unlikely Price would have approved wholeheartedly of any man who had married his only daughter.

Bryan contributed financially to Scott's winning senatorial campaign, which had a total budget of $60,000 and spoke kindly of him during the campaign, as he and Sanford became friends. Whatever Bryan did for Scott, it was enough to get him a seat in the special guest box beside Mrs. Scott at the swearing in ceremony.

Bryan later supported Sanford when Sanford ran for and was elected governor in the fall of 1960 and when Sanford was elected to the U.S. Senate in 1986. "Of course I had a lot of support among Greensboro voters so what Joe did for me didn't stand out like what he did for Scott when he was one of the very few people there willing to help," Sanford said with his familiar devious grin. It was not until almost a decade later that Sanford and Bryan had their first close encounter outside electoral politics involving a proposed business takeover that failed. But even that venture was cloaked in politics of the corporate world.

Sanford and Bryan didn't begin their really close and continuing association until after Sanford was chosen president of Duke University in December 1969. That was when Sanford, as only a smooth political charmer like him could do, began cultivating Bryan for financial help for the university. It was a cultivation that brought forth a bumper crop that, among other things, might one day help lead to a successful treatment if not a cure for the dreaded Alzheimer's disease.

That's a legacy any political figure or corporate executive could embrace. Sanford and Bryan were no exceptions. Ultimate success with such an historic and significant breakthrough on Alzheimer's is a long way away, of course, but progress being made at Duke in medical research, thanks in large part to the initial interest and support from Bryan, ranks among the best and brightest in the country.

It was students and not medicine, however, that put Bryan and Sanford together in the middle 1970s. More specifically, it was a Bryan granddaughter, a Duke student.

Granddaughter Mary Price (Pricey) Taylor had applied to both Duke and Princeton and had been turned down by the Ivy League School. "He couldn't understand, and frankly neither could I, that Princeton took such a high and mighty attitude," Sanford said. "Anyway she came to Duke and that sort of put me back in touch with him. I had him on my list as a prospect (to give money to Duke) and I went by to see him when I could."

Bryan wasn't an easy financial resource to tap, but Sanford took no back seat to anyone when it came to dealing the right cards at the right time. "I suggested to him that I wanted to make him a proposal to do for Duke what Mr. Morehead had done for UNC in Chapel Hill," Sanford of his initial plan. "That was my first rather ambitious and inflated proposal to him. I talked in terms of maybe $50 million. He listened politely to that, but he didn't even respond although it was pretty obvious to me he wasn't much interested and didn't have that kind of money anyway. Then I went back to see him again and mentioned some other projects, you know maybe in the $20 million category. Then I'd go back and reduce the figure a little bit. I just kept going back and mentioning projects and lowering the figure a little bit more each time. All that took more than a year and a dozen or so visits, but I was just trying to get to something that would appeal to him."

All this was taking place in the midst of Duke campus administrative infighting. While Sanford was massaging Bryan for money for his own projects, the Duke Medical School was itching to approach Bryan for money for that part of the campus. Sanford, not surprisingly, won the initial battle. "The people at the medical center just forgot who the president was," Sanford said, again with his familiar smile. The medical school officials waited, albeit impatiently, on the sidelines while Sanford wove his strains.

Bryan showed little enthusiasm for any of Sanford's bodacious building plans. Sanford had not given up, but each time he returned to his office in search of a project that he felt Bryan might support. His answer came unexpectedly with the help of Bryan granddaughter Pricey Taylor who casually mentioned to her grandfather that she was considering transferring off the Duke campus. He asked why.

"There's nothing to do on campus, no place for students to go, to be together," she replied.

"Well, about that same time I had been working on a plan for a $10 million student center that had petered out," Sanford said. "So I decided I'd just try that out on Joe. This was right after his granddaughter had complained to him of the need for such a center." That Duke gift from Bryan was but one example of the many generous acts on behalf of his grandchildren.

The Duke Student Center had actually been in the campus plans since the 1930s, first shuttled aside during World War II, then languishing during the lethargic 1950s and unable to generate any interest among alumni during the turbulent 1960s.

"Now you've finally mentioned something that gets my interest," a somewhat startled Sanford recalled Bryan responding when he mentioned the long-dormant student center. It wasn't until later that the Sanford learned about the granddaughter's complaint, but his timing could not have been better. Taylor also didn't learn until much later that it was her casual comment to her grandfather about the need for a student center that prompted him to act.

Sanford initially asked Bryan for $4 million, close enough to half the anticipated cost that Duke normally used to name a building after an individual donor. Bryan balked because, as was his custom, he had done his own research about the plans and learned that Sanford had offered to name the proposed facility after two other men — J. A. Jones of Charlotte or Thomas Finch of Thomasville — if either would contribute $3 million. Both Jones and Finch declined.

"How come you want me to give a million more than the other fellows you were asking for money," Bryan asked without hesitation. Sanford confessed, according to his then staff aide Jake Phelps, that he was just trying to get a much as he could. All he could get was $3 million, which Bryan promised to pay over a three-year period.

"Well, I hope you will allow us to put your name on the building," Sanford said to Bryan, knowing full well he would.

"Well, I assume that's the plan," Bryan replied with a smile.

Bryan made the $3 million pledge with the stipulation that the facility be named the Joseph M. and Kathleen Price Bryan University Center and the names be prominently displayed. He also was adamant that the facility should be called university center and not student center, but in reality that has never been the case. Students call it theirs.

Bryan later said with his touch of humor that his wife was

shocked at what he had agreed to do because he made the $3 million commitment without letting her know. "She told me she didn't realize we had that much money," he wrote in a letter to an oil investment friend. "I told her not to worry because we had three years to pay the pledge and if we could hit a good oil strike we would be OK."

Bryan paid parts of his pledge in cash, but donated to Duke some rental properties in Greensboro that he and his wife jointly owned to cover remainder of the commitment. The properties Bryan gave to Duke were part of a real estate company known as Kananjo, named for Bryan's three children (Kay, Nancy and Joe). The buildings included rental property that Mrs. Bryan had inherited from her father and were the same properties that Guilford College president William Rogers had earlier suggested unsuccessfully that Bryan donate to Guilford.

By the time Duke sold those properties, they had increased in value almost $250,000 beyond the value when the gift was made, so the school came out ahead. Furthermore, Bryan later agreed without public notice to contribute another $1 million to the center. That meant his total gifts far exceeded what he had pledged or that Sanford had requested and totaled more than $4.2 million. Sanford never complained about the surplus.

Pricey Taylor Harrison said in 1999 she really had planned to transfer from Duke, but felt compelled to stay after her grandfather's huge gift. "I didn't know until later that it was my comment that caused him to make the gift," Taylor said. "I was considering transferring to UNC for several reasons. I wasn't sure Duke was the right place for me. But after he made his gift I felt it would not appropriate to transfer. I thought it would be egg on my face to leave the school right after his gift. Unfortunately for me, though, the center wasn't completed until after I graduated."

But it was Duke that had egg on its face after granddaughter Taylor applied to the Duke Law School following receipt of her undergraduate degree. She was rejected by Duke Law admissions personnel and accepted by UNC.

Within a week of that rejection, however, Duke wrote her a letter of apology, explaining that the law school administrator who knew of those students with ties to Duke had been away when her application came in and her rejection was a mistake. When she was turned down, the letter said, the Duke Law School officials didn't realize she was Joe Bryan's granddaughter and that, once they realized who she was, they would be pleased to have her as a student. That episode, Sanford said later, embarrassed him. She declined the chance to remain at Duke and received a law degree from UNC.

Hanging in the foyer of the Bryan Center on the Duke campus down a hill behind the Duke Chapel is a large portrait of the Bryans with a commemorative plaque that reads: Joseph McKinley and Kathleen Price Bryan for their love, inspiration and support which made possible this university facility. The entire Duke family — students, faculty, staff, employees and all our friends — will forever be grateful to them."

The Center is a 169,000 square foot facility that serves students and visitors with a ticket office, drama theatre, bookstore, art gallery, film theatre and lab, meeting rooms, multiple food courts and administrative offices on three floors. The total cost was $17.6 million, plus another $7.5 million for an addition.

As promised, the Bryan's name was placed on what Sanford described as a "very attractive" sign in front of the building just as with names at other buildings on campus. But Bryan wanted something permanent; he wanted his name in concrete. The sign Sanford had planted in the ground out front didn't suit Bryan because it would have been possible to move or change it. Bryan complained.

"Joe, I'm not going to take your name off the sign," Sanford stressed when Bryan expressed dissatisfaction with the sign.

Joseph M. Bryan Sr. and former North Carolina governor and Duke University president Terry Sanford at the dedication of the Duke Student Center named for Bryan and his wife in 1982.

"I know you won't," Bryan said, "but I don't know about what some others might do." Bryan also complained about the sign to his then son-in-law Lauch Faircloth who was at the time a close Sanford associate.

"I called Terry and asked him to just get a damn tombstone mason over there and make the sign permanent," Faircloth said. "And that's what was done."

Sanford hired a stone mason to carve the Bryan name in the stone wall above the main entrance to the Center. His name will remain as long as the building stands.

Just as he did with most projects he supported, Bryan took a particular interest in the Duke Center, during and after its construction. He visited the site during the construction phase, asking probing questions about the design and why certain things were being

270

done a certain way. "The students even had a birthday party for him one time," Sanford said. "Joe had an association with our students that I'm sure he enjoyed." Once while visiting the Center after it was opened, Bryan was standing near his portrait when a student walked close, looked at the portrait then at him and exclaimed "that's you!" Bryan's smile lasted awhile after that remark as he and the student engaged in a conversation.

"I went to see him a little more often after that," Sanford said. "He would invite me to dinner. I probably went to see him 20 times during the time Mrs. Bryan was ill and after she died. He always had a bottle of real good wine with dinner. He didn't like to brag about it (the wine), but he'd sort of twist it around so I could see the label. I'd take the label and pretend I knew something about wine. I didn't, of course, but I knew damn well it was good wine. I always enjoyed those visits."

Sanford learned something else about Bryan in those visits and in his contributions to Duke. It was that although Bryan could and would be generous, he wanted value and results from his donations. "I was always impressed with the amount of thought that he gave to what to do with his money," Sanford explained. "He always gave careful consideration to how he handled his donations. He had logic on how best to utilize his resources. It always seemed to me that he took a great sense of responsibility to see that his money was properly utilized. I think that might have been because he didn't come from any great wealth."

Bryan's largest donation to Duke University would come later following his wife's losing battle with the ravages of Alzheimer's Disease. Sanford was involved with that gift, too, but not as directly as with the donation for the Bryan University Center. That story will come later.

Sanford's aborted private business venture with Bryan came in the spring of 1969, less than a year before the beginning of cultivation for the Duke gifts. Between leaving the governor's office in

1965 and becoming Duke president at the end of 1969, Sanford was in private law practice in Raleigh.

In February 1969, Sanford and his law partners were hired by Texas oil financier Walter Davis, a savvy investor with strong North Carolina business and political ties, to help pull off a corporate takeover of Jefferson Standard Insurance Company. Bryan was to be part of that plan, and Sanford thought he had that all worked out.

Davis and Sanford attempted to convince Bryan, his daughter Nancy and son-in-law Lauch Faircloth to pool their stock and add to stock that Davis and his then business partner Armand Hammer who controlled Occidental Petroleum had been quietly acquiring. The only way the deal would succeed was for Bryan to vote his and his wife's stock with that of Davis and others who were part of the plan. Jefferson management strongly opposed the plan, once they learned a deal was being attempted.

But unlike later attempted hostile takeovers in the corporate world, the Sanford/Davis plan never became public.

Bryan, who by then had retired from Jefferson, was originally for the plan and called a private meeting to discuss it at his Palm Beach rental unit. "It was at a place (Bryan) said he had been going to for 30 years and you could believe it when you saw it," Sanford said. "It was not very elaborate. We thought we had the Bryans stock, the Faircloth stock and enough others to make it work. But the old gal ties in Greensboro got to Joe. He was for it for awhile, although I wouldn't say he was enthusiastic. Then he changed his mind. Without his block of stock, there wasn't much point in continuing."

Sanford recalled Bryan's reversal of support to the plan after the Florida meeting. "Well, Kathleen plays bridge with all those women who are wives of people at Jefferson who oppose the plan," Sanford quoted Bryan as saying, "I just can't go along with it. It's just not worth it, getting into a fight with the wives." That's when the plan fell apart.

"He was talking about people like the wife of Roger Soles," Sanford said. "He just didn't want to get in a fight with the women. You know, Roger could be kind of a mean and nasty fellow. Of course, he had a reason to be that way to me. We tried to take over his company."

Shortly after that spring episode, Sanford sent Soles four tickets to an ACC tournament, apparently hoping to make amends for the failed business takeover. "I just stuck the damn tickets back in an envelope and mailed them back to him the same day," Soles said. "I didn't want his tickets and didn't want any obligation to him. Someone told me later that Sanford lost a lot of money on Jefferson stock after what he tried to do. I'm glad. He deserved it."

Sanford obviously maintained his friendship with Bryan after that thwarted business plan collapsed. All Bryan's contributions to Duke came during Sanford's Duke presidency. Bryan also supported Sanford when he made two unsuccessful attempts to become the Democratic nominee for president during the 1970s while he was at Duke and when Sanford was successful in being elected U.S. Senator in 1986. It was a U.S. Senate campaign that split them, however, in 1992 when Sanford's old political buddy and Bryan's former son-in-law Faircloth became a Republican candidate for Sanford's Senate seat and defeated Sanford for the job.

Prior to Sanford's first Senate race in 1986, he and Faircloth had several times discussed which one of them ought to be the Democratic candidate. Faircloth has said Sanford had assured him that he (Sanford) would not become a candidate that year. Faircloth felt mistreated and misled when Sanford filed as a candidate without giving Faircloth advance notice. Faircloth was also angered by reports that he received from Sanford's supporters that the former governor's campaign aides had snickered at Faircloth's chances of ever winning a Senate campaign. "That really set Lauch off," said Robert Scott, another former governor. "He just said that by God he'd show them." Six years later, Faircloth switched parties, became

the Republican nominee and beat his old Democratic friend Sanford for the Senate seat.

That campaign put Bryan in a personal and political bind. He
had been a supporter of Sanford for decades, but clearly didn't
want to campaign against Faircloth who, despite his divorce from
Bryan's daughter Nancy, was still close to Bryan.

"I knew he would find that a little embarrassing," Sanford said of
that campaign. "He had to be for Lauch. He liked Lauch because
Lauch paid attention to him. Early in the campaign, I wrote Joe a
letter and told him I understood the situation, that I'd see him after
the election. He didn't respond to that letter, but he didn't need to
and I didn't expect any response."

Bryan did work for Faircloth's election, lending him several hundred thousand dollars. Faircloth repaid the loan by turning over to
Bryan the deed to some farmland he owned.

Sanford and Faircloth were sharply divided for years after that
1992 Senate campaign. Only Bryan's death would bring them
together again.

Bryan had privately supported Sanford's 1986 senatorial campaign, despite Faircloth's unhappiness with Sanford's candidacy
that year. Bryan made two $3,000 contributions to that campaign,
telling Sanford he hoped Faircloth wouldn't find out.

At Bryan's 90th birthday party not long after Sanford's Senate
election in 1986, Sanford sent his former Duke staff aide and close
Bryan friend Jake Phelps to the celebration with the specific assignment to make contact with Faircloth in hopes of reconciliation.
Phelps learned at that occasion just how bitter Faircloth still was at
his old friend.

"We were at Mr. Bryan's home after the party," Phelps recalled.
"Lauch sort of moved away from the crowd at one point, I think
maybe just to blow his nose. I walked up to him and said that Terry
had asked if maybe he and Lauch could break bread together.
Lauch looked me straight in the eye and said it would be a (exple-

tive) cold day in hell before that ever happened." The two never did have lunch, but Bryan's death brought them together.

Sanford and Faircloth had their first face-to-face meeting following the bitter 1992 Senate campaign at Bryan's funeral in April 1995. As Sanford approached the church for the funeral, a reporter asked him for a comment about Faircloth. Sanford, without even the slightest hesitation responded: "The Lauch Faircloth once I knew is dead."

During the funeral, Sanford was seated at the aisle end of a pew in Greensboro's downtown First Presbyterian Church. As the family left the church, Nancy Bryan Faircloth stopped to give Sanford a hug. Faircloth, then the Senator, was following his ex-wife. He reached to shake Sanford's hand.

Sanford and Faircloth talked privately outside the church following the service. "I saw Sanford shaking his finger at Faircloth," Phelps said later. "On the way home to Durham, I asked Terry what they talked about. He said Lauch thanked him for coming to the funeral. Then he told me about the old Ed Koch line about asking voters of New York how he was doing as mayor. Terry said Lauch asked for an assessment of his Senate performance.

"Terry said he told Lauch he was getting a reputation in the Senate as a mean-spirited son of a bitch and that would not be a good legacy to have. He said Lauch thanked him for his candor. Then Terry laughed and said that's the first time he had ever called someone an S.O.B and been thanked for it."

Sanford's version of that conversation was a bit more diluted, but the message was the same. "I just told him a few things I thought he ought to be doing in the Senate," Sanford said. "I don't recall that he ever did any of them, but I suspect he did not."

Regardless of the exact words exchanged between the two old friends, Bryan would have been pleased that they actually had begun to speak again. Sanford and Faircloth were two of his favorite people.

The bitterness between the old adversaries lasted awhile after Bryan's death. Sanford's subsequent illness brought the two men together once more. Faircloth visited with Sanford in the spring of 1998 in last months of Sanford's life. Their conversation remains private. Faircloth told reporters, however, that he held no vendetta against Sanford. "Terry Sanford is a gentleman," he said. "I can say that as well as anyone, having known him for 40 years."

Faircloth visited with his old friend once more, on April 22, 1998. That was the day of Sanford's funeral in Duke Chapel. It was both a somber, yet uplifting service for the packed chapel. "He may not have been elected president of the United States, but he got buried like one," Sanford friend Hugh Morton said of that funeral.

Sanford's legacy to this state and to Duke lives on. So does Joe Bryan's. But Bryan has one thing Sanford never had at Duke: his name chiseled in stone.

17

PARTNERSHIP GIVING

W hen the Crash of 1929 hit Wall Street, Joe Bryan did
what a lot of other brokers in New York did. He
began to worry about his income and his family.
There was little business and a shortage of money.

As a previously thriving and aggressive member of the New York
Cotton Exchange, he had done well financially between his 1927
marriage and the collapse of commodity markets two years later.
But when the price of cotton fell to a nickel a pound, profits in the
brokerage business were as scarce as dollars in the hands of
investors.

Bryan and his young wife Kathleen and their two daughters Kay
and Nancy were far from destitute, of course. There was some limited business and father-in-law Julian Price back in Greensboro was
supplying a monthly family subsidy to ensure that the family had
what it needed, plus a few luxuries. But within 18 months of the
Wall Street collapse, the die was cast.

Bryan and his family would be coming to Greensboro for good.
Price wanted his daughter and grandchildren home and the way to
accomplish that was to offer son-in-law Bryan a job at Jefferson

Standard Insurance, even a make-shift one as a starter.

As tough as times were in New York, however, things didn't immediately get any better in terms of Bryan's paycheck when the family moved South. In fact, initially they got worse. Price, with an earned reputation for hard work and low pay among employees at Jefferson Standard, wanted his family back home, but he didn't cut his son-in-law any slack when it came to salary.

"It was quite a (economic) sacrifice for me to come to Greensboro," Bryan said of the move he made to pacify family patriarch Price. Indeed. His starting salary at Jefferson in 1931 was $65 a month, a paltry $16.50 a week.

Things, of course, got better over time. While Bryan never made top dollar in salary at Jefferson, he and his wife did quite well thanks to the rise in Jefferson stock prices and some shrewd investments on his own. He also didn't spent more than he had to in his early days in Greensboro.

He asked for his home on Sunset Drive to be built through construction connections at Jefferson subsidiary Pilot Life Insurance for cost of material and, even then, he cut some corners and left out features that wife Kathleen desired. She never got the large foyer and spiral staircase she wanted; Bryan said those fineries were too expensive. He didn't include a basement when the house was built, adding that later with less expensive manual labor with workmen who carried out dirt by the bucketsful because there wasn't room for equipment under the foundation. He much later added a wine cellar.

Twenty-five years after Bryan received his first Jefferson paycheck of $65 at the end of his first month on the job, he and Kathleen decided it was time to spread their resources, albeit on a relatively small scale. They established the Bryan Family Foundation Inc. in December 1955 with a meager amount of cash. But it was the start of what would become a major philanthropic undertaking in Greensboro and across North Carolina by Bryan, his wife, and their children and grandchildren and the foundation that Bryan carefully created.

The foundation was created with Bryan and his wife agreeing to sell 100 shares of jointly owned Jefferson stock. The price: $120 a share for a total initial contribution of $12,000. At Mrs. Bryan's death 29 years later, after hundreds of charitable donations, the market value of the foundation's assets was set at $1.6 million. After her death, the foundation assets ballooned from Mrs. Bryan's estate, valued at some $50 million, 45 percent of which went into the foundation. Within the first two years of Mrs. Bryan's death in October 1984, more than $23 million was distributed to the foundation from her estate. The remainder of the estate was split among Bryan (35 percent as the law allowed) and to Bryan grandchildren. With the assistance of Greensboro lawyer William Adams, Mrs. Bryan had rewritten her will — several times during the 1970s as she became increasingly ill — to ensure that the majority of her assets went to the family foundation or family members other than her husband.

Foundation assets continued to grow significantly during the 1980s and 1990s even as sizable donations were made each year. By the middle of 1999, foundation assets totaled approximately $60 million. Even with the phenomenal growth in the value of the organization, however, trouble lay ahead. Family friction abounded. Bryan had seen it coming a decade earlier.

"Joe wanted to start the foundation and use philanthropy through the family," said retired Greensboro lawyer Richard Wharton who drafted the original documents and served as foundation secretary-treasurer for many years. "Initially, Kathleen and (daughter) Kay put most of the money into the fund (after the original 100 shares of stock contributed by the Bryans). But Joe was the one who gave money away. Kathleen was not as inclined to contribute. Joe always laughed and said Kathleen thought $25 was a big gift."

Records of family giving do show that Bryan was generally more receptive to philanthropy in the early days of the foundation than his wife, except when it came to her church. Mrs. Bryan's devotion to her Catholic faith and her giving reflected her philosophy of giving. After her father gave the initial $400,000 to build Our Lady of Grace Church in Greensboro in memory of her mother Ethel Clay Price, she and her brother Ralph contributed heavily to finish the project. Mrs. Bryan and her brother Ralph Price personally contributed $300,000 toward the church rectory, school and convent.

The story of Our Lady of Grace Church actually may have begun around the Sunday dinner table at the home of Julian and Ethel Clay Price, many years before construction began. Catholics were few in Greensboro in the early 1930s the few Catholic parishes could afford full-time priests. History shows that a visiting priest would come to town on Sunday to deliver Mass at the lone Catholic place of worship that later became St. Benedict's near downtown Greensboro. Most often that priest was Abbot Vincent Taylor from Belmont Abby who, after services, would visit his Greensboro sisters Mary and Lucy Taylor. Mary Taylor was secretary to Julian Price at Jefferson Standard and Sunday dinners with the Taylor sisters and the priest were usually at the Price home.

The need for another Catholic Church was first discussed during those Sunday meals and Mrs. Price made known her desires for a new eye-catching place of worship. Her husband followed through after her death in her memory with his donation for Our Lady of Grace. Price, as was his late wife's wishes, wanted to spare no expense in building a cathedral.

Price met with Catholic leaders to review church designs and he chose as a model the Church of Our Lady of Refuge in Brooklyn. The model was scaled down by the architect of that church and Price contributed $400,000 in Jefferson stock to begin construction. But before the first bricks were laid, Price was killed in an auto accident in 1946.

Delays brought on by his death as well as shortage of materials because of World War II resulted in the need for another $300,000 to complete the building as Price had requested. Mrs. Bryan and her brother Ralph provided that money. George W. Kane Construction Company erected the church, on West Market Street west of downtown Greensboro. It is of Tudor Gothic architectural design with materials purchased from nine different states and several foreign countries.

Exterior walls are of granite mined from a site in Rowan County. More than 30,000 separate pieces of cut stained glass were imported from Belgium for the windows. Chairo marble from Italy was used for the Sanctuary and side altars. Artists from three states and Canada helped with the decorations. A special Legion of Mary Altar was included because of Mrs. Price's devotion to the Blessed Virgin Mary. Two marble plaques inside the front entrance to the church commemorate the life of Mrs. Price with the words "in loving memory of mother" as requested by Mrs. Bryan.

The first Mass at Our Lady of Grace was celebrated on July 13, 1952 and the church was dedicated on Sunday, September 14, 1952.

At the church's 25th anniversary celebration, a new Jubilee Organ was dedicated, again in memory of Mrs. Price with Mrs. Bryan and her husband being the primary donors of funds for the new organ. Mrs. Bryan also made frequent contributions for enhancements and upgrades for the church during her active membership. She was a stickler for details, even deciding on paint colors. She also had a reserved seat near the front. Her name wasn't on the pew, but parishioners knew where she always sat and that space was always left vacant for her use.

In 1956, Mrs. Bryan contributed substantially toward building St. Thomas More Catholic Church in Chapel Hill and to Our Lady of the Mountains Catholic Chapel, in Blowing Rock near where her parents had owned a home and abundant acreage that later became a federal park. Those contributions also were in memory of her mother.

Mrs. Bryan held obvious affection for her mother, which she expressed often in conversations and written correspondence, in addition to her Catholic contributions. On Mother's Day in 1930 while living in New York after her first child was born, Mrs. Bryan penned this note to her mom: "My Precious Mother, every night I thank God for having given me you as an inspiration, companion and example to my baby. I love you with all my heart and hope there will be innumerable mother's days for me to write you."

Mrs. Bryan also made substantial gifts to both St. Benedict's Catholic Church and St. Pius 10th Catholic Church in Greensboro. She gave to the College of Notre Dame in Baltimore where he mother earned a degree in 1892 and where Mrs. Bryan was awarded an honorary degree in June 1958. When she received that honorary degree, her friend Mose Kiser in Greensboro sent her note of congratulations along with a gift certificate for a half gallon of ice cream from Guilford Dairy where he was general manager of the farmers' cooperative. Mrs. Bryan also received honorary degrees from the University of North Carolina at Greensboro and from Converse College in Spartanburg, S.C. where she attended but did not receive an earned degree.

She gave generously to Belmont Abby College in Gaston County and to Maryfield, a Catholic retirement home between Greensboro and High Point. Her giving, in fact, once helped gain her an audience with the Pope after she had written letters to high-ranking church officials explaining her contributions to the church and asking for a personal visit with the Pope during a planned trip to Italy.

In an April 20, 1962 appeal to Cardinal Cicognanni, Secretary of State at the Vatican City in Rome, Mrs. Bryan outlined many of her contributions to the Catholic Church and sought his help in gaining a personal visit with the Pope.

"In the United States," she wrote to the man she had met a decade earlier when he came to Greensboro to help dedicate Our Lady of Grace Church, "all little boys grow up with the hope that one day they might be President. At the same time, all good little girls are fascinated by the hope that when they grow up they may go to Rome and have an audience with our Holy Father. That is the fond dream of my life and is a matter that is very personal and very close to my heart."

She explained in her letter that she and her husband would be in Rome for a week a month later. "This desire to see our Holy Father is not just an idle fancy, but a spiritual experience that my husband and I have yearned for, I might say worked for, for years. I am sending you my credentials of what I have tried to do in behalf of my faith. This would indeed be a real climax to an unforgettable experience."

Her appeal worked. In May 1962, Mrs. Bryan and her husband had an audience with Pope John XXIII. She had earlier received a pontifical order *Pro Ecclesia et Pontifice* award approved by Pope Pius XII and conferred in a pontifical high mass at Belmont Abby College on November 27, 1958.

In her allegiance to her Catholic faith, Mrs. Bryan was significantly different from her husband even though he was proud of gaining the visit with the Pope. Bryan, raised as an Episcopalian, drifted from that faith and others in his adult life. He never joined the Catholic Church and seldom attended with his wife and family. He was a member of Greensboro's Holy Trinity Episcopal Church at one time, but not a regular attendee and was not a member of any church at his death. Bryan did, however, leave $100,000 to Holy Trinity in his will and did the same for First Presbyterian Church where he requested his funeral to be held because he didn't feel Holy Trinity would be large enough.

Ironically, however, a religious service in the Catholic Church may have once saved the life of Bryan and his family. It was on Christmas Eve in 1954 that Bryan agreed to attend midnight mass with his family, something he seldom did. When the family returned home in the early morning hours, they discovered the house filled with smoke. Daughter Nancy was home alone and asleep upstairs. Joe Bryan Jr. ran inside, grabbed his sleeping sister and carried her outside to safety. If the family had not been at church that night, all would likely have been asleep when the malfunctioning furnace caused the home to fill with smoke. All could have died.

The giver and the spender in the early days of the Bryan Foundation were a matter of perspective. The only officers of the foundation other than Wharton were Bryan and his wife. They made all the decisions. "Whatever we gave, we gave together," Bryan said in a 1986 interview about the early days of the Family Foundation. "The major contributions would be in both our names. That's the way Kathleen wanted it. She was the primary (source) of the money."

Although Bryan was actively involved in the foundation's donations in the early years of its existence, he always planned to bow out in favor of his children. Bryan's influence became more apparent in early 1978 when his name was added with an official name change to the Kathleen Price and Joseph M. Bryan Family Foundation. "But Joe always wanted his children to take it over," Wharton said. That happened eventually, although not necessarily the way Bryan had preferred.

As Bryan's own wealth increased and his children and grandchildren became more involved in the Family Foundation, he became more disenchanted with the changing charitable philosophies of other family members. His philanthropic interests were different from those of his children and grandchildren.

Bryan by 1984, shortly before his wife's death, began formulating a different set of priorities. He didn't necessarily object to the worthiness of the charities the family foundation was helping, but he wanted something else for his own money. In late 1984, Bryan created his own separate foundation, voluntarily resigned from the family foundation and asked that his name be removed from the official title.

"He wasn't mad or anything," said Jim Melvin, president of the Joseph M. Bryan Foundation. "But he just planned it all out and chose to resign because he knew if it carried his name while his name was on his own foundation there would be a lot of confusion. It was all part of his plan. He didn't leave much to chance."

When Bryan resigned from the original family foundation, it officially became the Kathleen Price Bryan Family Fund.

Bryan had been generous to charities, particularly educational and medical, across the state and beyond during the earlier years of his giving. But his changing focus at the time of his wife's death brought more emphasis to more local issues and venues. He wanted his own philanthropy limited to Greater Greensboro. The original family fund was far more widespread and the family member's interest much more diverse.

Furthermore, the Family Fund accepted grant applications— hundreds of them. Bryan preferred to be proactive, deciding on his own what he wanted to help, not reactive based on some formulaic application.

The Family Fund had made contributions up and down the East Coast with amounts ranging from as little as $100 to more than $280,000 to a single institution. Between the years of 1991 and 1997, the fund awarded almost 600 grants totaling more than $11.6 million to more than 440 nonprofit organizations in North Carolina alone.

Grants during that period included public interest groups, human services, education, health, arts, culture and youth. Specific grants went for a wide variety of concerns dealing with access to health care, academic enrichment, affordable housing, domestic/sexual violence, AIDS research, persons with disabilities, and preservation of natural resources. Nonprofits in 10 North Carolina counties received 70 percent of the donations.

Eleven organizations received more than $100,000 each in the decade of the 1990s with Greensboro Urban Ministry and the Center for Community Self-Help each receiving $1 million. The Fund in the summer of 1999 also contributed $1 million to help create the Julian and Ethel Clay Price Park off New Garden Road in Greensboro on land previously owned by Jefferson-Pilot Corporation. Among the last donations of 1999, the Foundation contributed to the flood relief and rebuilding effort in eastern North Carolina.

With all the good works and all the positive results from the Family Fund, however, the changing and differing philosophies of family members would bring things to a halt in the months before 2000 began. The Fund was dissolved and split into three distinctly different parts. The reason: family disagreements.

"Certainly a lot of important philanthropy has occurred from the existence of the Fund," commented long-time trustee and Greensboro businessman Lanty Smith. "A lot of worthwhile things have happened. But board members were being asked to intervene in family relationships as well as being representatives of the community. There was no overall plan for designing and directing a philosophy for the fund's philanthropy. We spent far too much time on process. What was happening was not an acceptable way for a charitable organization to be operated. Everyone knew that something had to be done, and the family worked reasonably well together to accomplish the reorganization."

Smith and former Fund board trustees William Friday of Chapel Hill and Joel Fleishman of Durham all became concerned about family friction in the late 1990s. They led the effort for the restructuring as one way of reducing or eliminating family squabbles over grant requests.

Ironically, it was the involvement of more family members that Bryan had sought that brought the Fund to a halt and caused it to be split near the end of 1999. Joe Bryan Jr. had worked to bring the third generation Bryan grandchildren into the Fund as trustees on a rotating basis in order to give them exposure to and experience with philanthropy. But with nine grandchildren with strong personal motivations toward their own favorite causes, the topic of discussions in Fund meetings became one of personalities rather than philanthropy.

Bryan daughter Nancy Faircloth was the first to become frustrated with family infighting and resigned from the Fund board, telling friends she just couldn't take the family bickering. She has since created her own philanthropic organization, called the Stewards Fund. Joe Bryan Jr. also once left a Fund leadership post, later to return for awhile, but he has also now created a separate Fund.

The beginning of the end came in August 1998 when grandchildren on the Fund board fired executive director William Massey, an experienced and respected executive who now works with a national nonprofit organization in New York. After Massey's dismissal, the Fund was run on a part-time basis by Bryan's grandson and namesake, Joseph McKinley Bryan Taylor of Charlotte.

"It was really unfair and shabby the way Massey was treated," said Fund trustee Rebecca Anderson of Asheville who is now engaged professionally in nonprofit work in western North Carolina through an innovative program started by Massey and the original Bryan Foundation. "There were just so many varied interests among the third generation, everything was fragmented and splintered. There was no agreement on anything."

Massey received a severance package at the insistence of non-family trustees with the support of Bryan Jr.

Anderson was initially opposed to splitting the fund into three parts because it greatly reduced the potential influence and impact of charitable giving. But, she said, she reluctantly agreed out of necessity. "It grieved me to do it," she said. "I wanted (the original Fund) to have a seat at the table with other major philanthropic organizations like Reynolds and Babcock. That can't happen with the split, but it was the only way to continue. What we had wasn't working."

Former Fund trustees said that family squabbling in meetings became increasingly more divisive. One called the board meetings a cottage industry of intolerance and distrust. Another said disagreements among Bryan grandchildren over where to contribute turned into little less than family brawls. "It was eclectic philanthropy," said another.

Part of the problem, past trustees said, was that third generation members didn't understand the realities of the business or working world because many of them had not held steady jobs for long, if ever. "There often wasn't much of a touch of reality," trustee Anderson said.

The one Bryan grandchild who opted not to participate in the family feuding is Ann Faircloth. She declined to serve with other grandchildren on the board and has become head of her mother's own fund.

During the course of 1999, efforts of non-family trustees gradually brought about the restructuring of the Fund. Raleigh lawyer Walter Rogers, a member of the legal firm once presided over by North Carolina U.S. Senator Willis Smith, drafted new documents.

"There were some difficulties among family trustees with philanthropy," Rogers said. "Other trustees decided the existing structure wasn't a success and a new way would be better. All the Fund's assets will remain in philanthropic work, but will be distributed differently."

Rogers concurred that the differences in philosophy cost Massey his job as the lone Foundation executive. "Anytime you have these differing philosophies it will inevitably lead to differences with the executive director.

The dissolution of the Kathleen Price Bryan Family Fund came on a two to one vote among Bryan's three children. Nancy Faircloth and Joe Bryan Jr. supported the restructuring. Kay Edwards, the mother of the eight Bryan grandchildren who had served as trustees, opposed the change.

The assets of the Fund — some $60 million-plus when it was split at the end of 1999 — were split equally among the three Bryan children. This removes, at least directly, all the grandchildren from any involvement in money distribution for two-thirds of the assets.

Faircloth and Bryan Jr. will each have a nonprofit foundation to distribute their share of the Family Fund. Edwards created a charitable trust with her share, which she and her children will distribute.

"I regard this as an evolution, a step in the right direction," lawyer Rogers said. "It is really not that unusual in the world of family philanthropy. There is a store of wealth being preserved. The funds are essentially a public trust. The family is still involved, but the changes mean that there can be more time spent on philanthropy and less on negotiating among family members. All family members will no longer have to agree. It is a fact that Mrs. Edwards children will not be involved at all in two-thirds of the assets."

Nancy Faircloth has rolled her share of the Fund assets into her existing Stewards Fund. Articles of incorporation for the Stewards Fund, created in 1985, specify its primary purpose is to serve public interests in the areas of "traditional Western values and to emphasize the benefits to society accruing from such values."

The Stewards Fund, with offices in Chapel Hill and now run by Ann Faircloth as president, adopted its name from the Biblical philosophy of stewardship. "We all ought to be good stewards of what we have," Ann Faircloth said of the fund's philosophy. The Stewards Fund distributes money in Wake, Durham and Orange counties for basic needs of food, clothing, shelter and education. Fund directors decide on donations and do not accept unsolicited requests.

Bryan Jr. has created his fund with a unique name: "The Anonymous Fund." Purposes, according to fund documents, are to engage in charitable, scientific, literary, religious or educational activities.

The charitable trust created by Edwards is not required to file documents with the N. C. Secretary of State office outlining its purposes, but the name chosen is revealing of Mrs. Edwards' views on family. She picked the name Julian Price Family fund, focusing attention on her grandfather rather than her father. "That is where the money came from," Mrs. Edwards said. "It came from my grandparents, the Prices, not my parents.

Mrs. Edwards has not disclosed the specific purpose for or focus of her trust, but she said her children would continue to be involved in distribution decisions. "With my children of varying ages and in varying locations with varied interests, I think it will be better to give them some freedom in deciding where the donations will go," she said. "They will have a part in using the resources to foster their wishes."

While the exact future of the newly divided Bryan Fund is unclear with the separate entities, there is no doubt on the role of the Joseph M. Bryan Foundation's focus. It will be on Greater Greensboro, with everything specifically spelled out. That's the way the patriarch planned it, leaving nothing to chance or future personality conflicts. Bryan had, in fact, predicted the divisiveness among his family members, and he was determined to prevent any semblance of such unpleasantness with the Foundation that bears his name. In handpicking his Foundation trustees, he chose those who understood and accepted his philosophy of giving.

That was the Joe Bryan way. And that way has already led to another level of philanthropy that will continue to grow. It is a way that would have made Bryan proud and pleased.

18

MEDICAL MIRACLE IN THE MAKING

J oseph McKinley Bryan was clearly at a loss. He had overcome many obstacles in his life, but nothing like this.
As a child, he had endured desertion by his father and confinement of his mother into a psychiatric hospital. He survived a
war in Europe and armed bandits in Haiti. He struggled against
heavy odds as a young cotton broker in New York City during the
Great Depression. He had to prove himself capable over and over
as a Jefferson Standard Life Insurance executive among colleagues
who were filled with distrust because he was not one of them, a
native Southerner. Then with little to go on but gut instinct, he
started a television industry in this state from scratch.

He had done all that successfully. But now he felt, for the first
time, helplessness in fighting against an enemy he couldn't see or
touch. Nothing could compare to watching his devoted wife Kathleen sink slowly but surely into the depths of a fantasy world she
could not understand and he could not conquer. An insipid disease,
with no known cause or cure, was devouring her.

His resources and clout, always ample until now, couldn't solve
the problem. Mrs. Bryan gradually worsened. She was there in

body, but her mind and spirit were slipping away. She was being transformed before his very eyes from a vibrant personality who loved to communicate with hundreds of friends into an empty shell of a person who could hardly complete a sentence or remember the difference between lipstick and mascara or how to dress herself. She was becoming a person he could hardly recognize. It was as humiliating to her as it was frustrating to him. It was, he said, devastating.

Her downhill slide began gradually in the middle 1970s and lasted for another 10 years, becoming progressively worse. Kathleen Bryan was, tragically, becoming Greensboro's best-known victim of the little-known yet dreaded Alzheimer's Disease, a cruel killer with no known cure and, at the time, no accurate diagnosis.

At the beginning of the 21st Century, Alzheimer's — the loss of mental capacities among older people — was being recognized as one of the country's most dreaded diseases, but only 30 years earlier hardly anyone, including some of the country's leading physicians, was able to diagnose it.

Bryan sought the best treatment he could find among doctors in Greensboro, but nothing helped. Local doctors were as baffled as Bryan was. He tried the best and brightest at Duke Medical Center, only initially to come up with more questions than answers. First they said it was a heart problem, but that proved false. Then they said it was depression, but that was later discounted.

Then she was, needlessly as well as tragically it turned out, given physical shock treatments by a psychiatrist at Duke, a move that proved to be so debilitating that Bryan was brought to tears as he explained his regret for having agreed to putting his wife through that treatment.

"The word Alzheimer's never came up," Bryan said of the first series of treatments. "I didn't know what that disease was at the time and (Duke doctors) never did diagnose Kathleen's problem as Alzheimer's. But over a period of years, she went through a complete change in personality and her ability to remember. She had a nervousness that had not previously existed. Her condition gradually worsened. She was having an increasingly difficult time keeping things straight.

"It was a matter of great concern to me. The medical profession was floundering. I did some personal research on what was happening (to her) and I came to the conclusion that Alzheimer's was what was happening. I can't say I was responsible for diagnosing it, but from all I read, I had determined in my own mind that was what she had. I was just as sure, maybe more sure, than the doctors."

Bryan was subsequently proved right. His own independent research was right in step, actually a step ahead, of the Duke medical team. As Mrs. Bryan's condition continued to deteriorate, Bryan kept abreast of all he could find to read about the disease that even the best doctors were unable to explain.

Bryan and a team of private medical helpers cared for Mrs. Bryan for almost a decade in the couple's home that became, at times, a hospital ward. He was determined to provide the care at home rather than a nursing home. It was the depressing recollection of his one visit to his mother in a mental institution in New Jersey, he hinted without ever actually saying, that convinced him never to allow his wife to enter such a facility.

Mrs. Bryan's heart stopped on August 6, 1984, years after her mind slipped into a vegetative state. Bryan made his wife's final months and years as comfortable as possible, but he couldn't save her.

He made a commitment in her memory, however, to trying to save others from her dreaded plight.

Within a year of Mrs. Bryan's agonizing death, Bryan made the first of many steps leading to what he hoped — and others still hope — will be a medical miracle. That miracle would be a cure for Alzheimer's Disease with Duke Medical School researchers helping lead the way.

Alzheimer's Disease was first described in 1906 by German psychiatrist Dr. Alois Alzheimer and is named for him and his initial studies. As dreadful as the disease was when first identified, it wasn't taken seriously for more than half a century because it was a disease of old age. People were dying of other factors before they reached that demented stage of life.

Partly because of early deaths from other causes, when it comes to successful Alzheimer's treatment, the disease is still in its infancy. A cure could be generations away, at best, based on current research. At the end of the 20th Century, the nation's most famous Alzheimer's victim was former president Ronald Reagan whose mind had turned into a tangle of disjointed parts, none connected in the right order. Other well-known Alzheimer's victims have been Norman Rockwell and Rita Hayworth.

If and when a cure for Alzheimer's Disease comes, it may well be as a result of research on both human brains at the Joseph and Kathleen Bryan Neurobiology Research Center on the Duke University campus. Nowhere in the country has more medical research produced any better results than at Duke in terms of correct diagnosis of the cause. Duke research has determined that Alzheimer's is a genetic disease, a cause many earlier researchers discounted. It was Joe Bryan who first helped make the Duke research possible after suffering along with his wife Kathleen through her demise and death.

The Bryan Center at Duke is truly a symbol of hope for a cure among doctors there and elsewhere. Without Bryan's enthusiastic support, even his encouragement to speed the process along, the research facility likely would not exist and work on a cure would not be so advanced.

"Joe Bryan is my prototype of the ideal person," said Dr. Zovan Khachatorian, a renowned Alzheimer's researcher, former director of the National Institute of Health and current director of the Ronald and Nancy Reagan Alzheimer's Research Institute. "I was amazed at how sharp intellectually he was about the disease. Without him, I seriously doubt that the Duke Research would ever have been developed. What he did has helped to totally revolutionize the research field. He put Alzheimer's on the national scene. His gift to Duke was both timely and beneficial. Without him, we would not be nearly as far along in progress with research. He laid the foundation for being able to explain the disease. Duke is as far advanced as any research center. It is one of a kind in the country. Joe Bryan was the one who initially made that possible."

Bryan initially donated $250,000 to Duke for creation of a "brain bank" that allows medical researchers to study brains of Alzheimer's patients immediately after death. The quicker the research on brains, the better the diagnosis and the more accurate the conclusions. That brain bank paid for by Bryan was the first in the country when it was established in 1985.

Bryan then contributed $10 million as seed money to construct the neurological research facility that bears the Bryan names. The brain bank, part of the neurological center, and the medical research at the Bryan facility have moved diagnosis to new levels.

When asked for help on brain research by Duke representatives, Bryan readily agreed, but on his own terms, not theirs. "It was first suggested that I make a grant in my will for this purpose," Bryan said of the initial request. "But I knew if it was needed right away. It was needed in a hurry. I just thought it ought to be done much sooner than in my will. I wanted to see it being done while I was still alive, if I possibly could."

Alzheimer's is a progressive, degenerative disease of the brain and is the most common form of dementia, although not the only form. In January 2000, some four million people in the United States suffered from the disease, but almost 20 million family members were affected by persons with the disease because it eats away at caregivers as it does patients. By the middle of the 21st Century, some 14 million people will become victims unless science finds a way to prevent, postpone or cure the disease.

In Alzheimer's patients, the brain gradually deteriorates into a mass of tangles, not unlike the unraveling of a worn carpet. Brain fibers become frayed and entangled like the fabrics of a worn rug.

Victims of the disease suffer from memory loss, have difficulty performing familiar tasks, lose motor skills controlling speech and language, encounter rapid mood and emotional changes and lose initiative for normal daily and social obligations.

Alzheimer's is a disease only of older persons, retirement age and up. While few people under 65 have the disease, 50 percent of those 85 or older have symptoms. That means it is a disease that will only get worse and become more expensive and devastating as people live longer. The disease process can begin as much as 20 years before the symptoms appear and most Alzheimer's patients live from eight to 20 years with brains unable to function, three to four times as long as most victims of heart disease, cancer, or AIDS. The cost of treatment will become staggering.

The federal government spent an estimated $400 million on Alzheimer's research in 1999. While that may seem huge, by comparison the government spent more than three times that amount on AIDS research in the last year of the century. Regrettably, Alzheimer's doesn't yet have the political connections of some other diseases, thus research and funding lags behind despite the worsening need for treatment and cure.

The average lifetime cost of treating and caring for an Alzheimer's patient at the end of the 20th Century was $174,000. The total annual cost of treating Alzheimer's patients at the same period was $100 billion, making it the third most costly disease behind heart disease and cancer.

Bryan's gifts for medical research at Duke came from his heart because of the lingering suffering of his late wife, but they didn't come without difficulty because of the original misdiagnosis of Mrs. Bryan's illness as depression.

ADDING VALUE: The Joseph M. Bryan Story

"My first meeting with Mr. Bryan was not a pleasant experience," said Bucky Waters, Vice Chancellor of the Duke Medical Center and former Duke basketball coach. "In that first meeting, he scolded me because he was angry that his expectations of Duke had not been met with the incorrect diagnosis of his wife. He shook his finger at me, but it was heartfelt and he was hurt that Duke hadn't done what he expected. He had that gruff exterior, and with those steely eyes and big mustache he could really buffalo you. But that was just a façade. Underneath he was a wonderful, soft and caring person."

Bryan was upset that Duke had mistaken his wife's illness for something it wasn't. He was even more upset at himself, he said later, that he had allowed the shock treatments. "A good deal of the initial treatment seemed to be just drugs that would make her more docile, keep her sleeping and not aware of anything that was going on. I was looking for something that would help," Bryan said a decade after the treatments that failed. "I was, of course, a part of the shock treatments by agreeing to that because I was told it would help. But as I look back, it now seems pretty evident and obvious that those treatments were a very undesirable thing. I wish I hadn't allowed it."

The shock treatments to Mrs. Bryan were requested and administered by Dr. Bernard Bressler, a Duke psychiatrist, who would later be fired after being accused of criminal misconduct against some younger female patients. Dr. Bressler later moved to Virginia where he continued his medical practice. His son later joined the Duke medical faculty.

Those treatments, all members of the Bryan family familiar with the results agree, effectively robbed Mrs. Bryan of most of her remaining mental faculties. She became increasingly more childlike and emotionally unstable following the Bressler experiments. It was treatment that Bryan family members insist was unneeded at best, inhumane at worst. The only outcome was added misery to both the patient and her family.

Bryan's disappointment with Duke's initial treatment of his wife lingered for awhile, but it didn't last. His hurt was with the doctors who had misdiagnosed her illness, not the institution itself. He maintained his faith in the other leaders there. It was, in fact, a speech by legendary Duke football coach Wallace Wade that convinced Bryan many years earlier that Duke was something special and offered students and the state a quality of education that Bryan had never been able to get for himself as a child.

"I was quite impressed with that speech (by Wade)," Bryan said of his earliest recollections of Duke after he came to North Carolina. "He convinced me that Duke was not only interested in football, but in developing young people. I thought that was great. I developed a respect for the institution."

By the time Bryan encountered his difficulties with the Duke medical staff, he had already shown his generosity to the university through his $4 million gift to start the student center on campus. His daughter Nancy had served on the Duke trustee board, two of his granddaughters had been students there and his friendship with Duke President Terry Sanford, dating back almost three decades, had all served to foster the relationship.

But it was really a 20-minute conversation on Nov. 18, 1984 between Bryan and a Duke neurologist that unlocked the door for what would lie ahead for both Bryan and the Duke medical team dealing with Alzheimer's research. That brief conversation took place a mere three months after Mrs. Bryan's death. The timing was fortuitous; it was the eve of the Bryan's 57th wedding anniversary. It turned out to be an event that would forever change the way Alzheimer's research is done and forever alter the lives of thousands.

"It was a 20-minute appointment that changed medical research and essentially changed my life," said Dr. Allen Roses. And it changed a lot of other lives, too. But it almost didn't happen.

Duke Medical Center at the time, like most other medical centers across the country, had never done a lot of research into the causes and effects of Alzheimer's Disease. The National Institute of Aging was searching for biological causes of the disease and sought medical centers to apply for federal grants to foster research. Duke applied for one of five grants to be given. Duke's application didn't make the cut. It was judged to be the sixth best of 29 submitted, but only five were accepted.

To get the process started, Duke Medical dean Dr. William Anlyan had asked a little-known genetics researcher named Allen Roses to put together the request for funds. "I knew a little something about Alzheimer's, but it certainly wasn't my area of specialty," Roses acknowledged. "I also knew the application process was something of a (good old boys) club and I wasn't a member of the club. Dr. Anlyan didn't seem to be impressed with my protests and asked me to apply anyway."

Roses went against the political winds and prior medical research in his application. He set out to show that Alzheimer's was tied to genetic factors and susceptibility may well be hereditary. He explained how Duke would propose to conduct rapid autopsies of Alzheimer's patients' brains as one way of showing the genetic ties to the disease. That not only went against the grain of most previous research, but Duke was proposing to attempt rapid-fire autopsies without any facilities, equipment or personnel to do the work.

But the NIA staff was intrigued with the Roses proposal partly because it stood out as different from all the others. The NIA staff felt the plan that Roses described was "scientifically sound", but rejected it on the belief that Roses wouldn't be able to conduct rapid autopsies as he claimed. After all, no one in the entire country had ever done what he was proposing. But Roses was asked to rework his application — to make it more realistic and less fanciful — and submit it again.

"I talked with Dr. Anlyan about it," Roses said. "And he said, well

299

you know Mr. Bryan's wife just died of Alzheimer's Disease. Why don't you just go over and see if he would be interested in helping us get the ability to do the rapid autopsies during this year, so that when they (NIA) come back and say you can't do them, you might already have them done. That's how it all began."

Roses had never met Bryan and knew him only by reputation as a person who had helped Duke in the past. But he scheduled a first meeting with the assistance of then Duke staff member John Thomas. It was a meeting different from any he had ever had.

"He wasn't rude, but he was very direct," Roses said. "He sat down and listened to me for a while."

"What's your theory on Alzheimer's?" Bryan asked as his first question.

"I think it is genetic. We have a program that we want to start to prove my theory," Roses replied. Bryan stopped Roses and pulled out a copy of *Scientific American* magazine from his desk.

"There's a story here on Alzheimer's," Bryan said, "and it doesn't say anything about genetics." He proceeded to list other points in the story that differed from Roses' point of view.

"You asked me what I thought, not what everybody else thinks," Roses said with the same directness that Bryan had challenged him. "And I think it is genetic." Bryan just looked at Roses for a few seconds. "He sort of cocked his head back and surprised me with his next words."

"You know, I agree with you," Bryan said. "I also think it's genetic."

Bryan then talked briefly about the death of his wife and mentioned others in his wife's family who had similar symptoms.

"So, what do you want," Bryan asked.

"I told him," Roses said. "He wasn't gruff, but he was certainly challenging. I just said we have a study that is scientifically sound, but the only way of getting the materials we need, which are brains of dead people, we need to do what has never been done before. I told him we wanted to set up a brain bank to allow rapid autopsies. He asked how much that would cost to pull it off. I showed him a budget of $246,871. He looked at the figures, turned to his secretary and asked her to cut me a check for $250,000."

Roses pointed out to Bryan that the check was for almost $5,000 more than he had asked.

"I'm sure if there is anything left over, you'll make good use of it," Bryan replied.

The meeting consumed no more than 20 minutes. "That is literally how it all got started," Roses said. "That's how quickly he was willing to help because of what had happened with his wife. He was determined that what we were attempting would help others."

Roses immediately began shopping for brains of Alzheimer's patients, visiting nursing homes and interviewing family members of suffering victims and explaining what he wanted to do. By getting brains immediately after death, he explained to patients' family members, he was certain that research could be reliably enhanced in determining genetic ties, maybe even leading to cure.

Once Duke had the Bryan gift in hand, and the first family's permission was granted for the initial rapid autopsy, the dead person's brain was cut open within 17 minutes of death, in March 1985, even though research facilities were primitive. The second was done within 24 minutes. Ironically, the first brain examination was performed on a patient who was a close friend of the Bryans, although neither Roses nor Bryan knew it at the time.

As he scoured nursing homes near Durham in search of brains for instant study, Roses met Mrs. Margaret Lester whose mother was near death in Hill Haven Nursing Home from Alzheimer's and other complications. Roses explained his mission and Mrs. Lester agreed to donate her mother's brain immediately after death.

Lester's mother was Mrs. May Carmichael, widow of Joe and Kathleen Bryan's long-time friend Billy Carmichael. The Bryans and Carmichaels had been friends since the 1920s in New York and

301

it was Billy Carmichael who was the key to securing the Bryans support for creation of public television in this state and establishment of a women's studies program at UNCG.

"I didn't know of the family connections at the time," Roses said. "It just happened that way. But it was Mrs. Carmichael's brain that we tested first in our new experiment. Mrs. Lester, of course, knew of the family ties to the Bryans, but she didn't mention it to Roses. She was, in fact, wrestling within her own family to get approval for the brain experiment.

"It just seemed to me to be the obvious thing to do," Mrs. Lester said of the Roses request. "It was inconceivable not to allow it. It was something that might help others and it seemed both sweet and poignant because of the friendship between my mother and Mrs. Bryan. It was just fate that mother and Mrs. Bryan would end up with the same illness and die within such a short time of each other." Mrs. Carmichael died at age 85 on March 5, 1985, less than six months after Mrs. Bryan's death.

Lester's brother, Billy Carmichael Jr., felt differently about the brain probe on his mother. "He wasn't receptive. He didn't like the idea," Mrs. Lester explained. "He and I argued one day for more than hour about it. He finally said for me to just do what I wanted to do. I am glad I did it. I am glad we could help." The younger Carmichael would die four years later of similar symptoms.

The Bryan gift and the first few autopsies convinced NIA officials that Roses could walk the walk as well as talk the talk. When the next round of research grants were approved, Duke was head of the pact, receiving the first one for $5 million for research on rapid autopsies and genetic studies on brains. The Kathleen Bryan Brain Bank was created, but Joe Bryan wasn't satisfied.

As was his custom, Bryan took an active part in seeing all his donations were put to good use. He insisted on seeing the research facilities. "He often came see what we were doing," Roses said. "He was disappointed in the facilities. We were in a temporary building that I had been using for various kinds of research for many years. He looked around and saw how crowded and how substandard things were with no room for growth."

"Look, I'm a businessman," Bryan told Roses. "I made an investment in you and from my way of looking at it, it looks like a 20-fold payback. But you need a place to be able to bring this to the next level."

Roses said Bryan voluntarily offered to provide that space. "He wanted to build research space that would house the Alzheimer's Disease Research Center. It was amazing. He was 89 years old at the time. He knew we had received the federal grant, but he wasn't satisfied with that."

Bryan, dealing with Roses, Dr. Anlyan and other Duke officials, made the university an offer in the fall of 1985. He would contribute $10 million toward creation of a new medical research facility on campus, with one stipulation. One entire floor, Bryan insisted, must be reserved exclusively for Alzheimer's genetic research. Duke, of course, readily agreed to that ground rule. But that would later become a point of serious contention because Duke underestimated Bryan's dogged determination as well as his longevity. In short, Duke made promises it had not intended to fulfill.

"Well, it's hard to be loyal to Duke and not tell the truth about what happened," said Roses who has since left Duke for genetic research at nearby Glaxo-Wellcome pharmaceutical headquarters in the Research Triangle Park. "But the truth is that he was a man of 89 when he asked for that commitment for one floor for genetic research. There was a feeling (at Duke) that it would take four or five years to complete the building and, frankly, by that time Mr. Bryan would be gone and Duke could end up doing what it wanted to do. When it became clear that he was still very robust at age 93, and he was still insisting on one floor for genetic research, that became a problem.

"Mr. Bryan learned that Duke cut down the space for genetic

research. He fought that. He still owed $5 million on his $10 million pledge and he refused to pay until Duke fulfilled its promise. He had given his word and he wanted them to honor theirs. What Duke ended up doing was allowing part of that floor to be used by people who would be collaborative and involved in Alzheimer's research.

"Mr. Bryan paid his pledge, but what happened really did spoil his enthusiasm for what he had done, " Roses explained. "He had talked about doing a lot more for Duke, something like another $15 million in his will. But it never came about because he was so upset about what happened with the space allocation. He had gone from that $250,000 to $10 million and was going to do a lot more. But Duke just blew it. It's a pattern there on campus that they always think they know what's best. The bottom line is that this haughty action on the part of Duke probably cost the university another $14 million or $15 million."

Roses still maintains ties with Duke Alzheimer's research in his current post with Glaxo. Most of the original Roses colleagues at Duke are still there, one of them Roses' second wife, Dr. Ann Saunders. Roses' current research projects at Glaxo deal with genetics and contact is frequent between the campus labs and Roses' Glaxo research.

The Alzheimer's Research facility, named for Joe and Kathleen Bryan, cost some $26 million. Bryan's gift of $10 million was enough to get it named for the couple. Construction costs were higher than projections because of soil conditions that added to materials and time. The Bryan Center is recognized as being on the cutting edge of brain disease research. Had Duke not misled Bryan on allocated space, there may well have been more resources from his estate for even better research.

The brain bank at the research facility contained some 900 human brains at the end of the 20th Century. Autopsies on almost 200 of these brains were performed within hours, or less, of death. A team of researchers works five days a week examining brains of

Alzheimer's victims and conducting experiments on brains of mice in search of clues to causes, treatments and possible cures for the disease. Without Bryan's initial gift none of this might exist because it was his gift that allowed Dr. Roses to prove to the NIA that instant autopsies could be done successfully.

The brains of Alzheimer's patients gradually deteriorate, leaving essentially dead tangles and plaques with gaping holes where viable brain cells once functioned. Alzheimer-infested brains shrink and lose many of the components needed for normal function. The staff of the brain bank at the Bryan Center at Duke works to understand the plaques and tangles in brains as they cut and probe tiny particles as one means of determining a cause in search of a cure, including experiments on mice. They also work on research involving family members of Alzheimer patients in an effort to more accurately link genetic possibilities of the disease.

In memory of the Bryans, the Duke Medical Center each year holds an Alzheimer's Disease Conference to report on progress of research and to allow families of patients to discuss the dreaded disease and its impact on their lives. The conference is held in February, either on or close to Bryan's birthday.

Duke researchers were the first in the country to determine the connection between Alzheimer's and the APEO gene through work conducted by Dr. Peggy Vance with assistance from Dr. W. J. Strittmatter. Their team studies on the linkage of chromosome 19 and the APOE gene combination have provided a medical breakthrough that, as with Roses original studies on genetics, have given hope for successful treatment. Without the Duke studies, the connection between the gene tangles and chromosome 19 might well have been years away.

"It was basically this genetic epidemiology that brought this forward," Dr. Roses said of his former colleagues. We had been looking at other areas until Dr. Vance hit on this theory. APOE is still the only susceptibility polymorphic that has been identified for a major neurologic or other general medical illness. We know these genes exist now. The whole concept in genetics is APOE with Alzheimer's. Peggy Vance is due a lot of credit for the progress being made."

All humans have the presence of the APOE gene, one dose from the father and one from the mother. There are three forms of the gene: APOE 2,3, and 4. If a person has two doses of APOE4, the chances of contracting Alzheimer's are greatly increased. The higher the doses of the 4 gene, the earlier Alzheimer's is likely to occur. "We know this because of research conducted at Duke," Dr. Roses explained. "It was discovered there first through genetic research."

Aside from the gene connections, one other cause of Alzheimer's, based on research at Duke and other sites, is head injury. Persons with blows to the head are generally more susceptible to the disease.

Drugs have already been developed partly through Duke studies that initial research show could help postpone and delay the onset of Alzheimer's although a cure is far into the future.

Aricept is the most recognizable drug now prescribed for Alzheimer's patients. Marketed by a pharmaceutical company, the drug has fewer side effects than some other drugs. It doesn't prevent the disease, but it seems to slow the progression of brain deterioration. Vitamin E also has been shown to help slow brain cell death, as has estrogen.

In announcing the original Bryan grant, Dr. Roses enthusiastically overestimated the speed of successful treatment and cures. "This is the beginning of the end of Alzheimer's," Roses said. He now concedes that was overly optimistic, but he blames his exuberance on hope, not hyperbole.

"Allen Roses is a smart geneticist, but in his enthusiasm he greatly oversold the simplicity of finding a cure," commented Duke genetic researcher Dr. Don Schmechel, director of the Bryan Center. "We are still five to 15 years away from a cure. There are some 25 research centers in the country and they're very competitive in testing. Certainly Duke is one of the best and was given great momentum by Mr. Bryan's gift that has allowed us to pull people together. He has allowed us to be ahead of most other research centers. We now have names and faces on these genes and have some promising new theories. We're not there, but we're making good progress. If all this eventually works, it will put us out of business—thank God."

Dr. Schmechel's research colleague Dr. Kathleen Welsh-Bohmer, associate director at the Bryan Center, echoes that belief. "The instant autopsies allow us to be a leader in the knowledge in early changes in the brain," she said. "We can now work with research centers all over the world. We don't have a cure. There is no magic bullet, but good things are happening here through our research."

Duke's brain bank tissues, because of the volume and accuracy of past research there, are now used by other research centers in search of clues and cures.

Because of the specific interest in genetic ties to the tangles in Alzheimer's brains, researchers at Duke decided to conduct tests on both Bryan's immediate and extended families. There is a history of brain dysfunction on both sides of the Bryan family.

Bryan's mother suffered from mental illness for more than 50 years in an institution in New Jersey. His wife had Alzheimer's. Mrs. Bryan's brother Ralph Price had symptoms of the disease. The mother- in-law of Bryan's daughter Kay had symptoms.

Roses, with Bryan's support, secured blood samples of all members of the Bryan family and some from family members through marriage in an effort to determine possible links among family members and the likelihood of the onset of the disease. The results of the tests are confidential.

"All this was very troubling to him," Dr. Roses said. "He was concerned about his own family. He had received one report from Moses Cone Hospital in Greensboro saying that maybe his wife didn't have Alzheimer's. He found that troubling and asked me to look into it. I did that and what I found was that when they (Moses Cone doctors) put pieces of her brain on a block and cut it, they looked at the wrong parts. We cut the brain again, looked at the parts the right way and it was very clear she had Alzheimer's Disease. But it was a hard diagnosis. A lot of things got missed, particularly in neurological diseases where you don't have the expertise. Joe was very knowledgeable. He said, 'she had plaques and tangles in her brain'. He had seen the autopsy reports. He said he wanted to see a picture of plaques and tangles. I showed him a picture. Then he said he would like to see a picture of what Mrs. Bryan's brain looked like. I said this is your wife's brain. He was looking at her brain."

Bryan grew teary eyed when he realized it was his wife's brain he was viewing. "But he told me he felt relieved to know that we were on the right track after all those years of caring for her. Then he did something that I think was kind of remarkable. That same day he started talking with me about me and about other things. I think that was his beginning of an interchange at a different level with me rather than my just being a scientist and a supplicant for money versus someone who had done him a favor. I came to know the kinds of pressures on him with his own family, with friends and people he could trust and not trust. That discussion about his wife led to our becoming much closer. I think he picked out very, very few people he felt he could trust. There was just some sort of barrier due to the relationships he had with his children."

Bryan and Roses became close friends after that. Bryan, in fact, became a mentor of sorts. "He not only changed my professional life with the grant for research, but he changed my personal life, my entire life," Roses said. "Without him, I doubt I would even be alive." While working with Bryan, Roses was going through a nasty divorce, suffered a heart attack and underwent triple bypass surgery.

"When I got home from the hospital, I got a call from Mr. Bryan, basically castigating me for feeling so sorry for myself," Roses explained. "He told me I had a lot yet to do, that I didn't die and that I ought to just stop whining and get going with my life again. If it had not been for him and the Alzheimer's research, I don't think I would have had the drive to pull through. I think Joe Bryan saved my life."

Bryan and Roses personally had a lot in common outside Duke and Alzheimer's research. Both were deserted by their fathers when they were young, their mothers were both ill for a long time and both had to struggle to make a start in life. Both were also very direct, saying what was on their minds. Both were also great devotees of fine wines.

Roses acknowledged that at their dinners together, Bryan would open up bottles of fine wine, take a few sips and leave the rest for Roses to consume as the evening wore on.

Bryan's involvement with Duke has also brought forth an international connection. In Perth, Australia a major Alzheimer's research facility exists in the name of Joseph and Kathleen Bryan Laboratory. The new Perth lab opened in 1990 and works directly with Duke researchers on gene therapy. Bryan didn't contribute to the cost of the Australia facility, but Roses attached his name anyway. "He had always received credit and recognition for the things he paid for, so I just felt it would be appropriate to honor him for something dear to his heart that he didn't pay for," Roses said.

That research facility is one of two projects with Bryan's name attached that he didn't put any personal resources into. The other is a city street in his adopted hometown. Bryan Boulevard, stretching for 4.4 miles from near downtown Greensboro westward toward the regional airport where it becomes Airport Parkway, was named in honor of Bryan before it was opened in December 1996.

The Greensboro City Council considered renaming existing Wendover that loops around the city for Bryan at part of his 90th birthday celebration in 1986, but rejected that suggestion because of the cost of replacing signage. Instead, the council at the recommendation of then City Manager Tom Osborne unanimously agreed to name the new extension of existing Benjamin Parkway for Bryan.

Bryan's gifts to Duke have not been limited to Alzheimer's research or the student center. He also played a significant role in the advancement of eye research there and, in fact, presented Duke officials with some interesting challenges as he insisted the staff there not slack off on efforts to improve care and treatment for eye patients.

Bryan and Greensboro textile executive Allen Mebane have been two of the largest donors to eye research at Duke. It was in the spring of 1982, two years before Mrs. Bryan's death but after her initial treatment at Duke, that Bryan underwent treatment for glaucoma and made his first donation to Duke for sight research. Three years later, in July 1985, during a discussion with his own doctor at Duke, Dr. Bruce Shields, Bryan learned of the existence of a new machine in Germany — an optic nerve head analyzer — that greatly enhanced the way glaucoma patients could be treated. Believing that the machine would help patients, Bryan offered to purchase it with a donation of $110,000. He also made annual donations to the Duke Eye Center in subsequent years.

In early 1988, Bryan made a $100,000 challenge gift to the Eye Center with the stipulation that the Center staff would match it by the date of the scheduled groundbreaking for the new building. That day came on August 22, 1988, but the match was still $35,000 short.

"As the ceremony for the groundbreaking was about to begin, I was handed a message on a napkin to call Mr. Bryan," Eye Center director Sandy Scarlett said. "Well, you just did not fail to return his calls even under those circumstances. I phoned him and he wanted to know if we had met his challenge gift. I told him we were $35,000 short and he ordered me to raise that amount immediately or he wouldn't pay his pledge. I told him we couldn't do that because we were in the middle of the ceremony. He said he didn't care, but just to do it. I was scared not to and set a money-raising record that morning. I raised $35,000 in 15 minutes that day from the people participating in the ceremony, just to satisfy him. That's what he wanted. He knew it could be done. That's the way he was. He loved challenges. When we got that money raised from people who were there that day I ran down the hall and called to tell him. He could not have been happier. He said he knew it could be done if we worked at it. It would not have happened without his insistence and he was smart enough to know that.

"He paid his pledge right away. He has also given a lot of other money to the Eye Center. He was always willing to help provide resources knowing it would help future generations. He never demanded recognition, but he allowed us to recognize him, saying he hoped his actions would motivate others to give as well. He did motivate others and set an example. His money was wonderful, but his advice was even more important. He shared with us a perspective that we didn't have on things about the Eye Center. He was a special friend to a lot of people at Duke and to me. He was demanding of us, but he also was patient and kind. He had a gruff exterior, but he had a warm, fuzzy heart underneath."

Scarlett recalled one humorous event with Bryan when she was meeting with him in his office in Greensboro to discuss his offer to purchase the glaucoma machine. He had a question she couldn't answer and she offered to use her phone credit card to call Duke to get the answer. Bryan shrugged off her offer.

"If I can afford to buy the machine, I can damn well afford to pay for the phone call," he responded with a smile. She made the call on his nickel.

Bryan's gifts to Duke for Alzheimer's research resulted in what, for him at least, was one unplanned and somewhat unexpected friendship. It was through Duke that Bryan became a good friend with syndicated newspaper advice columnist Eppie Lederer, better known as Ann Landers. It was a friendship that blossomed and

311

Joseph M. Bryan Sr. and his one-time friend, newspaper advice columnist Eppie Lederer, better known as Ann Landers. Bryan and Landers, obviously fond of each other, carried on an affectionate letter-writing relationship for years after they met at Duke University.

flourished before turning sour. Bryan met Lederer through his Duke Medical School friend Dr. William Anlyan.

Bryan and Landers were obviously quite fond of each other as the letters in his personal papers can attest. He kept all her letters. Several of them reveal a fondness on her part that seemed to traverse well beyond mere friendship. "I think she was after him," one friend said.

Landers had written about Alzheimer's and other diseases in her newspaper column through the years and, as a result, had become friendly with Dr. Anlyan at Duke and others on the medical staff. At the dedication of the Bryan Alzheimer's Research facility, Dr. Anlyan invited the columnist and arranged to put Landers and Bryan at the same table.

"I thought they might like each other," Anlyan said. He didn't know how right he would be. The feelings of fondness between the two seemed instantaneous. They visited by mail for years, attended subsequent events at Duke together and Bryan arranged for Landers to speak at a Jefferson convention for her usual $10,000 fee.

Each of the letters from Landers to Bryan seemed to get a bit closer to her crush on him during the middle and late 1980s after the death of Mrs. Bryan. "You only live once," Landers wrote in one letter, "but if you do it right, once is enough. If I lived in Durham, I would pester you into being my steady date. Do fly to Chicago for dinner." Bryan's return letters to Landers were endearing, but he was not quite so bold as she was in her language, some of which was subject to multiple interpretations.

In a letter about her trip aboard the QE2 in July 1987, Landers wrote that she loved to fantasize and had been thinking what that trip would have been like 20 years earlier with Bryan as her partner. "The powers that be put in the wrong time warp," Landers wrote, "and you are one of the most elegant, interesting and delightful men I have ever met." In a subsequent letter, Landers wrote that she and Bryan would have had "a grand time" on that ship together regardless of their ages. She signed her letters "love and kisses, Eppie."

Landers even complained to Bryan about what she called the "notoriously cheap" newspaper editors in Greensboro who temporarily cancelled her column when the morning and afternoon newspapers merged, keeping instead the column of her sister Dear Abby. "Check this out for me, sweetie," she wrote Bryan in her condemnation of the editors' decision.

With reference to one of Bryan's planned trips to Lyford Cay in the Bahamas after his wife's death, Landers wrote that she only wished she were going with him. "I send more love than you can imagine," she wrote, "and it's only a small portion of what I feel."

In the spring of 1988, Landers wrote suggesting that Bryan should arrange for her to make a speech in Greensboro so she could see him after he sent her a photograph of himself in a UNCG

313

brochure. "But it doesn't show your eyes," she wrote. "I confess yours is the only mustache in the entire world that I really like. I have only kissed one man in my life with a mustache, but if I were closer to you I would make it two."

The letters stopped between the two in the early 1990s. Bryan's friends in Greensboro say he grew weary of her requests for favors. Landers first agreed to talk of her friendship with Bryan for this book, but later rescinded and said she would "take a pass" on talking.

∽

"I've never met a man quite like Joe Bryan," Dr. Roses said. "The Bryan Center is one of the major contributions in the world toward Alzheimer's research. Without his support, I wouldn't be involved in Alzheimer's work and the center at Duke wouldn't exist. There are people who just don't realize that except for him they would one day be suffering. He will have an impact on millions of people and billions of research dollars from that early beginning for the brain bank and then the research conducted in the building. He is class personified.

"We would not have been able to get started without the critical investment that he made when he made it for an experiment that he didn't really understand but that he was willing to risk helping with. He was thinking there were genetic factors and he was not afraid to invest. I have only a few heroes in my life, but Joe Bryan is certainly number one.

"I came to Glaxo from Duke because I have more freedom here. I came here because there is the chance of making a greater difference. Universities or institutes or governments don't make drugs. Drug companies do and I'm in a position now to actually push that agenda. I don't know what will happen or when. I don't think we will have a cure in 30 years, but I do think we will have drugs that will be able to prevent or limit Alzheimer's progression. And I believe that Joe Bryan will have played a large part in that happening."

314

19

GREENSBORO'S GREATEST GIFT

METICULOUS. *adj:* marked by extreme or excessive care in the consideration or treatment of details.

J oseph McKinley Bryan Sr. didn't invent the word, but he certainly qualified as a Southern distributor.

When he went on shooting and fishing excursions with wealthy friends, he planned the schedules, menus, wine selections, dinner hours and dress codes, and gun partners.

When he planned birthday parties for his wife, he selected the location, personally made out the guest list, chose the meals from salads to desserts, ordered the flowers of particular colors and even directed where they vases were placed.

When he went to the Masters Tournament each spring, he picked the place to stay, the people to stay with him and what they would do while there. When he bought new clothes — which he rarely did — his personal tailor came to him. Everything had to be letter perfect.

It was no surprise, then, when Bryan created his private philanthropic foundation in the fall of 1984, he carefully and repeatedly scrutinized every minute detail of its purposes, provisions and language. Nothing was left to chance or possible error of intent or result.

The Joseph M. Bryan Foundation of Greater Greensboro was officially created in October 1984, but it had a long gestation period because Bryan insisted on so much care and concern about it being done precisely the way he wanted.

"He regularly reviewed everything," said Bryan's long-time personal attorney Carole Bruce. "I would draft documents and he would review every word, making changes to ensure everything was exactly as he wanted it. He put a lot of time and thought into every aspect of the creation of the foundation."

Bryan created the foundation a mere two months after the death of his wife Kathleen with whom he had formed the Bryan Family Foundation (later changed to Fund) 29 years earlier. A large percentage of her money, some of which he helped earn through oil and gas investments in the Deep South, had gone into the original foundation. He established his own foundation so that his personal assets would go there, separate from those of other family members.

There has been continuing dissension within Bryan's family over where his assets should have gone, but people outside the family who are familiar with his wishes say Bryan was perfectly clear all along.

"It was always made clear to me that it was not Mr. Bryan's intention to leave any of his assets to (the original) fund," said William Massey, executive director of the Family Fund for four years. "I was advised when I accepted the job that I should not expect any of his assets to come to the family foundation. It was useful to me to know that our trustees did not expect his money to be used by the family. So there was no sense of disappointment, when Mr. Bryan died, that his estate did not have assets for the original family fund."

As one means of divorcing himself from the original foundation that he and his wife created in 1955, but before establishing his own foundation, Bryan resigned from the board of the family fund and asked that his name be dropped from the title. When that happened, the original family fund name was changed to the Kathleen Price Bryan Family Fund.

"He carefully planned this all out," said Jim Melvin, president of the Joseph M. Bryan Foundation. "He knew there would be confusion between the two if his name stayed on the original fund. It was just all part of his plan. You have give him high marks for thinking all this out the way he did."

In creating his own foundation, Bryan also set a new course and focus on his giving, significantly different from the philosophy of the original fund. "I don't think he agreed on the direction the original fund was taking," said lawyer Bruce. "He just did not agree on the way the assets were being used."

When Bryan and his wife established the original fund, their initial gifts were distributed mostly in Greensboro. Other donations were made to other areas, but not out of the fund account. As other Bryan family members became involved in distribution of assets, the variety and geographic region gradually expanded.

Bryan determined this scattershot approach wasn't what he wanted for his own assets. In setting up his own foundation, he made sure that wouldn't happen.

"You could sort of see the way he was wanting to go," Melvin said in explaining Bryan's thinking. "He wanted to focus on Greater Greensboro. That had to do with his great love affair for this town and community. His intention was that a substantial piece of money from his assets would be left here for the enhancement of this community. It is significant that he carefully planned it this way. He didn't leave it to chance and didn't want any uncertainties.

"He set his foundation up in 1984, but he was a visionary and was always thinking ahead. Even in his 99th year in 1995, he was

317

thinking as far ahead as 2050 and wondering what things might be like at that time. How many people do you know at age 99 are still thinking that far into the future? But that has a lot to do with our mission as trustees of his foundation. He thought this thing through very carefully. The original trustees that he personally selected had 10 years to watch and work with him, to understand his thinking. We didn't have much money in those years, but he gave us a feel for the kinds of things he wanted us to invest in for the benefit of this community. He knew the vast majority of his assets would someday be available for the foundation. He wanted us to know how he would have used those assets so we could fully understand his wishes. I think this was very visionary on his part. He was a man of few words, but when he spoke we knew we darn well better listen, and I believe we've done that and hope that future generations will continue to follow his wishes."

Melvin said that during Bryan's latter years, people seeking money for their favorite causes would frequently call and ask how to get to Bryan. "My response was always to have a good and worthy idea and not ask him for too much of what they were trying to raise," Melvin said. "One of his pet peeves was that people would come asking for his money without having made any significant commitment themselves to whatever it was they wanted. He just didn't like that kind of approach."

One example illustrates that point. Three local businessmen once went to Bryan to ask for money for a particular educational institution that was seeking $2 million. The trio made their sales pitch as Bryan listened intently.

"Well, you young fellows have a good idea there," Bryan said. "How much would you like me to give?"

The group talked about his responsibility and then asked him for $1 million. They had not once mentioned their own willingness to contribute.

"And that obviously ticked him off," Melvin said of the meeting.

"Well, I've got some good news for you," Bryan told the trio. "I'll give you $1 million, but I want you three to match it. I assume you can do that because each of you lives in a bigger home than I do and all three of you drive newer cars than I do. So you must have that kind of money. If the three of you will collectively commit to giving $1 million, I'll go over there right now and write you a check."

The three wouldn't agree to his offer, therefore neither would he for the larger amount. Bryan gave them $75,000, reluctantly because they had made no personal investment. They were merely seeking his dollars. He was bothered by their indifferent approach, despite what they said was the importance of the project.

"That pretty much sums up the way he was," Melvin said. "He didn't like giving big gifts to people who could have given more themselves and didn't. I think what he did to those three is a great fundraising story. I've used it many times to illustrate his approach to giving. He wanted people to make their own gift on behalf of the cause they wanted his help with if they felt it was significant and important."

A huge block of Bryan's assets were in Jefferson Pilot stock, some of which he inherited from his wife who was the daughter of the man who built the company but much of which he had purchased with his own money. Bryan began buying Jefferson stock shortly after he joined the company in the early 1930s. His faith in and performance with the company paid off handsomely because increasing stock values helped make him a wealthy man.

"He just always felt that Jefferson stock belonged here and ought to go back to the community," Bruce quoted Bryan as saying in creating his foundation using his Jefferson assets as well as profits from his oil investments. "He saw the company as part of this community and he wanted its success to remain part of the community."

The first personal donation Bryan made to his foundation was in December 1985, a gift of 10,200 shares of Jefferson stock valued at

$359,550. In late 1994, six months before his death, Bryan made a second significant donation of $750,000 in cash to the foundation account.

When Bryan died in April 1995, his total assets were valued at approximately $88 million, about 75 percent in Jefferson stock. His estate paid some $7 million in taxes and he had directed that at his death another $13 million be distributed among local educational institutions and charities, leaving some $65 million in the estate.

The rapid growth of the stock market between Bryan's death and the end of the 20th Century, even with the distributions, sent the Foundation assets skyrocketing. As of January 2000, the Foundation owned 1,250,000 million shares of Jefferson stock, plus bonds and other investments with a total value approaching $120 million.

By contrast, when the original Bryan Family Fund was dissolved in 1999 and broken into three separate entities (two non-profits and one charitable trust) among the three Bryan children, total assets of that fund were approximately $60 million.

As is made clear from the number of shares of Jefferson stock going to the Bryan Foundation account, the majority of Bryan's estate was in stock in the company. Bryan, of course, played a major role within the company in the broadcast growth even though his responsibilities in the insurance side were minimal.

But Bryan's shrewd investments, some of them risky, in oil in gas wells in several southern states significantly increased his own assets as well as those of Mrs. Bryan's. "Her estate was greatly enhanced by him through his investments outside Jefferson," Bruce commented.

Although Bryan's assets were enormous, he was not a heavy player in the stock market as might have been expected. Aside from his Jefferson stock and his holdings of shares in what was once N.C. National Bank, his stock portfolio contained only corporate bonds and two other Wall Street stocks in corporations outside North Carolina: General Electric and DuPont.

The Bryan Foundation's primary purpose, as defined in the articles of incorporation, is to support the city-owned park north of Greensboro that bears the Joseph M. and Kathleen Bryan name. "His primary concern and first interest was the enhancement of Bryan Park," Bruce said in explaining the details of the foundation's incorporation. "He had a dream that Bryan Park would become the foremost public park in the country, if not the world. But he didn't think it should be done solely with his money. He felt the city should maintain a commitment and carry out its role also. He never wanted the city to abandon the park. He wanted the city to do its share."

"The first thing (in writing) he directs us to do is making permanent improvements and significant enhancements to Bryan Park," Melvin said of Bryan Foundation directors. "Secondly, the language in the incorporation calls for the implementation and enhancement of other such programs, facilities, projects, and organizations which promote the economic, cultural and recreational lives of the citizens of Greater Greensboro. He wanted to be very focused on Greensboro."

No one disputes that Bryan's first recreational love in Greensboro is Bryan Park where he first made an investment in the early 1970s after the city council, at Melvin's recommendation, named it for the Bryans. Bryan subsequently poured millions into the park, for land, buildings, golf courses, soccer fields, physical enhancements and open space to be preserved.

A life-size statue of Bryan stands at the entrance to the park's enrichment center, which Bryan first paid for and then paid for remodeling. Some Bryan friends, led by Melvin, persuaded him to allow the statute to be sculptured at a cost of $36,000. Half of Bryan's ashes are buried at there. A stone walkway and base for the statue were added at a cost of $25,000, also paid by Bryan.

While Bryan approved of the statue, he later pointed out that when he agreed he didn't know he would be expected to pay for it. That fact shouldn't have surprised him, however, if it did. His money had paid for many of the other facilities at the park. Since Bryan's death, another $2 million of his assets have been used to pay for a new clubhouse, new greens and a new golf practice facility.

After limiting the use of foundation assets to Greater Greensboro and specifying distribution of funds for "economic, cultural and recreational" improvements, Bryan left other resource distribution decisions to his foundation directors.

The Bryan Foundation's approach to charitable giving has shifted from traditional practices used most often in the past by other philanthropic organizations. The Foundation does not accept requests for grants. Rather, directors unanimously choose projects on their own and decide whether to provide money. If any one of the six directors objects to a contribution suggested by another director, the project is rejected.

Other foundations, as a more efficient way of providing aid to charities, are adopting that approach. "I certainly see others realizing they would rather be more proactive than reactive," Bruce said. "Receiving hundreds of grant requests and sifting through them all instead of doing more meaningful things is a very difficult way to go about handling a business."

Interestingly, although Bryan never mentioned the word education in his written Foundation rules or purposes, the bulk of initial Foundation gifts since his death have been for that purpose in two public school programs in Guilford County. Directors approved those programs, Melvin said, because they support the economic and cultural aspects of lives of local people and, more significantly, because both Bryan and his wife were active supporters of educational enhancement programs during their lives. "That's why we've done so much with a strong emphasis on education," Melvin said.

The largest Bryan Foundation gift since Bryan's death was a $5 million grant to the privately-run Center for Creative Leadership in Greensboro, a business training institution created by the Richardson Family to improve leadership skills of corporate officials and military personnel. The Bryan gift allows Guilford County school teachers and principals to complete leadership training as one means of enhancing educational quality in local schools.

A second Bryan Foundation $1 million gift has been to finance four years of teacher training in the Paideia method of classroom instruction. Paideia stresses respect, civility, character building, listening skills and independent thinking among students in addition to regular classroom requirements. It also promotes increased active student participation in academic discussions.

Bryan's meticulousness in his approach to the purposes and language in creating his foundation extended to the selection of his directors, both in 1984 and in subsequent years. He made sure he chose people who would adopt his own philosophy. Three of the original five directors still serve: Melvin, Bruce, and local businessman Michael Haley. Those three along with Bryan and Bryan's personal friend Claibourne Darden made up the original board.

At Darden's death, community leader Shirley Frye joined the board. Since that time, businessman Mike Weaver and management consultant David DeVries have been added. Bryan personally picked all but DeVries who joined after Bryan's death.

Melvin and Bruce were picked because of their long personal and professional relationship with Bryan. He had full trust in their ability to follow his lead in their approaches to and philosophy of giving. It was Melvin, of course, who got Bryan started in charitable giving on a large scale and Bruce set up the foundation through her law office.

Haley said he was surprised during a business trip to Charlotte in 1984 to receive a call from Bryan asking him to serve on the foundation board. "He called me and said he would like to ask a big favor," Haley recalled. "He asked me to serve as a director of his new foundation. I was honored and accepted because I was in awe of the man. He was a great listener and I always felt he knew more about you than you knew about him. He is the most proper man I've ever known, always-impeccable even when walking his dogs. He was a perfect gentleman and always expressed his gratitude to me for serving. My association with him has made me a better person."

Haley said Bryan was a hero at Bryan Park when he visited there and children learned who he was because they were appreciative of the facilities he had provided for their pleasure. "He loved that attention when the children would come up and thank him for the park," Haley said. "He gave to that park because he felt he could make a difference. The things he and the foundation have done will have an impact on this community for a long time to come."

Weaver, a successful construction company owner, civic leader and philanthropist in his own right, said he felt Bryan asked him to serve as a director partly because of his friendship with Melvin and because of past associations on local project community projects. Weaver has his own foundation that was started by his father who was also a friend of Bryan's.

"Our foundations have traveled parallel courses," Weaver said. "I think Joe was very wise in the way he went about creating his foundation with his interests and his heart in Greensboro. He was willing to take some risks, but he monitored things closely to ensure his money was well spent. He was always proactive in keeping up with what was happening in this community. I think we have followed his lead and he would give us high marks for how his assets have been used (since his death)."

Weaver once worried that he would be competing with Bryan's love of Bryan Park when Weaver began the private development of a high-end housing neighborhood and golf course east of Greensboro. "He told me not to worry, that it was no problem," Weaver said.

Shirley Frye wanted to impress Bryan the first time she walked into his office at Jefferson Pilot in downtown Greensboro, but she

Joseph M. Bryan Sr., right, with N.C. A&T State University chancellor Dr. Lewis Dowdy on May 8, 1977, when Bryan was awarded an honorary degree from the university.

was gambling. Seeing a huge mounted fish on the wall, Frye casually turned to Bryan and asked if he had personally caught that marlin. "Why yes," Bryan replied with a wide smile. "And you're the first woman who ever knew what kind of fish that is." From that moment on, Frye was his friend.

"The thing is," Frye conceded with a laugh, "I didn't know the fish was a marlin. I was just guessing. I had no idea what a marlin looked like. I just knew that was the name of a fish. I really don't know why I said marlin. Thank goodness I guessed right."

Frye, a well-known and well-liked Greensboro community leader, first met Bryan through her husband, then state legislator and later state Supreme Court Chief Justice Henry Frye. Their friendship grew while she worked at A&T State University and Bryan made some gifts to the school.

Bryan asked her to serve as a director of his foundation because, he said, she knew the community needs well and knew specific needs of minorities. Personable and charming, Frye heaped flattery on Bryan at every opportunity. "I used to tell him the heavens opened up and he dropped out," she said of her camaraderie with the man she greatly admired. Bryan clearly loved the praise.

The first time Frye asked Bryan for a gift, before she became a Foundation director, was for the football stadium at A&T. He wasn't much interested. A football stadium wasn't his idea of a quality of life issue.

"Why should I do that?" he asked.

"Because I asked you and I know it's needed to help the university and the students," Frye responded. Bryan made the pledge, the first of many to the school for academic and athletic projects. That particular gift, however, caused a temporary touch of embarrassment when it was announced on campus. Then Chancellor Ed Fort, who at the time was relatively new to town, mispronounced Bryan's name, calling him Bryant.

"You see, even when you give money they can't get your name right," Bryan complained to Frye, only half in jest. A hastily written letter of apology healed the wound, if it ever existed.

Frye's relationship with Bryan was such that she could secure funds from him when members of his own family couldn't. Bryan's son Joe Jr. once wanted a donation from his father for the Eastern Music Festival at Guilford College, but he asked Frye to make the request because she could be more successful. She asked and Bryan gave.

"I always just thought he was a big teddy bear," Frye said. "He was always concerned about a lot of things, but he wanted immediate results. He never gave just to be giving, but gave where he could make a difference. He was a very caring person. Greensboro had been good to him and his big heart was in this community. Working with him and the foundation has been a great satisfaction in seeing what a volunteer can achieve in a community, to see what is meaningful and to see a quick turnaround and immediate results. Mr. Bryan loved things done this way."

Bryan confided to Frye that he was concerned that some people were seeking his foundation money without good reason or for wrong reasons out of greed and avarice. "Isn't in interesting what money can do to create controversy in people," Bryan said to Frye in predicting that the foundation would likely have problems with members of his family after his death. His forecast on that was accurate.

The Foundation's newest director, management consultant David DeVries, joined the foundation board after helping directors establish a process for consensus building in decision-making and improving effective ways directors could better work together more productively. After working initially with the board as a professional, DeVries became a believer in the Bryan approach to charitable contributions before he became a director. "Mr. Bryan didn't just give, he demanded accountability," DeVries stressed. "His whole modus operandi dominates what the board still does. We reflect regularly on his life and his giving in our own decisions. There are regular reviews of what the board does and what we as individuals do. There is no bureaucracy as some foundations have. I am pleased and intrigued with the way this board performs. Our guiding interest is in this community, just as (Bryan's) was. If we succeed as we hope, we hope others will follow."

That was clearly Bryan's desire, as a close look at his vast donations will attest. Bryan had a long-range goal with his giving as he carefully laid every piece in place even into his 99th year of life. When he died a few months short of his 100th birthday, he left a strict set of rules for his foundation directors to follow. His wishes have become their commands.

20

ADDING VALUE TO LIVES

A s one of Greensboro's best-known benefactors because of combined earned and inherited personal wealth, Joe Bryan Sr. entertained thousands of requests for his resources for more than a quarter century. Most were worthy. Some were frivolous.

He was easily able to sort out the difference because he listened intently and carefully scrutinized motivations. Many requests he warmly embraced for the betterment of his community and state if he saw they would add value to the lives of beneficiaries. Others he rejected as simply unworthy or of little value with the feeling that seekers were either self-serving or their interest was only for his cash with no personal commitment themselves.

Bryan was undoubtedly one of the wealthiest men in Greensboro, causing people to line up at his office door, more in his retirement years than ever before. He said he was both shocked and amused the day a lad walked into his office asking to get a look at the richest man in town.

"I was aghast," Bryan said at age 86 of that episode. "I wasn't and am not. I told him he could look at me, but he'd have to look elsewhere (for the richest)." Nevertheless, Bryan said he appreciated the compliment, even if exaggerated.

At the time, of course, Bryan was a millionaire many times over because of his past corporate status, wise investments and late wife's family wealth. And the word was out that he had already begun to give away many of his riches to numerous charitable causes for the benefit of others. And there is little dispute, despite Bryan's protestations about being the richest, that his vast resources put him at least near the top shelf among Greensboro's most affluent corporate citizens.

His contributions, it seemed, were constantly growing during his latter years and have continued through the Foundation he created. As often as not, he set a record among local givers for specific projects every time he opened his checkbook, although he said he didn't see it as any big deal.

He had more than ample resources, as did his various family members, he said, so it seemed only fitting that his assets ought to go to help others less fortunate. Pretty much, he made that his final career.

"If there is any kind of campaign going on, people go see Joe," said his shooting pal Claiborne Darden in 1982. "I mean (a campaign) for anything. He gets calls all the time and keeps stacks of requests on his desk. I've seen people follow him to the airport asking for money."

But as has been duly noted earlier, Bryan was no easy target unless he saw value added and he didn't just give money without good reason or logic. He wanted and insisted on positive, lasting results.

His philosophy, he said, was one that he wished others would adopt. Those with resources ought to be willing to help those without, but only as a means to bettering the lives of recipients.

He could have built philanthropic bonfires by handing out his resources without much thought, then walking away to let others worry about any misguided flames. But that wasn't the Bryan way.

Instead, he lit candles, one at a time and stayed to watch the glow enhance the fulfillment of his dreams and the lives of his recipients.

He was not just a time teller when it came to giving. Rather he favored building clocks that would last.

He was not content, using the old saw, to give somebody a fish or even just teach people how to fish. Rather he wanted to help build fisheries.

He was not satisfied with the unanswerable question of whether the glass was half empty or half full. Rather he simply most often simply asked for a bigger glass.

Partly that was because of his upbringing. He had to fight as a young man for his opportunities, but the challenges made him a better person. He wanted no less for those who received his help in his later life.

He knew he couldn't change everything, even for a few. But he was determined to change at least a few things for as many as possible.

He carried disdain for those who were content simply to seek his gifts in search of a free ride. But he was a soft touch for those committed to helping earn his benevolence through their own dedication.

He learned from where he had been as one means of better knowing where he wanted to go.

He was thoughtful and considerate among his friends and could elicit a devotion and respect that few were able to achieve. The only missing ingredient to this aspect of his life lay within his own family.

He felt solutions to problems lay in the head as much as in the heart. Services as a convenience were not good enough. He wanted to provide services that counted, to make a difference.

He set his sights higher than most and reached them more quickly than most through partnerships because he firmly believed that little of value was built in isolation.

He wanted his philanthropic seeds to help produce crops for many seasons, but he insisted on others adding their own ingredients, too.

He wanted his building blocks to serve as foundations, but he wanted others to add their own bricks and mortar to make the structures taller and stronger.

He was willing to lead, but only if others would follow.

He wanted answers, not just questions. And he demanded accountability.

He was an added value investor in the lives of those touched by his grace and benevolence.

What Joe Bryan was about was helping people help themselves and others. He was an investor in people and his return was in watching progress achieved with what, in a sense, was often a risk-taking approach to getting good works started.

These are among the descriptions given by those who knew him best or who watched his charitable giving closest over the longest periods of time, both during his three decades of corporate work and 35 years of productive retirement.

The Foundation Bryan created with his assets is designed to help the most people with the greatest needs. His constant goal was to spread the word of his benevolence so that others would pick up the cadence without missing a beat after he was gone.

The acronym among his Foundation directors is WWJD: What Would Joe Do?

"When you look at his life and how creative he was in how he did things," said Bryan's confidant and Foundation president Jim Melvin, "you realize how important it is to continue his interests. Five of us (directors) had the privilege of knowing him very well and are a privileged group because of that. But those who will follow will not have had that opportunity as we did. We have to ask ourselves what would Mr. Bryan have done? He gave us a pretty good feel for the kinds of things he had an interest in moving forward. What we are all about is causing his spirit to live on forever in what we do and our successors do.

"I heard him say many times that he always hoped some of his generosity would spark somebody else to do the same thing. He hoped and we hope that when other people with means and the desire to do worthwhile things would look at the kinds of things he did and say those were some good ideas and they would add to them. Going forward, we want people to have the ability to understand the person who made these gifts possible."

Bryan had ample resources to help worthy causes, and he did that over more than a 50-year span, first with the assistance of his wife whose initial assets far surpassed his, and then on his own. He also clearly took pleasure in the recognition he received for his large gifts, a fact he acknowledged without shame or apology, for the sake of his own ego as well as an inducement for others to do the same.

But he never learned to like the term philanthropy, calling it a meaningless label subject to as many different interpretations as interpreters. Rather, he often said, giving was simply an obligation for those like him whose lives had been blessed.

His philosophy of giving, Bryan told friends, was not to have a philosophy beyond seeing the need and responding so long as he could provide a helping hand rather than a hand out.

It was just something he did, a close friend said, as a matter of course, not just for a pat on the back — although he liked that. Bryan gained pleasure in seeing what his assistance and guidance could achieve and he was touched when those he had helped extended their praise. Even with his stiff and polished British persona intact, he would loosen up just enough to show obvious pride when was able to see that his help had allowed others to accomplish meaningful things. Giving, Bryan said, was his investment in the value of people and his dividend was in watching the positive result through partnerships. Bryan said he saw potential in everyone, but he also felt the greatest potential was when his resources could provide people a chance for accomplishment so he could later watch them and their projects grow on their own.

"He always felt that once things were up and running with his help, he ought to move on to something else," Melvin said. "That's the kind of thing Joe Bryan was all about. He wanted to help worthwhile projects get started and help people who were committed to ideas, but he also wanted them to stand on their own, to be self-supporting through their own commitment and dedication. He wanted to be the catalyst, but not the sole carrier."

That's the philosophy Bryan displayed in 1968, the first time Melvin asked him for a contribution of $25,000 to create an innovative public school enterprise program within the local United Way. Bryan gave the money, but gave the United Way leaders authority to use it wisely and productively for others. He did, however, watch for results. It was that gift, token though it was compared to his many later and larger donations, that convinced him people needed seeds to grow their own trees, not a ready-made forest ready for harvesting.

Bryan had given away a lot of money before he made that United Way gift, which has since been tripled by his foundation directors, but most of his earlier gifts had generally been through corporate connections or family ties. It was that initial enterprise grant to give school children with special needs a chance to develop on their own that eventually led to creation of the Bryan Foundation. That grant was also the motivation behind many of the numerous gifts Bryan made on his own and that his directors will make with the vast assets he left for distribution to others.

This philosophy is what Foundation director David DeVries calls Bryan's venture capitalist approach to giving. Bryan was willing to take risks, to think boldly and beyond the ordinary in an effort to increase the returns. He was what might be called a social entrepreneur, willing to break traditional molds to get things done more quickly and more definitively, provided all participants played a part.

"He didn't believe in giving to black holes," DeVries explained. "He demanded real accountability. His giving was an investment; it was a kind of venture capitalist approach. He felt if only one person thought something was a good idea, it might not be a very good idea. He wanted to forge long-term partnerships with others who had ideas for change."

Bryan did that when he gave $1 million to help create the innovative state School of Math and Science in Durham for talented students. He was the first private contributor to that effort, leading by example.

Bryan did that when he financed the creation of the $250,000 Duke Medical School's instant autopsy project for study brains of Alzheimer's patients. And he did the same when he contributed $10 million, to supplement a series of federal grants, for the Duke Alzheimer's Research Facility that bears the name of Bryan and his wife Kathleen. His initial gift was the beginning of tedious research in search of a cure or at least successful treatment for the dreaded disease that robs people of their dignity, as it did his wife.

Bryan carried that same philosophy forward with his lead $5 million gift for the School of Business at UNCG, to be pooled with other resources, as well as the scholarships at the same school that carry his name. To ensure his scholarship funds were being put to good use, he was a frequent visitor among and mentor to students receiving his financial aid. Foundation directors, at Bryan's suggestion, have turned over his Greensboro residence valued at $830,000 for use as the UNCG chancellor's home. The foundation paid for remodeling and refurbishing and retains ownership, but allows the university to continue use for the chancellor provided the school covers operational expenses.

Bryan did the same when he began adding millions to the enhancement of space and facilities at Bryan Park. He was willing to help with that park, he said, so long as the city also did its share. His resources, he stressed, could add value to the park, its facilities and space, but he shouldn't carry the whole load. The city maintains the park for the benefit of thousands, but it was resources from Bryan and his wife that made it possible.

Foundation directors have carried out that theme with their

largest gifts since Bryan's death in 1995. The $6 million given over several years for leadership training for school personnel and academic enhancement in classrooms is but one example. Foundation assets will provide the training and tools for higher student achievement, but the programs must carry forth without continued Bryan help once they are fully established.

That philanthropic thinking was a spin off of Bryan's corporate thinking from many years earlier when he was still perceived as a hard-charging bottom line executive. Partnering was the key to success, he said as far back as 1959 when he was asked as a Jefferson Broadcasting executive for time and money for a project. "Heaven knows I don't want to be against a liberal public service policy," Bryan wrote a colleague that summer, "and I advocate donation of time, leadership and money. But considering the time and talent we have spent on this very worthy program, I feel someone else ought to put up the dough. If Vick Chemical Company gives 100 cases of Vapo-Rub to the heathen Chinese, they could reasonably expect someone else to provide the transportation. Where we are giving substantial contributions of manpower, time and materials, we should let others do their share also."

Following Bryan's lead, helping people to help themselves remains a core value of the Foundation and its trustees. Examples of partnerships abound, several directed at helping to heal past wounds among Bryan family members who had complained they felt the senior Bryan was receiving too much personal recognition for contributions that came, in part, through his resources stemming from his wife's Price side of the family.

The Foundation has committed $433,000 to a two-year project in partnership with Goodwill Industries ($250,000) and the local social services department ($50,000) aimed as moving people from welfare to work. The project will assist up to 1,000 people to end welfare dependency through job training efforts and mentoring.

The Foundation provides $14,000 a year for an after-school program, called the Center for Champions, designed to help teach disadvantaged young people how to study and show respect.

The Foundation provides $10,000 a year for TYGR PAWS (Teaching Youngsters Golf for Recreation: Pride, Attitude, Wisdom and Self-Esteem) at Bryan Park in cooperation with the city, to teach golf skills as well as camaraderie among peers and self-improvement.

The Foundation put up $1.2 million, supplemented by $300,000 from a private businessman, to help create a Children's Museum downtown near the public library. A private non-profit foundation oversees the museum.

The Foundation contributed $115,000 for furnishing a new residence for the chancellor at N.C. A&T State University after the university purchased the home.

The Foundation has contributed $2.5 million for land and buildings as part of a new downtown Greensboro YMCA. The stipulation in the gift is that the building be named solely for Bryan's wife Kathleen. Bryan gifts to facilities bearing his name or the names of both he and his wife are many, but until the Y project was approved there was no single facility named just for Mrs. Bryan. Foundation directors agreed at the turn of the century that such a name was needed and appropriate.

The Foundation has approved contributing $1 million to the observatory at the new Frank Family Science Building at Guilford College in honor of Joe Bryan Jr. because of his long-time service and donations to that college.

Both the Y donation in memory of Kathleen Bryan and the Guilford College contribution honoring Bryan Jr. were approved as a step toward showing Bryan family members the Foundation considers them important parts of Bryan's assets and philanthropy.

The Foundation has contributed $100,000 to the Battleground Park fund in Greensboro in honor of former Congressman L. Richardson Preyer and his late wife Emily.

"Foundation trustees feel it would be appropriate to help the community with contributions and projects that do not bear Mr. Bryan's name," Foundation president Jim Melvin said of the partnership agreements. "He would have approved of that."

Twenty years before his death, Bryan read a newspaper story about a scheduled summer program for young people that had been dropped because promised federal money had been denied.

He offered to pay for the program himself at a cost of $100,000, with one proviso. He wanted any work done by teens to be worthwhile and meaningful. He was unwilling to pay for busy work that wasn't part of a learning experience. He was not interested in leaf-raking or unproductive work. (He was upset when he saw a newspaper photograph of four of the youths whose salaries he was paying huddled around a single fire hydrant with paint brushes in hand until he learned the photographer staged the shot and it was not taking four teens to paint one hydrant.) He was interested in helping give young people who wanted to work and learn a chance, but only if it added value to their lives for later life.

That, in a word, was the Joe Bryan philosophy of giving. Giving just to satisfy a request held no meaning and little value. Giving to add value to a life was what counted. That's the example he set and the goal his foundation trustees will follow.

If Bryan could get one more wish, it would be that others would do the same.

Bryan's philosophy of giving — and much of his life — was succinctly summed up in his funeral eulogy delivered by his friend the Rev. Joe Mullin at Greensboro's First Presbyterian Church. Mullin elaborated on that funeral message in a subsequent interview.

"He made this city greater," Mullin said. "Greater Greensboro was important to him and he was one of the city's greatest treasuries. There are not many institutions around here that he hasn't started, saved or improved. He opened his heart and hands to his community.

"He was a paradoxical man. He bought tailor made suits, but he wore them for 40 years. He could have owned a fleet of Ferraris and Rolls Royces, but he drove automobiles so long they verged on moving into the antique status. He moved with some of the high and mighty and associated with some of the most powerful people in the land, but he never dropped names. He treated everyone the same whatever their station in life. Indeed, there were fascinating paradoxes in this remarkable man.

"He came to Greensboro after he married Kathleen Price, but he fell in love with the city. He said he loved the greenness of the county, the openness and the people who took time to chat.

"He wore the green coat of the Greater Greensboro Open with great pride, and in that term 'Greater Greensboro' lay the dream of Joe Bryan. He wanted Greensboro to be better, to be the best city in the world and he was dedicated to making it happen. He profited from investments and got a kick out of accumulating wealth. But the paradox is that although he enjoyed earning money, he got a genuine satisfaction from giving it away."

Quoting from the 18th Chapter of the Gospel of Luke, Mullin in the funeral message recounted the story of Jesus who talked with his disciples of the difficulties of rich men getting into heaven because wealth, for some, becomes their God. Then he added, as quoted in the scriptures, that all things are possible with God.

"So far as I know, Joe Bryan was not affiliated with any particuar church," Mullin continued. "I do not know the motivation of his giving. I do not know his heart. No one knows another person's heart. Only the God who created us knows our hearts. But as Jesus said in his Sermon on the Mount, it is by their fruits that we shall know them. We can't know what's in a person's heart, but we can learn of their hearts by their actions. We know something about Joe Bryan's heart by what he did. He gave his wealth away. It was more than simply writing a check indiscriminately. He learned to give creatively. And like the other characteristics of his life, he gave with grace, style and flair.

"As the inscription (that Bryan wrote) at the base of his statue in Bryan Park says: 'When it comes to giving, man must tip his hat to nature. She gives joy, beauty and hope and excludes no one.' Joe Bryan truly tried not to exclude anyone and has brought joy, beauty and hope to so many.

"Joe Bryan, like all of us, had his faults, but what marvelous virtues and what a great heart. Because he lived among us, Greensboro and North Carolina will never be the same."

Bryan didn't write that eulogy, but he could have. He certainly would have given it thumbs up. It was, like he was: straightforward and on the mark.

JOSEPH M. BRYAN FOUNDATION

The Joseph M. Bryan Foundation was established on October 19, 1984. Its purpose is to commemorate the benevolence of Joseph M. Bryan Sr., a leader of both business and community projects, and to carry forth his philosophy of giving.

The mission of the Foundation, designed and carefully molded by Mr. Bryan, is simple and direct: to seek the implementation, improvement and enhancement of programs, facilities, projects and organizations which promote the economic, cultural, and recreational enrichment of the lives of Greater Greensboro citizens. By charter, the Foundation can only fund programs and organizations located within the Greater Greensboro area, but the limitations are only geographic. People served in the Greensboro area will have a positive impact on others far beyond the local community as they carry out initiatives that fit Mr. Bryan's vision of Greensboro.

The Foundation, funded primarily by Mr. Bryan's estate resources, started small with annual donations of as little as $1,000 to worthy causes. It has grown steadily and by the end of 1999 had assets in excess of $150 million. Foundation directors, in keeping with Mr. Bryan's wishes, were committed to annually donating millions every year for programs to benefit organizations, facilities and people in Greater Greensboro. During the final two years of the 20th Century, directors contributed $8.26 million to such causes.

A listing of the Bryan Foundation charitable grants during 1998:

Guilford County Schools for Paideia teaching
program (over four years a total of $1 million) $1,000,000

Center for Creative Leadership (to train school
personnel over five years a total of $5 million)
Center for Champions $32,854

Bryan Park land purchases. $1,772,122

Bryan Park general improvements $151,705

Greensboro Children's Museum $1,224,014

N.C. A&T State University Field House $400,000

Greensboro United Way $300,000

Goodwill Industries (multi-year) employment project . . . $52,071

UNC-Greensboro Chancellor's residence maintenance . . $30,442

United Arts Council $50,000

National Women's Collegiate Golf Tournament $36,642

Rotary Foundation $1,000

Greensboro Community Foundation $5,000

Salvation Army. $250,000

North Carolina Department of Transportation
for Beautification of Bryan Boulevard $50,000

Greensboro YMCA (in addition to a commitment
of $2.5 million for the proposed
Kathleen Bryan downtown Y facility) $900

A listing of the Foundation charitable grants for 1999:

Bryan Park improvements...$745,016

Guilford County Schools Paideia Project $250,000

Guilford County Schools Leadership Project $895,140

Goodwill Industries..$227,566

UNCG, Fred Chappell Endowment $50,000

Old North State Boy Scouts capital campaign..................$37,500

N.C. Department of Transportation
Beautification Project along Bryan Blvd. $50,000

Greensboro Garden Club Council $75,000

Community Foundation of Greater Greensboro....................$800

National Conference for Community and Justice $1,500

Greensboro Chamber of Commerce..................................$1,050

United Arts Council of Greensboro $50,000

Rotary Foundation $1,000

N.C. A&T State University..$1,500

Grassroots Productions Festival of Lights...........................$5,000

UNC-Chapel Hill (for Greensboro educational project) $4,000

National Women's Collegiate
Golf Tournament, Bryan Park $32,282

Chamber of Commerce Economic
Report for Federal Express Impact Study $90,132

N.C. Business Court, Greensboro $69,965

Bryan Speakers Bureau brochure
encouraging volunteerism $12,092

Bryan Leadership Development Initiative...........................$1,250

BRYAN CHARITABLE BEQUESTS

In the latter years of his long life, Joseph M. Bryan Sr.— who died in April 1995 just a few months shy of his 100th birthday — carefully chose organizations to receive bequests from his estate at his death. He arranged these gifts through his meticulously crafted Will beyond what his charitable foundation had already given or might give in the future.

These bequests, totaling almost $13 million, and the purpose of each as specified by Mr. Bryan are listed below.

UNC at Greensboro Bryan School of Business ....$5 million
To be used for programs, scholarships, and fellowships and professorships at the school. The income is to be used for programs and not for buildings.

N.C. School of Math and Science ....$1 million
To establish the Joseph M. Bryan Endowment Fund with the income to be used for special activities of the school, including recreational and extracurricular activities.

UNC Public Television ....$1 million
To be used for the enhancement of facilities at the Joseph and
Kathleen Bryan Communications Center, including the purchase of
equipment to be used by the center.

Bennett College $500,000
To be used in the discretion of the college president for the benefit
of the school.

Guilford College...$500,000
To establish the Joseph M. Bryan Sr. Scholarship Fund with the
income to be used for scholarships.

N.C. A&T State University...$500,000
To establish the Joseph M. Bryan Sr. Scholarship Fund with the
income to be used for scholarships.

Greensboro College $500,000
To establish the Joseph M. Bryan Sr. Scholarship Fund with the
income to be used for scholarships.

Wake Forest University $500,000
To establish the Joseph M. Bryan Sr. Scholarship Fund with one
half of the income to be used for athletic scholarships and one half
to be used for general scholarships.

Hospice of Greensboro, Inc. $500,000
To establish the Joseph M. Bryan Sr. Endowment Fund with the
income to be used for the care of Hospice patients who are unable
to pay for their own care and who do not have insurance that ade-
quately pays for their care.

Greensboro Urban Ministry $500,000
To establish the Joseph M. Bryan Endowment Fund with income to be used for providing shelter and food for the homeless.

United Way of Greensboro $500,000
To become part of the Kathleen Price and Joseph M. Bryan Community Enrichment and Venture Grant with the income to be used for the purposes of the original grant.

Mount Hermon School...$250,000
To establish the Joseph M. Bryan Sr. Scholarship Fund with income to be used for scholarships.

Central Greensboro YMCA $250,000
To be used for additions to and maintenance of the facilities.

Hayes-Taylor YMCA...$250,000
To be used for additions to and maintenance of the facilities.

Davidson College $250,000
To establish the Joseph M. Bryan Sr. Scholarship Fund with income to be used for scholarships.

Foundation of Greater Greensboro $200,000
To be held as an unrestricted endowment fund named for Mr. Bryan.

Our Lady of Grace Catholic Church.............................$200,000
To establish the Joseph M. Bryan Sr. Endowment Fund with the income to be used for maintenance and enhancement of church property.

Humane Society of Guilford County $200,000
To establish the Joseph M. Bryan Fund with the income to be used
for purposes of the Society.

Holy Trinity Episcopal Church...$100,000
To become part of the church endowment fund.

First Presbyterian Church $100,000
To become part of the church endowment fund.

Canterbury School $100,000
No purpose specified

NOTES AND SOURCES

Chapter 1

Joseph Bryan Sr. multiple video interviews with Kevin von der Lippe in UNCG Jackson Library Special Collections, June 1992.

Author interview with Katherine Springs, February 11, 1999

Author interviews with Jim Melvin, October 9, 1998, and May 11, 1999

Author interview with Carole Bruce, May 11, 1999

Bryan family historical records and personal papers in UNCG archives

Author interview with Ted Ely Jr., August 29, 1999

Greensboro Record, November 20, 1927

Author interviews with Greta Medlin, October 27 and November 4, 1999

Author interview with Kay Edwards, February 24, 1999

Author interview with Ann Rambeaut, November 4, 1999

Joe Bryan interview with Duke University archivist Jim Gifford, February 26, 1986

Author interviews with Duke Alzheimer's researchers Dr. Don

Schmechel and Kathleen Welsh-Bohmer and with former National Institutes of Health director Dr. Zovin Khachatorian, March 1999

Author interview with Charles Crutchfield in Charlotte, June 30, 1998

Author interview with Augusta National member Blake Clark, March 29, 1999

Author interviews with various Bryan family members, Bryan Foundation trustees and attorneys in civil suit during 1999

Chapter 2

Bryan family birth records in Special Collections archives at UNCG Jackson Library

Bartholomew and Caroline Bryan marriage certificate

Lorain, Ohio, newspaper clippings, spring 1896

Bryan family historical military records at UNCG, dated February 16, 1864

Series of Bryan family historical correspondence and genealogical records among Bryan papers at UNCG

Civil War military records for Joseph and Lawrence Bryan, dated between May 1864 and May 1865

Author correspondence with Columbia University admissions officer Jocelyn Wilk, October 7, 1999

Joe Bryan video with archivist Kevin von der Lippe, June 16, 1992

Moxham family history compiled May 12, 1957, and published in Sydney, Nova Scotia, history booklet among Bryan family records at UNCG

Series of Bartholomew Bryan letters to his sisters Annie and Dora, December 1902 and January 1903

Author correspondence with Greystone Park Cemetery, spring 1999

Caroline Bryan death certificate, May 1, 1954

Author interview with Bryan archivist Gary Parks, August 25, 1999

Author interview with Ted Ely Jr., May 5, 1999

Bartholomew Bryan letter to Ted Ely Sr., 1938

Bartholomew Bryan death certificate

Joe and Kathleen Price Bryan wedding story in Greensboro Record, November 19, 1927

Joe Bryan grammar school diploma

Joe Bryan academic grade records from Mount Hermon School

Author interview with Greta Medlin, November 4, 1999

Chapter 3

Joe Bryan video interview with archivist Kevin von der Lippe, June 16, 1992

Bryan family correspondence, circa 1914, in Special Collection archives at UNCG Jackson Library

Mount Hermon School correspondence in archives at UNCG

Military records among Bryan family papers at UNCG

Financial records and correspondence between Joe Bryan and William Bryan in archives at UNCG

Author interview with Katherine Springs, February 11, 1999

Author interview with Georgia Kyser, February 17, 1999

Author review of series of Bryan family records dated from 1914 through 1920 in archives at UNCG

Chapter 4

Author interview with Katherine Springs, February 11, 1999

Joe and Kathleen Bryan marriage certificate

Kay Bryan Edwards birth records in archives at UNCG

Joe Bryan video interview with archivist Kevin von der Lippe, June 18, 1992
 Author interview with Kay Bryan Edwards, February 25, 1999
 Author interview with Elise Franklin, November 2, 1998
 Author interview with Seth Macon, April 28, 1999
 Author review of Jefferson Standard business documents among Bryan papers at UNCG Jackson Library
 Undated author interview with Clara Mae Hines
 Author interview with Roger Soles, October 2, 1998
 Joe Bryan taped audio interview with unidentified Jefferson Broadcasting representative, August 4, 1980
 Author interview with Mary Gee, December 16, 1998
 Author interview with Marjorie Warren, August 18, 1999

Chapter 5

Author review of Julian Price business records among Bryan papers in archives at UNCG Jackson Library
 Gayle Fripp, "Greensboro A Chosen Center," page 118
 Author interview with Jefferson Pilot public relations staff personnel
 Author interview with Charles Crutchfield, June 30, 1998
 Review of Jefferson Standard business documents relating to purchase of WBT
 Review of Jefferson Standard history compiled by James Fox, July 1982
 Author interview with William C. Friday, September 5, 1998
 Author interview with Kay Edwards, February 24, 1999
 Review of series of Greensboro News & Record clips pertaining to Jefferson Standard history
 Author interviews with Greensboro business leaders, summer 1999

Author interview with Adelaide Holderness, fall 1999
Jack Scism, Greensboro News & Record, August 8, 1995
Aubrey Lee Brooks, "A Southern Lawyer," page 102
Julian Price obituary, Greensboro Daily News, October 26, 1946
Undated Greensboro News & Record clips on renaming of city streets
Author interview with Gayle Fripp, fall 1999
Author interview with Horace Kornegay, June 22, 1999
Author interview with Seth Macon, April 28, 1999
Julian Price personal letter, July 29, 1946, in archives at UNCG

Chapter 6

Jefferson Standard business documents dated 1940s and 1950s in Special Collection archives at UNCG Jackson Library
Author interview with Dudley Hughes in Jackson, Miss., December 14-15, 1998
Author interview with Roger Soles, October 2, 1998
Jefferson history compiled by James Fox, July 1982
Undated Bryan family records at UNCG
Author interview with Elise Franklin, November 2, 1998
Author interview with Mary Gee, December 16, 1998
Author interview with Seth Macon, April 28, 1999
Greensboro News & Record clips, January 1920 and 1923
Author interviews with Jefferson public relations department personnel, fall 1999
Review, fall 1999, of undated Price family history compiled by Margaret G. Hill Price, in the possession of Virginia L. Price Hill.
Undated Julian Price interview in Greensboro Record
Julian Price interview in Greensboro Democrat, November 26, 1942
Ethel Clay Price family records at UNCG

Author interview with Greensboro Historical Museum director William Moore, January 12, 1999
Ethel Clay Price birth certificate
Author interview with archivist Gary Parks, August 25, 1999
Review of DeBritt Research documents at UNCG
Author interview with Kevin von der Lippe, March 24, 1999
Author interview with Lauch Faircloth, February 2, 1999

Chapter 7

Joe Bryan interview with unidentified Jefferson Standard Broadcasting representative, 1982
Bryan interview with archivist Kevin von der Lippe, June 18, 1992
Jefferson business records among Bryan family papers at UNCG Special Collections Division in Jackson Library
Author interview with Lauch Faircloth, February 2, 1999
Gene Autry correspondence with Bryan in archives at UNCG
Author interview with Roger Soles, October 2, 1998
Bryan conversation with unidentified Jefferson representative, 1980
Bryan business records in archives at UNCG
Bryan personal correspondence in archives at UNCG
Undated Asheville newspaper clippings from the 1950s and unidentified magazine profiles of Sen. Robert Reynolds
Correspondence between Bryan and Howard Holderness, 1959, at UNCG
Julian Price personal papers among Bryan business documents at UNCG
Author interview with William Jones, June 15, 1999
Author interview with Federal Judge N. Carlton "Woody" Tilley, September 17, 1999
Correspondence between Bryan and Gov. Luther Hodges, 1959

Author interview with Ann Rambeaut, November 4, 1999
Bryan correspondence with Pilot Life Insurance President Emry Green, fall 1934
Public real estate records, Guilford County Register of Deeds office
Author interview with Norman Wiggins, fall 1999
Public records in Guilford Clerk of Court office
Author interview with Seth Macon, April 28, 1999
News stories on death of Julian Price, October 25, 1946

Chapter 8

Author interview with Lauch Faircloth, February 2, 1999
Author interviews with Janie Price, November 4, 1998
Review of Jefferson Standard business documents in Special Sections Division at UNCG Jackson Library.
Author interview with Charles Crutchfield, June 30, 1998
Bryan correspondence with Crutchfield in archives at UNCG
Review of official papers of UNC president Gordon Gray and of Charles Crutchfield papers in North Carolina Collection at Wilson Library, UNC Chapel Hill
Author interview with Georgia Kyser, February 17, 1999
History of Jefferson Broadcasting compiled by James Fox, July 1982
Lew Powell, "On This Day in North Carolina," page 79
Bryan video interview with archivist Kevin von der Lippe, June, 1992
Review of Bryan business records relating to WBT purchase, archives at UNCG
Undated Joe Bryan correspondence with his brother Bart, early 1950s
Author interview with Louis Stephens, October 21, 1998
Author interview with Doug Mayes, January 7, 1999

Author interview with Loonis McGlohon, January 7, 1999
Author interview with William C. Friday, September 5, 1998

Chapter 9

Review of official papers of Gordon Gray and Charles Crutch-
field in Wilson Library, UNC Chapel Hill
Author interview with Georgia Kyser, February 17, 1999
Author interview with Margaret Lester, February 10, 1999
Various readings on the careers of Billy Carmichael and Kaye
Kyser
Personal correspondence between Billy Carmichael and Kath-
leen Bryan, circa 1950s, in Special Collections Division of archives
at UNCG Jackson Library
Review of history of creation of UNC-TV in Wilson Library,
UNC Chapel Hill
Author interview with Jake Dunlop in Beaufort, N.C., May 20,
1999
Author interview with Alan MacIntyre in Chapel Hill, February
17, 1999
Author interview with John Young in Chapel Hill, October 23,
1998
Author telephone interview with Mrs. Earl Wynn of Chapel
Hill, spring 1999
Author interview and correspondence with WBTV archivist
David Eades, spring 1999
Author telephone interview with Wesley Wallace of Chapel Hill,
March 5, 1999
Author interview with Bob Schenkkan of Texas, October 21, 1998
Author interview with Charles Crutchfield, June 30, 1998
Author interview with William C. Friday, September 5, 1998
Author interview with W.O. "Bo" Carter, December 1, 1998

Chapter 10

Author interview with Seth Macon, January 5, 1999

Author interview with Roger Soles, October 2, 1998

Author interview with Janie Price, November 4, 1998

Author interview with Greta Medlin, March 27, 2000

Author interview with Julian Price of Asheville, spring 1999

Author interviews with Bob and Joe Gorrell, May 5, May 13, 1999

Author interview with Turner Lindley, June 30, 1999

Author interview with Bob Koonts, November 22, 1998

Review of Jefferson business records among Bryan papers in Special Collections Division at UNCG Jackson Library

Jefferson history compiled by James Fox, July 1982

Author interview with Walker Rucker, September 30, 1999

Ralph Price correspondence in Jefferson history records, circa 1950s, at UNCG

Aubrey Lee Brooks, "A Southern Lawyer," pages 100-105

Julian Price personal papers in archives at UNCG

Author interview with Richard Wharton, September 8, 1999

Author telephone interview with McNeill Smith, September 2, 1999

Author interview with Julius Smith III, September 1, 1999

Author interview with Walter Davis in Chapel Hill, October 23, 1998

Author interview with Terry Sanford, February 20, 1998

Author interview with Lauch Faircloth, February 2, 1999

Author telephone interview with Hugh Cannon of Charleston, S.C., April 30, 1999

Author interview with Cope Livingstone, grandson of Jack Lindley, June 25, 1999

Chapter 11

Author interview with Bill Burns of Durham, May 3, 1999

Author interview with Jim Spearman of Marshallberg, N.C., May 21, 1999

Author interview with Jim Melvin, August 5 and October 9, 1998

Author interview with Tom Storrs in Charlotte, January 7, 1999

J. Van Lindley interview with NCNB public relations representative, July 11, 1983

History of Jefferson Standard compiled by James Fox, July 1982

Author interview with Cope Livingstone, June 25, 1999

Author interview with William Jones, June 15, 1999

Author telephone interview with Neil Vanstory Jr. of Raleigh, February 22, 1999

Author interview with Seth Macon, April 28, 1999

Author interview with William Rogers, May 27, 1999

"The Story of NationsBank" by Howard Covington and Marion Ellis

"McColl: The Man with America's Money" by Ross Yockey

Author interview with Allen Watkins April 26, 1999

Review of Security Bank records among Bryan papers at UNCG

Joe Bryan video interview with archivist Kevin von der Lippe, June 18, 1992

Bryan correspondence concerning Security Bank and NCNB among his personal papers at UNCG

Chapter 12

Greensboro Daily News story by Greta Tilley, July 18, 1982
Author interview with Seth Macon, Jan. 5, 1999
Bryan family papers in Special Collection Section of archives at UNCG Jackson Library
Author interview with Lauch Faircloth, February 2, 1999
Author interview with Greta Medlin, November 8, 1999
Author interview with Jim Melvin, October 9, 1998
Author interview with L. Richardson and Emily Preyer, spring 1999
Review of Bryan Park records among Bryan family papers in archives at UNCG
Greensboro News & Record clips on Bryan statute dedication
Author interview with Carole Bruce, February 5, 1999
Author interview with Ken Eiler, fall 1998
Author interview with Dudley Hughes in Jackson, Miss., December 14, 1998
Author interview with Kemp Reece, November 10, 1998

Chapter 13

Author interview with Greta Medlin, March 10, 2000
Author interview with Terry Sanford, February 20, 1998
Author interview with Dr. Allen Roses, October 23, 1998
Bryan family papers in Special Collection Section of archives in UNCG Jackson Library
Author interview with Jim Melvin, October 9, 1998
Author interview with Shahane Taylor, June 2, 1999
Author interview with Ann Rambeaut, November 8, 1999
Author interview with Blake Clark, March 29, 1999
Author interview with Mrs. Frances Carr, September 22, 1998

Author telephone interview with James Becher, fall 1999

"The Making of The Masters" by David Owen

Author telephone interview with Allen Medlin in Columbia, S.C., December 21, 1999

Author telephone interview with Billy Joe Patton in Florida, January 27, 2000

Author telephone interview with John Derr, March 29, 2000

Author interview with Dave Phillips, April 14, 1999

Author interview with Dudley Hughes in Jackson, Miss., December 14, 1998

Author interview with Jack Rochelle in High Point, N.C., spring 1999

Author telephone interview with Mrs. Roy Hay in Paris, France, November 4, 1998

Author telephone interview with Jere Ayers, spring 1999

Author telephone interview with Tristan Colket Jr., October 12, 1999

Author telephone interview with John Haughton in Canada, October 12, 1999

Author telephone interview with Mrs. Margie McBain in New York, December 17, 1999

Author telephone interview with Mrs. Lucy Sharp in Kennebunk, Maine, December, 17, 1999

Author interview with Dr. David Patterson, March 1, 1999

Author telephone interview with Tim Ireland in Thomasville, Ga., December 7, 1999

Chapter 14

Greensboro Daily News story by Greta Tilley, July 18, 1982

Series of author interviews with Mrs. Kay Edwards, December 1998 and February 1999

News & Observer story, 1986

Series of author interviews with Joseph M. Bryan Jr., February 1999

Author interview with Mary Price (Pricey) Taylor Harrison, May 16, 1999

Author interview with Bryan Taylor, April 29, 1999

Author telephone interview with Howard Taylor in Great Falls, Va., Sept. 30, 1999

Author telephone interview with John Taylor in Madison, Wis., September 24, 1999

Author interview with Kathy Evatt, October 26, 1999

Author interview with Laura Edwards in Chapel Hill, June 21, 1999

Series of author telephone interviews with Ann Faircloth in Chapel Hill, summer and fall, 1999

Author interview with Greta Medlin, September 27, 1999

Author interview with Bynum Hunter, August 12, 1999

Review of foundation records in Secretary of State office, Raleigh, N.C., January 6, 2000

Author interview with Mrs. Frances Carr, September 22, 1998

Author interview with Mrs. Mell Clemmons, August 13, 1999

Author interview with Mrs. Jerri Darden , spring 1999

Bryan family papers in Special Collection Section of archives at UNCG Jackson Library

Author interview with Mrs. Judy Davis , October 27, 1998

Author interview with Carole Bruce and Jim Melvin, May 11, 1999

Court records in Guilford County Courthouse

Author interview with lawyers Wade Smith and Randall Roden, fall 1999 and spring 2000

Author interview with William Massey, August 28, 1998

Author telephone interview with Gary Parks. August 25, 1998

Author interview with Mrs. Elise Franklin, November 2, 1998

Author interview with Ann Rambeaut, November 8, 1999
Visit to Green Hill Cemetery, fall 1999
Author interview with Mrs. Margaret Brooks, September, 1, 1999

Chapter 15

Author interviews with Ann Rambeaut and Greta Medlin, November 8, 1999
Joseph Bryan death certificate
Author interviews with Jim Melvin and Carole Bruce, May 11, 1999
Review of news clippings from Greensboro Record, circa 1920s
Author interview with Walter (Sticky) Burch, fall 1999
Public property records in Guilford Register of Deeds office
Author telephone interview with Ken Eiler, spring 1999
Author interviews with L. Richardson and Emily Preyer, summer 1999
Author interview with Kay Edwards, February 2, 1999
Author interview with Joe Bryan Jr. February 18, 1999
Bryan family records in Special Collections Section of archives at UNCG Jackson Library
Author interview with Mrs. Margaret Lester in Chapel Hill, February 10, 1999
Joseph M. Bryan video interview with archivist Kevin von der Lippe, June 18, 1992
Author interview with Gov. James Hunt, February 3, 1999
Author interview with Seth Macon, January 5, 1999
Author interview with William Jones, June 15, 1999
Greensboro Daily News, Giles Lambertson editorial column, November 1983
Author interview with Ed Fort, April 13, 1999

Author interview with Dr. David Patterson , March 1, 1999
Visit to Bryan School of Business, UNCG
Bryan family records in archives at UNCG
Author interview with Gloria Scott, fall 1999

Chapter 16

Author interview with Gov. Terry Sanford, February 20, 1998
North Carolina Manual during Kerr Scott years in public office
Author interview with Pricey Taylor Harrison, May 16, 1999
Bryan family records in archives at UNCG
Joe Bryan video interview with archivist Kevin von der Lippe, June 1992
Author interview with Jake Phelps, June 16, 1999
Author interview with Carole Bruce, February 5, 1999
Author interview with Lauch Faircloth, February 2, 1999
Author interview with Walter Davis in Chapel Hill, October 23 , 1998
Author interview with Roger Soles, October 2, 1998
Terry Sanford biography, quote by Hugh Morton at Sanford funeral

Chapter 17

Bryan family records in Special Collection Section archives at UNCG Jackson Library
Joe Bryan video interview with archivist Kevin von der Lippe, June 18, 1992
Author interview with Ann Rambeaut, November 8, 1999
Bryan Family Foundation records
Author interview with Richard Wharton, September 8, 1999

Review of Our Lady of Grace historical documents

Author telephone interview with Our Lady of Grace historian Jim Patton, fall 1999

Author telephone interview with the Rev. John Akers, summer 1999

Author interview with Joe Bryan Jr., February 18, 1999

Author interview with Jim Melvin, October 9, 1998

Author interview with Lanty Smith, September 8, 1999

Author telephone interview with Joel Fleishman in New York, fall 1999

Author interview with William C. Friday, September 5, 1998

Author telephone interview with Rebecca Anderson , January 6, 2000

Author telephone interview with Ann Faircloth in Chapel Hill, January 8, 2000

Author interview with Walter Rogers in Raleigh, August 19, 1999

Author interview with Kay Edwards, February 10, 1999

Chapter 18

Joseph M. Bryan video interview with archivist Kevin von der Lippe, June 1992

Joseph M. Bryan oral interview with Duke Medical Center archivist Jim Gifford, August 26, 1986

Author interviews with Dr. Allen Roses in Durham, August 23, 1998, and May 3, 1999

Author interview with Bucky Waters, February 9, 1999

Author telephone interview with Dr. Zovan Khachatorian, March 30, 1999

Review of medical studies of Alzheimer's disease at Duke Medical Center, et al

Author interview with Dr. William Anlyon in Durham, September 25, 1998

Author interview with John Thomas in Durham, May 3, 1999

Author interview with Mrs. Margaret Lester, February 10, 1999

Author interview with Dr. Don Schemechel, March 19, 1999

Author interview with Dr. Kathleen Welsh-Bohmer, March 18, 1999

Author attendance at Bryan Alzheimer's Conference in February 1998 and February 1999

Author tour of Bryan Neurology Center on Duke University campus, fall 1999

Author interview with Dr. Sandy Scarlette at Duke Eye Center, March 29, 1999

Author review of written correspondence between Joe Bryan and Eppie Lederer (Ann Landers), circa 1986-1990

Author interviews with Jim Melvin and Carole Bruce, May 11, 1999

Chapter 19

Author interviews with family members, friends and past employees

Bryan family records in Special Collection Section of archives at UNCG Jackson Library

Author interviews with Jim Melvin and Carole Bruce, May 11, 1999

Author interview with William Massey, August 28, 1998

Review of historical and current records of both Bryan Family Fund and Joseph M. Bryan Foundation

Author interview with Michael Haley, June 25, 1999

Author interview with Shirley Frye, June 25, 1999

Author interview with Michael Weaver, June 22, 1999

Author interview with David DeVries, January 2000

Chapter 20

Series of author interviews with Jim Melvin, October 1998 and May 1999

Author interview with Greta Medlin, March 10, 2000

Joseph M. Bryan Foundation documents, historical records and IRS returns

"The Cathedral Within" by Bill Shore on the significance of philanthropy

Audio tape of Bryan funeral by Rev. Joseph Mullin and author interview with Rev. Mullin

Series of interviews with Bryan family friends during fall 1998 and spring 1999

BIBLIOGRAPHY

Official Documents and Collections:

Papers of UNC president Gordon Gray and of WBTV broadcast executive Charles Crutchfield in North Carolina Room of Wilson Library at the University of North Carolina, Chapel Hill

Papers and family records of the Bryan family history and correspondence, dated from pre-1900 through the early 1990s, donated to the Special Collection Department of the archives in Jackson Library at the University of North Carolina at Greensboro

Records of the Bryan Family Fund and Joseph M. Bryan Foundation, including listing of charitable contributions

Papers of Gov. Terry Sanford

Authorized history of Jefferson Standard Life Insurance compiled by James F. Fox Public Relations Inc., June 1982

Series of videos by archivist Kevin von der Lippe with Joseph M. Bryan Sr. conducted in June, 1992

UNC Television videos of Joseph M. Bryan Sr. contributions to UNC-TV, to the School of Business at UNCG and of testimonials at his death

Duke University videos of Joseph M. Bryan's contributions to Duke

Published sources:

TERRY SANFORD, Politics, Progress & Outrageous Ambition, by Howard E. Covington Jr. and Marion A. Ellis, Duke University Press, 1999

Across Fortune's Tracks, a biography of William Rand Kenan Jr. by Walter E. Campbell, UNC Press, 1996

The Meaning Of Honor, The Life of Frank Hawkins Kenan, by Marion Ellis, Chapel Hill, 1994

WILLIAM FRIDAY, Power, Purpose & American Higher Education, by William A. Link, UNC Press, 1995

Oil in the Deep South: History of the oil business in Mississippi, Alabama and Florida, 1859-1945 by Dudley Hughes, University of Mississippi Press, 1993

The Cathedral Within, Transforming Your Life by Giving Something Back, by Bill Shore, Random House, 1999

Singing My Song, the memoirs of Katherine Wooten Springs , Springfield Press, 1994

North Carolina Manuals

On This Day in North Carolina, by Lew Powell, John. F. Blair, 1996

Interviews by author:

Interviewed between February 10, 1998 and December 1, 1998:

Dr. William Anlyan, Ed Armfield, Bill Blackwell, Frances Carr, Charles Crutchfield, Arnie Culbeth, Jerri Darden, Judy Davis, Walter Davis, Elise Franklin, William Friday, Adelaide Holderness, John Hopkins, Bob Koonts, Kevin von der Lippe, William Massey, Jim Melvin, Janie Pace Price, Jim Pridgen, Kemp Reece, Dr. Allen Roses, Terry Sanford, Roger Soles, Bob Schenkkan, Louis Stephens and John Young

Interviewed between December 1, 1998, and March 1, 1999:

James Babb, John Broome, Carole Bruce, Joe Bryan Jr., W.O. Carter Jr., Kay Edwards, Lauch Faircloth, Mary Gee, Dudley Hughes, Jim Hunt, Bob Koonts, Georgia Kyser, Margaret Lester, John Lindley, Alan MacIntyre, Seth Macon, Cecil Martin, Doug Mayes, Loonis McGlohon, Beverly Moore, William Moore, Joe Mullin, Charles Myers, Linville Roach, James Spearman, Katherine Springs, Tom Storrs and Bucky Waters

Interviewed between March 1, 1999, and June 1, 1999:

Jere Ayers, Bob Beall, Dr. Katherine Welsh-Bohmer, Carole Bruce, Bill Burns, Hugh Cannon, Caddy Carson, Blake Clark, Patsy Davidson, Jake Dunlop, Penny Sansing-Edwards, Ted Ely Jr., Ed Fort, William Friday, Lloyd Gordon, Bob Gorrell, Joe Gorrell, Pricey Taylor Harrison, Nat Hayes, Dr. Zoven Khachatorian, Kevin von der Lippe, Cope Livingstone, Seth Macon, Jim Melvin, Charles Patterson, Dr. David Patterson, Jim Patton, Dave Phillips, L. Richardson Preyer, Emily Preyer, Jack Rochelle, William Rogers, Dr. Allen Roses, Sandy Scarlett, Dr. Don Schmechel, James Spearman, Bryan Taylor, John Thomas, Wesley Wallace and Alan Watkins

Interviewed between June 1, 1999, and September 1, 1999:

William Black Jr., Mell Clemmons, Laura Edwards, Ted Ely Jr., Elise Franklin, Shirley Frye, Michael Haley, Bynum Hunter, William Jones, Horace Kornegay, Turner Lindley, Cope Livingston III, Seth Macon, Jim Melvin, Gary Parks, Jake Phelps, Julian Price, Walter Rogers, Dr. Don Schmechel, James Slaughter, Shahane Taylor, Marjorie Warren, Michael Weaver and Norman Wiggins

Interviewed between September 1, 1999, and December 31, 1999:

Dr. William Anlyan, James Becher, Margaret Brooks, Walter Burch, William Bryan, Bill Carr, Steve Catlett, Tris Colket, Clyde Collins, Howard Covington Jr., Kay Edwards, John Ehle, Kathy Evatt, Joel Fleishman, Elise Franklin, Mary Gee, James Gifford, Mrs. Roy Hay, John Haughton, Sister Lucy Hennessy, Tim Ireland, William King, Tom Lindley, Margie McBain, Alex McMahon, Allen Medlin, Greta Medlin, William Moran, Walker Rucker, Lucy Sharp, Lanty Smith, McNeill Smith, Julius Smith Jr., Ann Rambeaut, Roger Soles, Charles Sullivan, Howard Taylor, John Taylor, N. Carlton Tilley, Kevin von der Lippe, Virginia Waller and Richard Wharton

12

INDEX

C

P